P9-DFS-773

AT REAGAN'S SIDE

BOOKS BY HELENE VON DAMM

Sincerely, Ronald Reagan (edited by Helene von Damm)
Wirf die Angst weg, Helene

AT REAGAN'S SIDE

HELENE VON DAMM

Doubleday

NEW YORK · LONDON · TORONTO · SYDNEY · AUCKLAND

Published by Doubleday, a division of
Bantam Doubleday Dell Publishing Group, Inc.
666 Fifth Avenue, New York, New York 10103

DOUBLEDAY and the portrayal of an anchor with a dolphin are trade-
marks of Doubleday, a division of Bantam Doubleday Dell Publishing
Group, Inc.

Library of Congress Cataloging-in-Publication Data

Von Damm, Helene, 1938-
    At Reagan's side / Helene von Damm. — 1st ed.
      p.   cm.
    Includes index.
    ISBN 0-385-24445-2 :
      1. Von Damm, Helene, 1938-   . 2. Reagan, Ronald—Friends and
associates.   3. Ambassadors—United States—Biography.   I. Title.
E840.8.V66A3 1989
327.2'092'4—dc19
[B]   88-25653
                                         CIP

ISBN 0-385-24445-2
Copyright © 1989 by Helene von Damm
All Rights Reserved
Printed in the United States of America
January 1989
FIRST EDITION

Designed by: Diane Stevenson/SNAP • HAUS GRAPHICS

CONTENTS

Prologue   vii

Chapter 1   Childhood   1

Chapter 2   Breaking Away   14

Chapter 3   The New World: America, Here I Come   26

Chapter 4   New Horizons: Joining Ronald Reagan   42

Chapter 5   Happy Days   73

Chapter 6   Searching   88

Chapter 7   A Mission   97

Chapter 8   The Making of a President   110

Chapter 9   The Work Begins: The Kitchen Cabinet and
             Transitions   126

Chapter 10   A New Beginning: The Inauguration and
             the First Days at the White House   153

CONTENTS

Chapter 11   Learning the Ropes: Life in Washington   171

Chapter 12   Politics Is Not a Rose Garden   181

Chapter 13   How the Game Is Really Played   192

Chapter 14   Growing Wise to the Ways of Washington   210

Chapter 15   We're Losing Our Grip   222

Chapter 16   Troubles Ahead   235

Chapter 17   The Challenge: Tough Days   250

Chapter 18   The Reward: United States Ambassador to Austria   262

Chapter 19   Arriving in Vienna: The Fairy Tale   278

Chapter 20   Disappointments Everywhere   289

Chapter 21   The Fall from Grace   305

Epilogue   316

I MUST HAVE LOOKED AT MY WATCH A HUNDRED TIMES on Monday morning, May 16, 1983. Would everyone be on time? Would the rain stop so that we could hold the ceremony outside in the Rose Garden instead of in the State Dining Room? What would the President say? Would Mrs. Reagan attend?

My watch gave me none of those answers, of course. It simply crawled along at what seemed to be an unusually slow pace.

The rain did not stop. I tried to keep busy in my White House office but I was too excited and the words on the papers I held swam before my eyes. At last, at a little before 4 P.M., the White House receptionist phoned to tell me that my husband, Byron Leeds, had arrived. I smoothed my skirt, combed my hair, and hurried down to the Reception Room on the first floor to greet him. The wait would soon be over. In a few minutes, I'd stand next to the President of the United States, place my hand on the Bible, and take the oath of office as the U.S. Ambassador to Austria.

Byron winked at me as I entered the reception area of the

West Wing. "Have you forgotten the oath?" he teased. I needed humoring. My heart was pounding. "Is it four yet?" I asked. He nodded and gave me his arm and we headed off to the State Dining Room. Well, I thought, if I can't have the Rose Garden, the gracious State Dining Room was a wonderful substitute. Most ambassadors get sworn in at the State Department or in an office. I was getting special treatment and I felt very pampered indeed.

When Byron and I entered the room I was overwhelmed. It was packed. Just about everyone who had been important in life in the twenty years since I had arrived as a poor immigrant from Austria was there.

The chief of protocol, Selwa (Lucky) Roosevelt, announced the President of the United States. Everyone rose and applauded. The two of us made our way to the podium and the President whispered to me, "You know, Helene, I had a carefully prepared speech, but looking around this room, I think I'll discard it. This turnout really tells your story."

True to his word, he spoke extemporaneously, as I had seen him do thousands of times in the eighteen years I had worked for him, but never before were the words all for me.

"Helene von Damm is the most American human being I know," said the President. "More American than Patrick Henry. If you doubt it, just try criticizing the United States in her vicinity." He then reminisced about how he had hired me when I just a young, eager secretary. He spoke of how he had grown to rely on me, and of how I had grown into a professional.

The President then explained how I had been mentioned for the post of ambassador. "When our last Ambassador to Austria discovered that he was very ill, he told me that if for any reason he couldn't return to his post, the one person he thought would be best for the job was Helene von Damm. I have to admit, I greeted this news with mixed feelings. How do you say goodbye to someone who has been so important in your life for eighteen years? I know she will be a great diplomat. She has tact. She has great dependability. And there's something else that adds to my joy at this appointment. In spite of my sorrow at her leaving, I'm very, very glad that from now on she'll have a chauffeur to drive her around. If there's one thing about America Helene never mastered it's traffic!" Everyone roared. They were all my friends and the laughter was affectionate.

Then he looked at me and said, "We still have a string on you."

"I hope so, Mr. President," I replied.

Bill Clark, who had been Chief Justice of the Supreme Court of California, stood up to administer the oath. Byron held the Bible for me and I swore to defend the Constitution of the United States and faithfully execute the office of Ambassador to Austria. Then it was my turn to speak.

I looked out at the faces before me—all of my mentors and friends. Bill Clark, National Security Adviser to the President, Lee Ann Elliott, former associate director of the American Medical Political Action Committee (AMPAC) and my first American boss to take an interest in me, Lyn Nofziger, Ed Meese, Cap Weinberger, Dan Terra, Bill Casey, Ray Donovan, Drew Lewis, Dick Darman, Lynn Wood, Tad Tharp, Dennis Patrick, Larry Eagleburger, Lionel Olmer, and many, many more.

"I hope it's all right for an ambassador to show emotion," I said, my voice quivering a little, "because if not, I just flunked my first test of diplomacy. It is overwhelming to think that in less than twenty-five years, a humble immigrant can rise to the office of ambassador to the country from which she came. I hope Mrs. Reagan will forgive me for stealing her line, but my life too began with Ronald Reagan."

Mrs. Reagan might forgive me for stealing her line, but she might not forgive me for accepting the post of ambassador. As I looked around the room, I noticed that neither she nor Mike Deaver, my friend for eighteen years, was present. The rise had not been cost-free.

"In looking back," I continued, "what I cherish most about the American people is their incredible generosity. With all the initial handicaps of a new immigrant—especially a thick accent!—I never felt anything but total acceptance and support as I struggled to make my way as a citizen here in the United States. Whenever there was a bridge to cross, there were outstretched hands to help. And most of all, there was Ronald Reagan, who didn't just talk about equal opportunity in the abstract, he made it a reality for me. God bless you all.''

CHILDHOOD

"**A**REN'T YOU A LITTLE YOUNG TO BE WRITING your memoirs?" asked a friend who heard about this project. I thanked him for the compliment, but then also reflected on why I want to tell my story as it has unfolded so far. I guess the main reason is that I've experienced more than I ever dreamed possible in the past fifty years. My life, which ought to have begun and ended in a small village in Austria, has instead propelled me to the highest levels of the United States government and to the rank of ambassador. And further, I want to write about my experiences as a way of thanking my country, the United States of America, and Ronald Reagan for making it a place where dreams can come true.

———

In 1938, Hitler absorbed Austria into the Third Reich in what came to be known as the Anschluss. Austria was not a conquered enemy, but rather became an ally of Hitler's, though there were many Austrians, just as there were many

Germans, who were to varying degrees anti-Nazi. My mother's father was one of them. My father was blindsided by them, I'm sorry to say. Nineteen thirty-eight was also the year of my birth. It was a strange start for Helene Antonia Winter, who would devote twenty years of her life to Ronald Reagan.

My first enemy was the United States of America. One of my earliest memories, from age five, was of kneeling on the cold, hardwood floor of our apartment in Ulmerfeld-Hausmening to say my prayers, and having them interrupted by the piercing wail of air-raid sirens. My mother, who had left me in privacy for prayer, rushed back into the room, swept me into her arms, grabbed my older brother Pepi by the hand, and rushed into the cellar of the building. There we three would huddle, hearing the blasts and feeling the ground shake, sometimes far, sometimes near, until at last we heard the all clear. The American bombers were gone.

Because my first association with airplanes was of bombing and death, I felt uncomfortable around planes long into my adult years.

Ulmerfeld-Hausmening is a village in what's called the Lower Region of Austria. There was nothing much there worth bombing, and though we were frightened night after night, only one bomb actually fell on our village. We all figured it must have been meant for Amstetten down the road. My mother, brother, and I didn't always wait out the raids in our basement. As I grew older, the bombing intensified and we were herded into a "safer" shelter, a cavern near the Ybbs, the local river. The cavern must have been formed by a stream centuries before. Water no longer surged through the tunnel-like interior—but it remained damp and very cold. Icy droplets fell from the ceiling. We sat on rough wooden benches. Babies cried. Adults complained. All of us shivered. We sometimes were forced to remain for hours in that dark, cold tunnel of rock with bats flying over our heads.

When we got home my mother would heat a basin of water on the stove (we had no hot running water) so that Pepi and I could wash our hands and faces. A full bath was much too extravagant to imagine. And then, if it wasn't close to dawn, we'd grab what little sleep we could.

I wasn't aware of deprivation, though. Our apartment house was among the nicest in the village. I believe it was once a grand estate. The rooms were large with high ceilings, and there was a lovely park outside our windows. Or perhaps I just fantasized that it had once been part of a great estate. When we lived there, in the early and middle 1940s, it was owned by the local paper mill. My father had worked as an engineer in the paper mill, and though he was now disabled with tuberculosis and unable to work, they allowed us to go on living in the same building.

I never really knew my father. By the time I was out of infancy he was already very sick. The antibiotics that can cure tuberculosis were not yet available. My memories of him are very dim. The sanatorium was several days' journey away, so we never visited him. What I knew of him I knew through my mother's descriptions.

If I went to school then, I don't remember it. I do recall that Pepi went to school because the image of my mother with her finger to her lips whenever I made too much noise is still vivid. "Pepi has to study." I wanted to play with Pepi. What child doesn't crave the attention of the older siblings? But I made do with girlfriends when he was at the books.

The pattern of daytime play and nighttime terror in bomb shelters went on until I was seven. In 1945, the Allies began their final push into Germany and Austria. The Americans were moving across the Rhine in the west and the Russians were pouring in from the east. My mother was extremely frightened. The stories of atrocities by conquering soldiers were on everyone's lips, and as a woman alone with two children, my mother felt especially vulnerable. The only escape she could think of was to flee to the area where the sanatorium was located. It wasn't that my father could protect us, but I suppose she thought being near him would provide comfort.

There were a few problems. In the first place, my mother was a country woman who had scarcely ever been out of our village and was not wise in the ways of travel. Besides, trains operated only sporadically because long stretches of track had been bombed. Nor did she have any idea of how she would support us once we did arrive or where we would live. But she knew one thing: we were going southwest, toward the Americans and away from the Russians. I was confused. Frankly, the foreigners I feared most were the Americans. It was their bombs which had shattered my childhood nights. But my mother had her mind made up. Only when I was older did I understand the wisdom of her move.

We did manage the journey, though it was difficult. The roads and trains were flooded with refugees moving in all directions, with pickpockets and charlatans trying to profit off the misery of others. Everything was chaotic. When we finally reached our destination, we had nowhere to stay. We slept outside the first night, with our bundles of clothes for pillows.

The following day my mother found a place for us at a nearby farmhouse. The owner was willing to allow us to sleep in a loft over the barn if we worked for our room and board. Mother readily agreed. We soon discovered that privacy did not come with the contract. There were already several other families of refugees living in the loft and they did not welcome our presence. I don't think we spoke to them once in the entire summer we were there.

My mother and brother worked in the fields during the day. I was too young for manual labor, so I just wandered around. I'd never been on a farm before, so everything interested me. The owner's daughter became my friend and showed me how cows are milked and pigs are slaughtered. I watched her father slit the pigs' throats and hang them in the yard to drain off the blood before skinning them and slicing them up. It was such a revolting sight for a seven-year-old that for years I had trouble eating meat of any kind. This, of course, was to Pepi's benefit, since meat was scarce.

But things seemed safe enough for the human inhabitants of the farm. The war seemed far away—until one day we saw several American military policemen approaching in a jeep. I was afraid of anyone in uniform and ran to the loft to hide. I looked out from between a crack in the boards to watch what they would do. They were looking for something. One had a cigarette dangling from his mouth—a scarce commodity in Austria at the time. They were shouting to one another as they poked around. At last they seemed to find what they were looking for at a certain spot near a tree. They went back to the jeep and returned with pickaxes and shovels. They dug quickly and efficiently, coming to their object without difficulty. It was a large wooden box with brass handles. They lifted it out and broke open the lock with the ax handle. It was filled with shiny silverware and china.

I'll never forget what happened next. By this time the farmer and his family had assembled outside to watch the digging and were waiting anxiously. When the American soldiers saw that the box contained only the family's valuables and not (as it was explained to me later) the cache of guns and hand grenades they had been led to expect, they handed the box back to farmer and went on their way. The family was incredulous. They hugged one another with joy. It was unheard of for soldiers to pass up an opportunity for looting. There was something special about these Americans, I decided.

Our family had also buried our valuables in a box in the garden before we left Ulmerfeld-Hausmening. But we were not so lucky. I don't know who got to them: it could have been fellow Austrians, or Russian soldiers, or even our neighbors. But when we returned, our box was gone.

We spent the summer of 1945 at the farm. I had no sense of time at that age. If someone had told me we had lived there for a year it wouldn't have surprised me. Time moves slowly for children. One morning I came upon my mother packing our meager belongings into a duffel bag. "The war is over," she said, smiling. "We're going home."

Going home proved to be far more difficult than we had imagined. The roads were choked with people going in all directions: refugees from Eastern Europe, Austrians of all regions, soldiers on their way home in tattered uniforms or on crutches. Everyone was on foot, unless you were fortunate enough to catch a short ride on top of a horse-drawn wagon or you could pile into a train. Only the military had cars.

At the start of our journey, I recall, we had a guard. I wasn't sure what his function was but I knew it was his decision that we traveled only at night. He went ahead of us and then came back to say whether or not the coast was clear. I was told to be silent, which is difficult for a child. I remember the guide coming over to me once after I had whispered to my mother. He grabbed me around the waist with one hand and clamped his hand over my mouth with the other. He must have carried me that way for half a mile. I learned to keep silent after that.

After a few days, our guide disappeared. The three of us then began to trek during daylight again. Like Germany, Austria was divided after the war into four zones: American, British, French, and Soviet. Our home was in the Soviet zone. The Soviets had set up checkpoints everywhere. People were obliged to line up while the Soviet soldiers examined whatever identification papers they had. They were purportedly looking for ex-Nazis, but since they had total power, they also carted off anyone they chose. I remember standing at many such checkpoints, my knees trembling in complete terror. What if they took my mother? What would I do? What if they took me? My mother was powerless to prevent it.

When, after several weeks of walking, we did finally reach home, my mother broke into tears. And they were not tears of joy. Our building, like many others, had been appropriated by the Russian soldiers. Everything in our apartment was now theirs, and we were told that we had no claim on our own home, we'd have to find lodgings elsewhere. We wandered about the village after getting the news about our apartment. We wanted to appeal our case to a higher authority. But there was no higher authority. The Russians and the Allied forces elsewhere were in charge.

Our neighbors told horrifying stories about the Russians. Apparently the first wave of Soviet soldiers who had been sent in to "liberate" Austria had been elite troops. They were civilized, many spoke German, and they were skilled propagandists for the U.S.S.R. as well. But they were on the move to "liberate" other territories. The soldiers in the second wave were the ones everyone was talking about. They were so primitive, most had never seen such ordinary Western conveniences as toilets, stoves, or even bicycles. They were curious, but more than that they were greedy. Most of them were full of hate and behaved like barbarians. They stole everything they could get their hands on, including, because they were eager for Western technology, entire factories, which they disassembled and shipped back to the U.S.S.R. in pieces.

While some of this is endemic to war, the other zones of Austria were not suffering nearly as much, because the British, French, and Americans did not consider themselves licensed to rape, pillage, and kill.

Without an apartment to live in we turned to my grandmother, who lived in a three-room apartment on the second floor of a farmhouse. The kitchen was the only warm room. It housed the wood-burning stove, whose warmth made it the center of the house. At night, my grandmother slept in one of the freezing-cold bedrooms, and my brother, my mother, and I slept in the other. Waking up in the middle of the night with an urge to use the bathroom was a bad idea. The flat had no bathroom and no running water. There was a toilet in the hall but to get there you'd have to get out of a warm bed and step onto the icy floorboards.

In the morning my mother heated a pot of water on the stove, just as she had done in my early childhood, so that we could wash our hands and faces. One day a week, she'd make enough hot water for a bath in a small, portable aluminum tub. Pepi and I used to fight over who would get into the small tub first before the water became cold and dirty.

During the war we had lived in constant fear of American bombing. Now, under Soviet occupation, there were more personal harms to be dreaded. A knock on the door at night could be a Russian soldier looking for schnapps. We'd heard stories that after the frightened tenants had given up whatever liquor they had, the soldiers would rape all the women in the apartment, old and young. If you failed to respond to the knock, they'd shoot the door open. Beatings were so common on the streets that people never walked anywhere alone. And young girls would attempt to disguise themselves as boys or go into hiding to avoid rape.

One night there was a fight at a local bar and a Russian soldier was beaten and then thrown into the river, where he drowned. There was no inquest. The following morning the Russians simply assembled everyone who had been involved in the bar brawl that night and shipped them all to Siberia.

In time, a semblance of normality set in and things improved, but Soviet rule remained terribly capricious. One never knew what pretext they'd find to deport or execute someone. Living for those ten years knowing that the smallest offense, or no offense at all, could lead to death or disaster, I developed a lifelong sympathy for people around the world living under Communism.

The violence touched even our close neighbors. My best girlfriend's mother and brother were both randomly murdered one afternoon by soldiers while they were out berry picking. We never found out who was responsible. In the chaos of postwar Austria, random violence was common. A murder trial would have seemed extraordinary. So profound was the fear of the Russians that people were driven to insane acts. Our next-door neighbor heard that the Russians were coming to execute him. He panicked, shot his two children, then his wife, and then himself. The shock was staggering. But even worse is the memory of how my starved and frightened fellow villagers reacted: before the blood of the bodies was cold, the house had been picked clean by its "neighbors."

I was terrified most of the time. I used to lie awake at night in the cold bedroom of Grandmother's apartment and imagine being beaten or murdered by the Russians, or by anyone in a uniform. I would cry, unable to slide gently into sleep as most children naturally do. But I couldn't tell my mother how I felt. I loved her very much, and depended on her utterly of course, but somehow I felt that she couldn't provide the comfort I needed.

———

Mother was a loving, giving, but simple person. Her father had been a game warden and she had grown up miles from other children. That's probably why she remained extremely shy and withdrawn her whole life. Her family were the sort who worked hard and spoke little. She received an elementary school education, but her horizons were quite limited. I doubt whether she ever read much beyond a popular novel or the town's newspaper. This is not to disparage her role as mother. I knew she would do anything to ensure that Pepi and I were safe, warm (well, as warm as possible under the circumstances), and well fed. And she succeeded. She had some money from my father's disability pay and she made it go a long way. Even during the worst shortages following the war, we never went hungry. While most women didn't dare venture out on country roads alone for fear of rape, my mother used to walk an hour each day to the surrounding farmers in hopes of getting fresh milk for us. Sometimes she even managed to find us some meat. She was truly brave and she never complained.

Nor did I ever feel deprived vis-à-vis the other girls in the village. Even after my father died when I was twelve, and we had to make ends meet on his meager pension. She taught herself to sew and obtained modern dress patterns to outfit me as though I had been shopping in a fine Vienna store (or so I felt at that age). And she found ways and means to get me dolls, and hair ribbons, and glossy American magazines, and other trinkets so important to little girls.

The one thing she couldn't be was a soul mate. When I would try to tell her what I was feeling, she would respond with one of the clichés she'd heard from her own mother. "Never put off to tomorrow what you can do today." "A penny saved is a penny earned." And so on. I grew frustrated and stopped turning to her with my thoughts.

My real world was harsh and unsatisfying, so I fled into the realm of fantasy. I gobbled up all of the romance fiction I could find, and eagerly watched for each film from America. In my early teens, I developed a fascination for all things American. Ever since we had seen those American soldiers turn back the farmer's goods to him, we had all changed our opinion of Americans. They now represented to me a glittering world of comfort and pleasure. I combed the movie fan magazines and cut out photographs of my favorite stars for my scrapbook. I particularly loved Clark Gable and Cary Grant. When I played with my dolls, I made them Rita Hayworth or Betty Grable in my imagination, and they always lived in the United States. For a time I was able to interest some girlfriends in my imaginary games, but they soon lost interest. They were interested, naturally enough, in the local boys, not in the celluloid images which enraptured me.

I couldn't really turn to my brother either. In the first place, he was seven years older, and therefore not interested in the same things. Besides, my brother was quiet and withdrawn like my mother—though, unlike her, he was very bookish and intellectual from a young age. He was kind to me, saving up to buy me my first watch and my first bicycle, but there was no real intimacy, no sharing of secrets or sorrows between us then.

I wish I had known my father better. People said I was very much like him: curious and striving. But tuberculosis kept us apart. After the war he was released from the sanatorium, but his job in the paper mill had long since been given to someone else. They had no other work for him in our village and so they sent him to another plant in another city. We couldn't go with him because there were no apartments for rent. He was able to find only a room with another family and tried to visit us every other weekend. But he was still a stranger. The visits were short and he was usually extremely tired. The only consequence I can recall of his limited presence in our lives at the time was his decision that I, at age ten, ought to attend a convent school for a proper education. Until then, I had been attending the local grammar school.

I was enrolled in Gleiss, a few miles from our town. For the first time in my life, I was challenged by learning, and blossomed—at least for a short while. The world, of which I had had too much experience and too little knowledge in my short life, now unfolded some of its riches before me. The nuns taught me to paint and play the piano. I read history, learned a few phrases of Latin, learned spelling, and how to stand absolutely erect with a book on my head. Alas, my convent education came to an abrupt end after one year when my father died. After that there wasn't enough money to afford it.

I was heartbroken to have to leave the convent school; it had expanded my horizons amazingly. But in one way I wasn't sorry to leave. It relieved me of the endless church visits and calls for prayers which bored me.

My brother was nineteen when my father died, and while he was now the nominal "head of the family" (in patriarchal Austria that saying carried great weight), he was away at the University of Vienna. Somehow, my mother found the money for my brother's education. Mine wasn't considered so important. It wasn't intended as favoritism, and I didn't take it that way. It was simply an unchallenged assumption that education was more important for boys back then.

I enrolled again at the local school and remained there until I was ready for secretarial school. I had returned to an uninspiring setting for someone who was eager to know more about the larger world. My teachers were terribly parochial and limited. There was never any give-and-take between students and teachers.

Secretarial school was next, but not better. It was about thirty minutes away by train, and though I had the company of other girls from the village who were attending the same school and shared the ride with me daily, I remember it as a dreary experience. I had to get up before dawn and make it down to the freezing-cold railway station. It hadn't been painted since before the war and was lit only by bare, grimy light bulbs spaced several yards apart. We stamped our feet and waited for the equally dirty and unwholesome trains. The school was in an old building in the city of Waidhofen. The curriculum included typing, shorthand, dictation, business-letter writing, and some bookkeeping. We also learned English—which was always my worst subject. I was so hopeless in English that one of my teachers took me aside and kindly inquired why I was doing so poorly in one subject and fairly well in all the others. "Because I know I'll never get a chance to use it," I replied gloomily.

————

I completed secretarial school at the age of sixteen. The next stage of my life was by no means clear. Other girls in the village were considering local posts and eyeing local boys for potential husbands. I was different. I knew I had to get away from the stifling atmosphere of our village. I had no money and no prospects of getting any money. Nonetheless, soon after my graduation from secretarial school, I announced that I was moving to Vienna. My poor mother was dumbfounded. Though she knew I had an adventuresome spirit, she never thought I would dare make such a dramatic move at so young an age. She tried to talk me into staying closer to home and finding a local job, but I shook my head. She protested, "But you don't know anyone in Vienna."

"I know Pepi," I replied. "And soon I'll know others."

I was excited but terribly scared. My mother had given me the equivalent of thirty dollars to start out with—I'm sure it was all of her savings. It meant that, at least for a time, I could manage. Rent for my first room was only eight dollars a month.

When I arrived in Vienna after a two-hour train ride, carrying all of my worldly goods in two suitcases and one satchel, I discovered that Pepi couldn't offer me a place to stay. "You nut," he said as he shouldered my bags, "how did you expect to live when you got here?" I just shrugged and looked foolish. As an engineering student at the university, he had a dorm room the size of a closet, not large enough for one person and certainly too small for two. Moreover, it was for men only. But he had seen a notice on a bulletin board advertising a room to rent in the sixteenth district. A Czechoslovakian woman had a tiny fourth-floor walk-up to rent. I had thought my grandmother's apartment was cramped, but this room was minuscule. There was barely room for the small bed and nightstand. Nor was there any privacy. I had to go through the landlady's entire apartment, even her bedroom, to reach my room and the only running water was in the hall.

BREAKING AWAY

VIENNA WAS A MAGNIFICENT CITY, IF SLIGHTLY THE worse for wear. Before World War I it was the capital of the vast Austro-Hungarian Empire. It was considered the second most sophisticated city in Europe, after Paris. Its boulevards, parks, and stately buildings made it Paris's rival in beauty as well. But by the time I moved there in the mid-1950s, it had the look of faded glory. Large portions of the city were still bombed-out and desolate.

Not that I was in any position to enjoy it. For me, Vienna was no better than Ulmerfeld-Hausmening. I found a job quickly and set to work as a typist for an export company. For the first month, I received no paycheck. But I was sixteen and didn't know how to assert my rights. Maybe no one gets paid for the first month, I thought. But my employer didn't pay me the second month or the third month either. By that time, the money my mother had given me was gone and I quit.

I wandered the streets of Vienna looking for any kind of

work. I inquired for a salesgirl position in a department store but was told that my English was too poor and that it was important to be able to communicate with foreigners (Vienna had been divided into four sections by the Allies after the war). After several more rejections I was finally able to land a job in the bookkeeping department at a pipe company.

Work began at 8 A.M. sharp—if you were even one minute late, you were called before the boss for an explanation. I made entries in the accounts receivable books. We got a half hour for lunch and I was able to make friends with some of the other girls who were in the same boat. At least at this job, dreadfully dull as it was, I was paid.

But not enough. I wasn't making ends meet. If I wanted to go out in the evening with some of my girlfriends from the shop, I had to choose between ordering espresso or going to the movies and taking the streetcar home. I couldn't afford both. Usually, to avoid the appearance of desperation, I would order the espresso and walk the hour home from downtown. I wasn't starving, but when my mother sent me packages of homemade pastry wrapped in brown paper I would rip open the bag and devour all the strudel at once. My usual diet consisted of muffins and bread, which were affordable, but no meat. I began to gain weight. My mother noticed this when I made my monthly visits back home, but I could never admit to her how unhappy I was and how much I wished I had never left home.

At least back at home I had been able to look forward to life after school. That gave me courage and something to shoot for. But now, in Vienna, I felt despair. What was there to look forward to? Was this all life could offer?

I was so unhappy with my lot that I began to look at newspaper advertisements where men were looking for devoted wives. I responded to one of the ads (why not? he said he had an apartment!) and found to my chagrin that I would have to go through an agency and pay a fee of twenty dollars for the referral to the man. At the time, I was earning only twenty-five dollars net per month, so I couldn't afford it.

Oh, what dreary memories I have of those days! I was so unhappy. My room was depressing and so tiny that I couldn't even fit an easy chair into it. It was icy cold and miserable in winter. I was making so little money that most entertainments, such as the famous Vienna opera and symphony, were beyond my reach. The only thing that made life bearable was the institution of the Vienna coffeehouse. For the price of an espresso I could sit all afternoon on weekends and read the newspapers and magazines of the day (which I could never afford to buy).

Deliverance from the gloom of Vienna life came only on Wednesdays, when the son of a friend of my grandmother's, Karl Böhm, and his wife, Lisl, invited me to stay for the evening and then spend the night. They welcomed me as a constant guest in their home. Karl was an engineer and they lived comfortably, if humbly, in a small apartment. They had no children of their own and they more or less adopted me and looked after me. I always gorged myself on food and enjoyed my weekly bath. It was luxurious. Hot running water and clean white tile. Lisl would scrub my back for me and wash my hair. She became my substitute mother, sometimes sewing dresses for me and deciding when the day had come to get my pigtails cut off. With a short, fashionably shaped blunt haircut, I suddenly looked more like a young woman and less like a girl.

That was not, as it turned out, an unmixed blessing. At the pipe company, my immediate supervisor was making advances toward me, and they were not subtle passes. He threatened me with force. I was repelled and frightened. But when I spoke to some of the other girls in my department, I discovered that they had had similar experiences and that this was a pattern with him. At that point, I went to the boss in the front office to complain. I explained what was happening to me and what had happened to the other girls. He looked up at me and said, "Well, are you still a virgin?"

This was long before the feminist movement and it was inconceivable at that time to tell him that his question was totally inappropriate. But I did press the issue about my superior, asking that something be done to stop him. But the boss was unmoved. He told me bluntly that while it was too bad he was harassing the girls, "he's more important to the company than you."

As it turned out, through sheer stubbornness and persistence I was able to fend him off. I was determined not to be a victim—at least, not again. I had still not recovered emotionally from a teenage experience.

Back in my early teens, my mother had sent me to stay with my paternal grandmother one summer in Klagenfurt, a town near the Yugoslavian border. It was a nice change of scene for me. But it led to one of the most traumatic experiences of my youth. Near the town was a lovely lake surrounded by fir trees and flowers. It was secluded, the perfect place to swim. I had no companions that summer and was just out one day swimming by myself when I saw a young man, a little older than I was, on the shore of the lake. He said hello. I said hello back.

At the time I was incredibly naïve. The convent school experience had made me quite shy and withdrawn. I was still a complete child emotionally. In fact, I was literally still playing with dolls. While I no longer believed in the stork, I had only the vaguest notion (which I didn't dare to think through) of how babies wound up in women's bellies. When I asked my mother once, she replied, "When you're old enough you'll know."

After the boy and I said hello, we began to play ball and horse around. This alone was more of a thrill than I'd ever had before! Then he offered to walk me home. The path led through a patch of woods. When we had gone a little way into the forest, he suddenly (in my young eyes) turned into a monster. He pulled me off the path and into the bushes and began trying to kiss me and fondle my body. I was beside myself. When he pulled his pants down, I was disgusted at the sight and had no idea what he was trying to do. I struggled as if my life depended on it. Somehow I succeeded in breaking free. I ran as fast as my trembling legs would carry me to my grandmother's home and rushed to my room. I must have cried all afternoon.

Perhaps if there had been someone to talk to, I would have recovered from that experience more easily. But there was no one. In a way, that marked the beginning of a very difficult teenage period. I felt like two people. On the one hand, I was quite mature and capable of earning my own living at the age of sixteen. Yet emotionally I was thwarted. I'm certain that the effects of that split surfaced again and again throughout my life.

———

I don't know if my experiences were typical of a young defenseless girl in the big city or if there was something different about me or about Vienna. With hindsight, I'd have to say that it was both. I was much too willing to take foolish risks as a teenager—going off to a big city without any money—but Vienna was no city to be defenseless in either. It was still traumatized after the war and occupation. The moral fiber of the country had eroded to a frightening extent. I believe that general breakdown of morality was why I had the experiences I did, and why I found myself dating a small-time hood at seventeen. (I didn't know it when I met him, of course.) I had an innate sense of right and wrong. Well, perhaps it wasn't innate, it may have come also from my mother. But in any case, my views about morality, honesty, and fairness were not widely shared by the people I met.

I was constantly lending friends money and not being paid back. One girl whom I had befriended was engaged to a young law student. I couldn't believe my ears when she told me that he had been convicted of gang-raping a girl he and some friends had met at a bar. She married him anyway.

Vienna, once a princely city, was turning into a raw place for me. I was eighteen, overwhelmed by my experiences, and frightened. I just wanted to leave!

———

But where to turn? I just couldn't face going back home with my tail between my legs. Pepi was my only hope. He had received his degree and was working for the Siemens Corporation in Erlangen, Germany. I called him and asked if I could come. He must have been amused at his tag-along little sister. But he didn't show it. I must have sounded sufficiently desperate on the phone for him to take my situation seriously. He said, "Of course you can come."

I was so thrilled to be getting out of Vienna that I just packed up my belongings, bought a train ticket, and headed north. Once again, Pepi greeted me at the station. This time, he did have room to put me up, but not much. He was subletting a room in someone else's apartment, and the landlady made it quite clear that she did not want me there. I'm sure she didn't believe that I was Pepi's sister.

Erlangen was also the site of an American army base. After poking around looking for work, I was able to find a position as a maid for an American captain and his family. The personnel were housed in the American compound just outside the base. It consisted of a cluster of modern apartment buildings. Everything was clean and new.

I moved in with them, and for the first time in my life I didn't have to worry about getting enough to eat, I had hot and cold running water, and I even started to enjoy myself and have some fun.

Captain Arnold and his wife were completely kind to me. They spoke some German, and contrary to my fears, didn't mind at all that my English was so halting. I had no worries that Captain Arnold would make a pass at me. He was a gentleman. In fact, the amazing thing to me was that all of the Americans I met on the base seemed to be exactly the way I had imagined Americans to be during my early teens when I used to moon over movie magazines. Everyone was unbelievably friendly and polite. The hard edge that I'd seen so much of in my own country didn't seem to afflict Americans at all. I drank in their friendship with gratitude.

Since my brother lived close by, we often had dinner together. I also began to socialize with some of the American soldiers at the Prinz Heinrich tavern. Lots of the girls who worked in the American compound gathered there after hours. It was considered perfectly respectable. And so I did.

One night I met a very handsome, intelligent young American soldier named Byron Leeds. I gazed at him from across the room and giggled with my girlfriends about how handsome he was. Soon we had turned our attention to other matters and were watching a couple in a booth toward the back who seemed to be falling in love. We speculated as to whether he'd take her to America if they got married. Suddenly, I felt a tap on my shoulder. It was Byron asking me to dance. I was nonplussed. I stammered and finally said no.

It wasn't that I didn't like him, I told him later, after we had become close; it was just that I considered myself a terrible dancer and didn't want him to see me in a bad light. But at the time, his ego was hurt, and though I kept going back to the Prinz Heinrich in hopes that he'd ask me out, he didn't. Finally, after two weeks of unbearable tension, Emmy, the waitress, interceded. She told Byron that I liked him and he asked me out. I was ecstatic. After two weeks of waiting my initial interest had grown into a huge crush. Our first date was scheduled for my eighteenth birthday.

When the great evening arrived, my brother showed up at my door carrying a bottle of French cognac. The captain's wife was helping me dress. I must have tried on everything in my closet at least three times. Nothing seemed right. At last I settled on a pink dress with a wide skirt—very fashionable for the 1950s. If I had been a dancer it would have been a dress to do the jitterbug in. Some of my girlfriends who had been waiting with me throughout the previous two weeks stopped by to keep me company before the appointed time of Byron's arrival. We decided to try the cognac. I ceremoniously poured for everyone, feeling pretty and alive and full of hope. Before long we were all giggling and telling jokes. We decided to have another round of cognac. It was delicious. Those French sure knew how to make liquor. We had another round. The bottle was gone. When the room began to spin around me I knew that I was the stupidest girl in the world. By the time

Byron arrived I was in the bathroom being sick. Instead of getting angry or disgusted, when I finally emerged, my skin blotchy and my feet unsteady, Byron kissed me tenderly on the forehead and told me to go to bed. At that moment, I knew I was in love with him.

Our next dates followed in rapid succession. We wanted to be together all the time. Byron treated me with so much respect that I was almost taken aback. For the first time in my life I had dates like the ones I had seen in the movies. He picked me up and saw me home. We went to dinner and the movies—my favorite was *High Society* and the song "True Love" became ours. Byron indulged me in American junk food, which I loved, especially banana splits! No one outside my family had ever been so kind to me. Byron never raised his voice, never seemed peeved or impatient with me, and always treated my mistakes in English with a broad grin and a gentle correction. He tried to learn German from me too. But either I was a poor teacher or he was a poor student. Anyway, I learned more English than he did German.

Byron was six years older than I, and he seemed so much more worldly. He had read so many books. He used to tell me the stories of great novels he had read in college as we walked around Erlangen. He told me the story of *Anna Karenina,* and *Gone With the Wind,* and *A Tale of Two Cities.* I was falling more in love with each passing day.

Yet the fond hopes I nurtured about the future were not to be. When Byron's tour of duty was coming to an end, he took me out for a lovely dinner and explained that he loved me but he couldn't marry me. I was devastated. I couldn't stop the tears. He tried to make me understand.

He said it would hurt his family terribly if he married someone who wasn't Jewish.

He explained that it wasn't my religion (or lack of it) so much as it was his family's feelings that he was worried about. I tried to understand but it was difficult for me.

For one thing, as strange as it may seem, I was still quite ignorant at that point in my life about the Holocaust. In fact,

Byron was the first Jew I'd ever met. In grammar school, when we studied history, we never got up to modern times. I kept hoping that the following term would bring some information about the war and so on, but it never did. In my village, there were no Jews. The only people I knew who were dragged off or killed by the Nazis were Austrians of the Catholic faith.

I recall that after the war I did question my mother about Mauthausen, a camp just a few miles from our village. She said she had heard that "unspeakable things happened there." But she didn't say, and perhaps she never knew, that it was particularly for Jews. And among the other people of the village, no one discussed the Holocaust—not because they were avoiding the subject, but because, like most simple people, they were concerned with their own daily survival and were content to leave politics and other larger issues to others. Perhaps if they had more of an interest in politics, which affects everyone, history would not have taken such a tragic turn. The one and only time I had ever heard an anti-Semitic remark was from one of the other maids at Erlangen when she heard I was dating Byron. She said something like "Oh God, how can you? You'll spoil your blood!" But other than that, I was like a sleepwalker on the subject of prejudice.

So when the man I loved told me he couldn't marry me because he was Jewish, I was baffled and hurt. But there was nothing I could do.

It was over. We didn't see each other again. I knew when he was scheduled to fly out of Erlangen but I didn't see him off. It would have been too painful. For days I walked around like a zombie. All of the girls who had watched our romance blossom from the beginning were sympathetic but it was no use. I was so unhappy that I did what by then had become a pattern in my life. I decided I needed a change of scene.

I spent the summer in Sweden as an au pair. When I returned to Germany in the fall I didn't want to resume my old job with Captain Arnold; the house was filled with too many memories of Byron. But I still didn't have working papers for

German offices, so when Helga, a former maid in the American compound and a good friend, told me she had lined up a job at an insane asylum for good money, I agreed to sign up too.

They assigned me to work in the cafeteria making hash. The job wasn't exactly challenging but the money was more than I'd ever earned before, so at first I was content. But that contentment didn't last. The employees of the asylum had quarters in the same area as the patients. Only those who were considered dangerous to themselves or others were kept segregated. If I thought I was going to be able to get some peace of mind after the disappointment with Byron, I certainly picked a hell of a place to do it.

Imagine a young girl with a vivid imagination, after a long day in the kitchen, trying to drift off to sleep hearing the rantings of the mental patients! (This was before the days of antipsychotic drugs.) I felt as if I had wandered into an Emily Brontë novel. There was, of course, nothing to fear, but I lasted only a few weeks there. By the time I left I had huge dark rings under my eyes. I could handle being cold and hungry and poor. But handling my own imagination was much harder.

My working papers had finally come through and I was able to get a job in the bookkeeping department of a small stocking factory in Erlangen. My standard of living plummeted again. The pay was less than I'd been making at the asylum, so I could only afford to rent an attic room in a farmhouse on the outskirts of town. It was back to basics. No running water. No indoor bathroom. The toilet was an honest-to-goodness outhouse, standing by itself behind the *Misthaufen,* or dung heap. The shortest way to it was through the cow barn, and I can't count the number of times I stepped in, ahem, fertilizer on my way!

I kept a bucket of water in my room, but sometimes in winter the top would freeze and I'd have to break the ice with an ice pick in the morning to be able to wash my face. Fortunately, my brother was living in his own apartment then, so I showered at his place as often as I could. More depressing than anything else was the woman who rented a room below me with her two illegitimate children. She believed that one of the American fathers would be coming back any day to take them all to America. Not every American behaved as they did in the movies, I reflected ruefully.

After a few months, I had gotten over Byron for the most part and decided to start going out again. I went back to the Prinz Heinrich and met lots of new people, some German and some American. I liked a young American named Charles McDonald very much. When I was with him I could almost forget about Byron—though not completely. He was an orphan and had also been poor, but nonetheless had gone to college (something I respected very much since my formal education was so limited). After a few months I realized that we were seeing quite a bit of each other. I wasn't really concentrating. I seemed to be on autopilot. When we had known each other about a year, Charles proposed and I accepted.

Why not? I was almost twenty. I wanted change badly. Europe, while it had rebounded from the war to some extent, was still suffering. In the United States at that time, mothers were telling their children to clear their plates because there were "starving children in Europe." That was in some cases literally true (though the Marshall Plan helped tremendously). My horizons in Austria or Germany seemed so constricted. Charles was a sweet-tempered man and I liked him very much. I wasn't mature enough to consider that I was making a serious and hopefully lifelong commitment. I didn't want to say no.

We were married in the chapel at the army base. Afterward, there was a party for us at the Prinz Heinrich. We managed, on a shoestring, to go to Paris for our honeymoon.

Since Charles's tour of duty would be finished in a few months, I remained living where I had been and he stayed on the base. He then flew to the States ahead of me to look for a job and a place to live. We thought that would smooth the transition and also give me a chance to say goodbye to my mother. I would follow by boat three months later.

My mother cried, but I told her I was happy and so she managed a smile. She wrapped some things she was sure I'd never be able to get in America: warm stockings, a good pair of sewing scissors, and delicious Austrian strudel. She was right about the strudel.

I made my way to Amsterdam by train. I'd seen so little of Europe that I spent the entire train ride with my face pressed against the glass. Charles had given me enough money to handle all necessary expenses, so I was able to sit back and enjoy the adventure. The boat was not the *Queen Elizabeth,* nor the accommodations first class, but it didn't matter. I felt like a million dollars in my windowless dorm room on the lowest deck. The Atlantic crossing can be difficult in the autumn, but we were lucky with the weather. Only one day was really choppy. But I had no symptoms of seasickness. I think I was probably too delirious already dreaming about America. My fantasy to go and live in the country where my childhood dolls had always played was coming true. My bitter prediction to my teacher in secretarial school that I'd never get a chance to use my English was proving false. I was as excited as the millions of immigrants who had made the trip before me when I saw the Statue of Liberty welcoming us to New York Harbor. Seeing the New York skyline for real was more awe-inspiring than any picture.

When Charles greeted me at the pier I was agog. I asked if we'd have time to see the sights in New York but he said that wouldn't be possible. His job, as a salesman for a printing company, required that we get on a bus immediately for Detroit. I was disappointed. But I figured there'd be lots of opportunities to come back to New York. After all, I was now an American and all things were possible.

THE NEW WORLD: AMERICA, HERE I COME

I HADN'T QUITE BARGAINED ON DETROIT. CHARLES had rented a furnished apartment for us in a lower-middle-class neighborhood on the outskirts of town. There were no rolling green lawns such as I'd seen in the movies, and certainly no dazzling night life. Since Detroit was the world capital of car production, there was little public transportation and I felt stranded. The only way for me to get around was on foot and everything was so spread out that I couldn't get far that way.

Charles was in a car pool which picked him up every day at seven-thirty and returned him home around five-thirty. Other than household duties, I had nothing to do, and no one to talk to. My English was still quite limited and my Austrian accent was very strong, so it was difficult to make friends. When we socialized with Charles's friends, I might as well have been from Mars as from Austria. They didn't talk much. Not just to me. They scarcely talked to each other. Their idea of fun was gathering around the television set eating potato chips and watching sports.

I tried to focus on the good things. Charles was kind to me. I now had all the amenities I had pined for so long: a modern bathroom, a kitchen, central heating, but it wasn't enough. No matter how long you want something, it's amazing how quickly you take it for granted once you have it.

I realized that I had never really gotten to know Charles before we married. I'd never asked him about his aspirations for the future, his hopes or dreams. Now I was discovering that, unlike most Americans who strive to rise above the level they were born at, Charles had little ambition. He didn't want to own his own house. He didn't want a career, just a job. He didn't want children. It was as if his life was in suspended animation.

I reverted back to what was familiar. I decided to look for a job despite my poor English. I thought my best bet would be a job as a typist—even if I couldn't recognize the meaning of the words, I could still type what others had written. After several job interviews—which required a full day's journey by bus—I landed a job at the Hartford Steam Boiler Insurance and Inspection Company. I must have a talent for getting the worst jobs.

The pay was dreadful and the working atmosphere worse. We typists all sat in rows, typing out policies. We were required to sit with our backs ramrod straight. Talking was not permitted except during a ten-minute break in the morning and another in the afternoon. For reasons which I cannot to this day fathom, they didn't permit erasures on insurance policies, so if we made one mistake, we had to start over. I never absorbed anything I was typing. Even if my life depended upon it, I could not say what a steam boiler is.

But I was used to dreadful jobs and I didn't see any alternatives. Eventually, I was moved up to the status of underwriter (though with only a very small raise). It wasn't easy work. I had to assemble the actual insurance policy that the salesman had sold and give it to the typist to type. After it was typed I had to find all of the fee schedules and paste the proper fees next to the level of insurance purchased. Next I had to total up what the premiums would be. Frequently that was complicated. The insurance policy for General Motors, for example, was several inches thick. It was the kind of thing that could make a saint pull out his hair: complicated and boring. If it hadn't been for some lovely people who worked there, notably Evelyn Savickas, who became a lifelong friend, I'd have gone crazier than those patients in the asylum in Germany.

Life with Charles was uncomplicated but also boring. When I got home in the evenings we found little to talk about. He would read or watch television. I went grocery shopping and cooked and cleaned—the standard housewife. The only time we ever seemed intimate was in bed—but that was misleading. There was no deeper relationship upon which the sexual interaction was based and so ultimately it too was an empty gesture. The one bright spot was Charles's sister Marie and her three children. The youngest, Lynn, was born after my arrival in the family and they made me the proud godmother. Charles was good with the children also and our weekends with them were the only times I really felt that we were a family.

But day to day my natural curiosity had no outlets and my gregariousness was stifled. Detroit came to seem like a prison. But I wasn't ready to accept failure yet. Especially not when my mother was coming to visit me. It was now 1963. I decided to focus on the things I thought would impress her the most: all of my creature comforts. I arranged to get five afternoons off from work for the week of her visit, and, trying out my new driving skills on our new turquoise Ford, decided to show her the sights of Detroit and its environs. It was an incredible feeling to be taking my mother around America. I got a new infusion of enthusiasm. I resolved that we both needed to see more than the Detroit area, so I asked for more time off from work (I was pushing my luck but I think part of me wanted to get fired) and took off for Chicago. From there we traveled by train to Niagara Falls and then down to New York City.

For the first time in the almost four years I'd been in America, I stood on top of the Empire State Building. I put my arm around my mother and gazed at the modern wonders man had created on that spectacular island called Manhattan and something inside me burst free. I knew I would never be happy with the limited life and shut-in world with Charles McDonald.

My mother and I parted tearfully at the pier. I didn't tell her how her visit had changed my outlook. I just hugged her close and promised to write as all daughters do. Somehow, even though my mother was a simple person, there was something about our relationship which made me always want to do better to make her proud of me.

When I returned to Detroit, my perspective had changed. I was looking for ways to expand my horizons and I found them through a neighbor of ours named Marvin Lowe.

We had moved into a new apartment complex which had a swimming pool and children's playground. I met Marvin one afternoon by the pool. We became fast friends. His life story fascinated me, because it seemed so much the opposite of my own.

Marvin was born into wealth and privilege. His family owned a chain of movie theaters. But he was also gifted with intelligence. He had earned a law degree with honors and was a member of Mensa, a society for people with high IQs (which, at the time, impressed me very much). But Marvin's life was not all smooth sailing. The family business had been extremely successful in its heyday, but when television came on the scene they underestimated its appeal, failed to react to the changing times, and wound up losing everything. When I met Marvin in 1961 he had just moved from Chicago to Detroit, where he had gotten involved in television programming. Though he was no longer wealthy, as evidenced by the fact that he was living in the same apartment complex as Charles and I, he had an elegant bearing, and more sophistication than anyone I had ever known before.

We spent hours talking—first just the two of us; later, his

gentle wife, Sylva, joined in when she had the time. No subject was off-limits. We discussed religion, politics, marriage, jobs, and even sex. No one I admired so much had ever spoken to me this way before. It was like finding a father at age twenty-four. The first time Marv told me that I was too intelligent and talented to waste away at the Hartford Steam Boiler Insurance and Inspection Company, I thought he was joking. No one had ever told me I was smart.

But Marv was not joking and soon I began to reevaluate my self-image. With constant encouragement from Marv, I started to question things I had always taken for granted. I had no real ambitions for a career—not because I didn't want one but because I really didn't grasp that one was possible. Marv helped me to understand that in the United States people judge you by what you prove you can do more than by birth or social status. He also explained that there were lots of ladders up. "Why don't you go to school?" he asked me.

My memories of school were so dismal—that gray, cold, uninspiring secretarial school in Austria was my most recent memory—that I didn't jump at the opportunity. But it began to percolate in the back of my mind.

The other great challenge Marv laid before me concerned my marriage. It was pretty clear that he thought I had made a mistake marrying Charles. We discussed it. "Are you happy with him?" he asked one day by the pool. My eyes filled with tears. I couldn't speak. I just shrugged my shoulders.

"There is divorce, you know."

I protested that marriage was forever. But Marv gently suggested that if there were no children involved, divorce could sometimes prevent two lives from being needlessly wasted. It was frightening yet exciting to hear someone say that. Freedom from the dry and empty life with Charles suddenly loomed as a possibility instead of just something I dreamed about.

I was bitterly disappointed when Marv and Sylva were transferred back to Chicago. It was as if someone were pulling a black curtain down on the only window in my dark little cell.

They promised to write but I assumed that was mere politeness and never expected to see them again.

I was wrong. They wrote at least once a week from the very first. Some days on my way home from work I would run from the bus stop to the mailbox. I didn't want Charles to see the letters first. I would read them in the bathroom. They all made the same point in varying ways: Marv wanted me to move to Chicago, find a job, and build a new life for myself. He didn't have to twist my arm. I was aching for a challenge.

When I told Charles that I needed a change of scene and was going to Chicago, he didn't seem to mind at all. There was no talk of divorce. He seemed to take my words at face value. So we parted on friendly terms.

I packed two suitcases and got on a bus going west. The parallel to my similar flight from Vienna to Erlangen was obvious. I suppose I've always been a bit of a nomad at heart. Charles and I didn't speak again for two years. We exchanged Christmas cards and occasional letters about tax documents which had to be jointly signed but that was it. At the end of two years, I called to say that I had decided to remain in Chicago and thought we ought to get divorced. "Okay," he said, as if I'd suggested that we order out for pizza. He invited me to come back to Detroit to pick up my remaining belongings but I never took him up on it. I just couldn't bear to see that apartment again under any circumstances.

As usual when arriving in a new city, the first priority was to find a place to stay. Marv and Sylva lived in the Near North, a section with well-maintained brownstones, a few high rises, and tree-lined streets along Lake Michigan. It was well beyond my price range, but as Marvin pointed out the various sights, I allowed myself to fantasize about what it would be like not to have to scrimp and save every penny. After a morning of tourism, Marv suggested that we stop for lunch at his tennis club, which was managed by a friend of his. I readily agreed—it would be a chance to extend the fantasy I was enjoying. I'd imagine myself as a wealthy socialite with a club of my own.

Lunch was served on a white tablecloth. Each table was adorned by a large orchid in the center. As we ate, Marv introduced me to the club's manager as "one of my bright, rising stars." He told the manager I was looking for an apartment. The manager raised his eyebrows. "Oh, really? Are you neat?" I was a little shocked by his familiarity, but I answered that yes, I was neat. "And responsible?" I nodded, smiling. "And can you water plants?" I was getting puzzled. "Great," he announced, "I've got a free apartment for you."

A husband and wife who were club members (she was a former Wimbledon player named Mary Hare) had gone to England for an extended stay and had prevailed upon the poor manager to water their plants during their absence. He was only too glad to be relieved of his chore—and in return I got a free place to live.

Their apartment was in the Near North section. It was the most elegant place I'd ever lived in: high ceilings, polished wood floors, and a huge kitchen. I started work at the Chicago branch of the Hartford Steam Boiler Insurance and Inspection Company right away, and spent most evenings with the Lowes just a few blocks away. The fantasy didn't last long, though.

One night, as I was getting ready for bed, I heard footsteps in the hall outside my bedroom. Every childhood fear of midnight knocks on the door came flooding back to me. In my panic I reached for the first thing I found (which was a hairbrush) and stood frozen in the middle of the room, hairbrush poised in the air, waiting. The steps came closer. The door swung open slowly. A nicely dressed man with a shocked expression on his face said, "What the hell are you doing in my house?" It was the rightful tenant. He had seen a light on in the apartment and left his wife in the car outside while he came up to confront the "burglar."

We sorted things out. It was wrong of the tennis club manager not to tell them that I'd be there when they returned. Once all the appropriate phone calls had been made and explanations delivered, we settled down for a much-needed glass of wine. They were very sweet. In fact, they offered to let me stay until I found a place of my own. I told them I'd already imposed on them too much. But they insisted that there was plenty of room, and I did stay another week or so.

I found a room in a residential hotel nearby. It reminded me of the efficiencies I'd seen in so many Hollywood comedies. There was a Murphy bed (the kind that folds into the wall), a toilet in a closet, a sink, a hot plate, and one window. It wasn't the luxurious section of the Near North but it wasn't grim either.

The job at the boiler company was, though. Basically, I was still doing underwriting, as I had in Detroit. It was as numbing as ever. Marv came to the rescue again. He kept assuring me that I was ready for something better. He boosted my confidence every day. "You should be looking for a secretarial position," he urged. I wanted to move up to being a secretary, but my English still embarrassed me. Marv dismissed my misgivings and insisted that my English was fine—better than that of many native speakers. I accepted the compliment but pointed out that I frequently missed words people used in conversation and figured out what they meant by the context. "Okay," said Marv. "If you're taking dictation and you don't recognize a word, write it down phonetically and look it up later."

It sounded logical. I did it. In fact, I do it to this day. What phonetic spelling can't solve, however, are idiomatic expressions. Years later, in California, Mike Deaver gave me directions to his house. He said, "Make a right at the light and then take a dogleg." I had no idea what he was talking about but figured it would be clear when I got there. When someone else in the office needed directions to Mike's that same afternoon, I volunteered to explain. "You go to the light," make a right, and then you take a fire hydrant."

Marv finally persuaded me to come for an interview at a firm in his office building on North Michigan Avenue, right next to the Wrigley Building. The associate director of the American Medical Political Action Committee (AMPAC), Lee

Ann Elliott, needed a secretary. I was a wreck on the day of the interview. My boss at the Hartford Boiler Company had looked very severe when I asked for some time off in the middle of the day. I had never missed work before for any reason and I think he guessed that I must have a job interview. I was somewhat worried that I wouldn't get the job at AMPAC and then I'd get fired from the boiler company for having the temerity to ask for time off.

I had been too nervous to eat that morning, so by the time of the interview at 3 P.M. my stomach was grumbling so loudly I was convinced others would hear it and I'd make a fool of myself. As I waited in the reception area I noticed a drinking fountain. I hoped that the water would silence my unruly stomach, so I kept drinking and drinking. The receptionist smiled at me kindly but quizzically. I looked around. The office was carpeted, quiet, and well furnished. I had never worked in such comfortable surroundings.

At last, Lee Ann Elliott came out to greet me. We shook hands and I followed her back to her office. By this time all the water I had been drinking in the reception area had followed its normal course through the body and I was now in increasingly urgent need of a rest room. But I didn't ask. I was too nervous. I don't remember anything that was said in the interview. It didn't take long, perhaps fifteen minutes. Lee Ann told me later that she hired me over more qualified candidates because I seemed like the kind of person who would stay until midnight if a job needed doing. "Your eagerness served you well," she said.

I gave the Hartford Steam Boiler Insurance and Inspection Company three weeks' notice, but they were willing to let me go sooner. I was thrilled to be getting out of there and wound up finishing out the week and saying goodbye. That was the last time in my life I ever worked a job I hated. I was twenty-five years old and I had begun to carve out a niche for myself in the world instead of letting the world control me. It was one of the most important steps in my professional career.

AMPAC was a whole new world. It was like moving from

one culture to another. People were friendly and open. There wasn't the omnipresent feeling of suspicion that had been so much a part of my former working environment. I no longer felt that someone was always looking over my shoulder. I discovered the great American institution of the lunch hour. Until then, I had always had to eat at my desk or had gotten only a half hour for lunch. The other secretaries were incredibly friendly and introduced me to lots of customs and mores which I had not yet discovered about my new country. I remember one day when we were talking about Illinois politics and someone mentioned the name of a candidate who was from an aristocratic family. "Political death in Chicago," they all agreed. I was intrigued. They filled me in on how much American politics is still infused by the "humble origins" mystique.

They also explained the role of women, which was far more enlightened than what I had known in Austria. The secretaries were quite surprised when I told them that my brother had gone to the University of Vienna whereas my doing so was never even discussed. It wasn't that American women were treated exactly like American men, but I did think they had a much healthier self-image than the women I had grown up with who hoped to marry the local florist.

Now that I was moving ahead professionally, I was more inclined to look about me and appreciate my surroundings. Chicago is a beautiful city—though the cold took some getting used to; I would wear three layers of clothes in the winter. I began to go out regularly and indulge a playful side of myself which I hadn't been aware of before. After work most evenings, a bunch of us from the office would go out for drinks. We swapped stories. I told them about my childhood in Austria and they would look shocked. They couldn't believe the kind of suffering that had become routine in my home country. And then they'd tell me stories about their lives: relations with their parents, current boyfriends and husbands, vacation trips. I saw that the kind of life they were leading wasn't beyond my reach.

———

Marv was still a constant ally and friend. He would pop his head into the office on occasion to say hi. And on weekends, he and Sylva would often have me over for dinner or drinks. I was bursting with excitement about my new job.

"How's your English problem?" Marv asked teasingly.

"It good," I said, laughing.

But then I told Marv about a persistent feeling of insecurity that did truly bother me. Education. Marv said just one word: "Northwestern." Within a week I had enrolled in evening and weekend classes at Northwestern's campus in downtown Chicago. I focused on English, one course in grammar and another in writing, but I also took courses in American history, literature, and even in algebra. I went on a self-improvement binge. People laughed at the dogged, Germanic way I went about it. But I didn't mind. It was what came naturally.

First I discovered real books. I had always loved to read, but I had been wasting time with trashy novels. Now I began to dig into biographies: Churchill, Disraeli, Elizabeth I, Lincoln, Napoleon. By this time, I had developed a warm, long-distance relationship with my brother Pepi and he helped me make selections. I read voraciously, skipping around centuries and topics as I chose. "What era are we in this week?" my boss, Lee Ann Elliott, would ask as she passed my desk and glanced over the stack of books I had borrowed from the library.

The self-improvement regimen wasn't just intellectual. I also enrolled in sports classes to learn to ski and play tennis. I had all of my activities set out on a calendar. I still have it. It shows that I played tennis from seven to eight in the morning, worked from nine to five, studied for my classes from five to seven, and attended classes in the evening. I even had my weekly night with the women from work penciled in for Tuesdays. Years later, at a party, my girlfriends from that time—Carol Kazanjian and Shirley Shoup—did a skit on my structured life in Chicago. I must admit, it was pretty hilarious.

That rigidity may have helped me accomplish a lot in my Chicago days—though it didn't always stand me in good stead. Years later, when I was in Sacramento (and still clinging to the same regimented lifestyle), I met and got a huge crush on Pete Wilson, who was then a California assemblyman and an eligible bachelor (he is now a United States senator). After months of daydreaming about him I managed to wangle an invitation to a reception I knew he was going to. We hit it off immediately and he asked me to join him for dinner afterward. I was delighted. But after one drink, I remembered that my regimen required me to go home and do my laundry. And I left. I was sure he'd understand. He didn't, of course. And that was the beginning of the end of Helene the automator.

During my years in Chicago, my love for America really blossomed. I suppose back when I was a teenager in Austria reading American movie magazines, I had had a crush on the United States. But in Chicago that crush grew into real love. I wasn't at all interested in politics, but I did appreciate the amazing openness of American society. I never expected, with so little formal education and no connections, to be able to do better than the Hartford Steam Boiler Insurance and Inspection Company. I certainly never expected to be able to work in so refined a place as the American Medical Association PAC.

After I had been with AMPAC for about eleven months, I approached Lee Ann Elliott and told her I was going to apply for United States citizenship and wanted her to sponsor me. She said she'd be honored. It turned out to be more complicated than I expected. There was a written test which required a knowledge of all the U.S. Presidents and when they'd served, all the states in the Union, the Bill of Rights, and the Preamble to the Constitution. The other secretaries saw me studying during lunch hours and commented that none of them could pass the test. They got American citizenship as a birthright, I reflected, and therefore they take it for granted. For me, it was worth ten times as much effort as I was putting into it. I would have memorized all the emperors of Rome and all their mistresses if that had been required. I desperately wanted to be able to call myself an American.

When the day came for my swearing-in, I invited several friends from work and Marvin and Sylva to attend the ceremony. It was held at a Chicago courthouse. With me among the new citizens were about fifty other people from everywhere from India to Mexico to the Philippines. We all recited the pledge of allegiance together and also renounced all ties to other governments or "kings." I felt a thrill down my spine as the judge said, "Congratulations. Now register to vote."

I had never really thought much about politics—a fact which became glaringly obvious at AMPAC. Our mission was to lobby for private health care, but I didn't believe in it. Like most people, I simply assumed that the system I had grown up with was best. I never seriously considered alternatives. After twenty years in politics I must say that I think most people approach politics that way. They vote the way their parents voted or the way their college professors taught them. They never seriously consider that there may be a better way.

I made no secret of my views about medical care. I told Lee Ann Elliott that I believed in socialized medicine such as we had in Austria. She didn't try to talk me out of it but she did give me some books to read. AMPAC was then heavily involved in the Goldwater for President campaign. I read Goldwater's campaign book, *The Conscience of a Conservative,* and suddenly saw that I didn't know what I was talking about when I touted socialized medicine. Much of Goldwater's book was over my head—I wasn't at that stage politically sophisticated enough to understand everything he was saying, but it began something. After that, I had a context into which I could put the things I read in the newspapers and heard on radio and television.

I began to question which tasks should be handled by government and which by the private sector. Not surprisingly, the first area I decided was better left private was medicine.

About a year after the election, I was invited by Lee Ann to accompany her to a dinner sponsored by AMPAC. She said I might enjoy some of the speakers. It was my night for American history, we were just about to discuss the Battle of Antietam, but I decided to skip class and go to the dinner. Lee Ann said she thought I'd be particularly interested since one of the speakers had been a Hollywood actor and was now a rising star on the political horizon.

We sat near the head table, and I was fascinated to see a handsome, dark-haired man with twinkling blue eyes seated near the podium. I nudged Lee Ann. "He looks familiar. Who is he?"

"That's our speaker, the movie actor I mentioned to you," she replied. "His name is Ronald Reagan."

When he rose to speak, he dominated the room. I suppose it was partly his movie star aura which got people's attention, but it was much more than that. I've since met dozens of actors who have no stage presence off camera. They can walk into a room and be completely ignored. That was never the case with Ronald Reagan. When he was in a room he was always the center of attention. There is just a kind of magnetism about the man. But I wasn't feeling star-struck that evening. I was intent upon his speech. So much of what he was saying fit right into my stage of political development. He talked about the virtues of free enterprise and the dangers of intrusive government. I was just starting to understand how damaging government bureaucracies can be. Ronald Reagan quoted Thomas Jefferson: "That government is best which governs least." Yes, I thought. That is the ideal.

Mr. Reagan also went into a long and passionate description of totalitarianism. I was rapt. He was describing things I had lived with and seen with my own eyes. I had lived under two forms of totalitarianism: first Nazism and then Communism. I knew that when he described them as "assaults upon the human mind, the human body, and the human soul," he was absolutely right. It was all becoming extremely clear suddenly. Until that moment, I had thought that America was wonderful but had considered it more or less an accident of history. A nice accident, but still an accident. Now Ronald

Reagan was making me see that it was no accident. America was wonderful because it was founded on and lived by certain immutable principles.

At the speech's conclusion, I didn't rush up to Mr. Reagan like a groupie seeking an autograph, but I made a decision. I resolved then and there that I was going to work for that man and help him, should he ever seek political office.

I consulted with everyone I knew through AMPAC and at Northwestern about Ronald Reagan. I researched him at the library and came home with a file full of articles. Mr. Reagan had just come to national attention as a political figure when he made a famous speech on behalf of Barry Goldwater in the 1964 presidential campaign. He was now on the lecture circuit, but rumors abounded that he might be making a run for the Governor's office in California.

Did I really want to go out West? I was twenty-seven years old and I was going to turn my life upside down for a man I'd only seen once and never met. It seemed like lunacy. But I had taken far greater risks in my short life. I thought it over carefully. I had enough confidence by now in my abilities, so I wasn't concerned that the campaign wouldn't hire me. I did consider, however, what would happen to me if the campaign collapsed after a little while and left me without a job. What would I do then?

My fallback position would be to go to the Sierras and become a skibum for a winter—something I'd fantasized about ever since I'd learned to ski. I figured I could always wait tables if it came to that. Just to practice my skills, I got two waitressing jobs in Chicago at two very different restaurants so that I'd have some experience to claim when I reached California. One was a short-order place, a coffee shop, the kind you used to find in every city before the explosion of McDonald's and Burger King. The other was the London House, one of the city's finest restaurants, where I worked weekends. I had figured out other aspects of the risk I was taking as well. Where would I live? I didn't know a soul in California except for John Galvin, a young engineer I had dated in Chicago before he took a job out West. No problem. I'd live in cheap residential hotels. It wouldn't be the first time.

My job at the London House came to an abrupt end one day when I accidentally dumped an entire tray of cocktails into a patron's lap. I was fired on the spot. But I wasn't upset (except about the poor man's three-hundred-dollar suit). I was so tired from working two extra jobs and also trying to manage my principal job at AMPAC that I was relieved.

NEW HORIZONS: JOINING RONALD REAGAN

IN JANUARY 1966, I HEARD A RADIO REPORT THAT FOR-
mer movie star Ronald Reagan had announced his intention to
run for Governor. I gave two weeks' notice, and started studying California road maps.

First I had to find out where the Reagan for Governor
headquarters was located. I spent a fortune in long-distance
calls finding out that there were two headquarters: one in Los
Angeles and one in San Francisco. I knew that one couldn't
survive in L.A. without a car, so I plumped for San Francisco.

Since all of my belongings fit into two suitcases, I decided
to waste no time and I flew to San Francisco. When I arrived, I
was feeling flush enough to take a cab to a residential hotel on
Bush Street, close to the campaign headquarters. The man at
the desk asked me if I wanted to share a room with others (the
cheapest way) or rent a room for myself alone. "Alone," I
declared. I was on the brink of a great adventure—making

Ronald Reagan the next Governor of the state—this was no time for sharing rooms with strangers!

I got my key, dumped all of my baggage in the middle of the room, and made my way to the Reagan headquarters. There wasn't as much to it as I was expecting. There were only three or four people. They had one typewriter (that I could see) and only two telephones. I told them that I was ready to go to work. They looked over my résumé, handed it back to me, and said, "Sorry, we're not hiring right now."

I was devastated. It wasn't that I thought my credentials were so overwhelming that they'd be sure to hire me. I suppose it was that I was so taken with the romance of my own story I couldn't see that others might be less so. A young woman of twenty-seven comes halfway across a continent, with no friends or relatives in California, just out of devotion to Ronald Reagan . . . was that not an irresistible story? They managed to resist it.

I was mortified. What was I going to tell all of my friends in Chicago? I had told anyone who'd listen that I was going to work for Ronald Reagan. There was only one thing to do: keep trying. I figured I'd get some part-time work with Kelly Girls, which wouldn't require a commitment, and then I'd check back with the Reagan campaign every week.

There was only one problem. I was almost starving. Kelly Girls paid very low wages. I was forced to accept a roommate at the boardinghouse, and I was worried that I'd soon have to move into a foursome if things didn't improve.

Why was I willing to put up with all that? Why didn't I get huffy after the initial rejection and return to Chicago? There are many reasons. The first, I suppose, is that my life experience had not led me to expect acceptance. Being a poor girl with little education was still the self-image I carried with me, despite the college courses and other self-improvements I'd undertaken in Chicago. I therefore expected to have to prove myself every step of the way. I was hurt, naturally, when the Reagan campaign turned me down. But I didn't interpret that rejection as a commentary on me, Helene McDonald. It was only a rejection of a secretary with a strong Austrian accent who had shown up one morning looking for work. I'd have to show them what else I had to offer.

The second reason I persisted was that Ronald Reagan had come to symbolize everything I believed in. It was so much more than a job. His belief in America's special mission, to be, as he would later put it, "a light unto the nations," thrilled me. Moreover, he seemed to understand how unusual America's freedoms were. I thought then and still think that in a world which is governed mostly by despots of one stripe or another, an appreciation of freedom is crucial. And finally, his anti-Communism wasn't just a slogan to me. I had lived under Soviet occupation. I had seen the truth about Communism up close—that it's just another form of Nazism. The big difference was that the Communists weren't in such a hurry as Hitler had been, which meant that the democracies would have to stay vigilant for a much longer stretch of time. I believed in all of these things with my whole heart—and I wasn't going to let an initial rejection deter me.

I kept going back, and the weeks stretched into months. My money wasn't holding out. I began to scan the classified advertisements in the *San Francisco Chronicle.* I applied to TWA for a stewardess job (you had to know two languages and I figured I might as well play to my strengths), but they rejected me.

My luck changed in June. Ronald Reagan defeated San Francisco mayor George Christopher in the Republican primary and his campaign was gearing up for the general election.

I had been seeing the same woman each and every week when I came to inquire about jobs. When I came in after the primary she didn't smile, but she did tell me that a job had opened up, and though they'd gotten many applications, she held it for me, sure that I would be back on Friday as always. I was jubilant.

It was a typist position in the scheduling department. In the pre-word processor days, being a typist in scheduling meant doing schedules not once, not twice, but as many as twenty times until the day of the trip. It was the nature of the business; schedules were always changing.

It was exciting to be on the campaign at last. The people were very friendly, and though I didn't get nearly the amount of attention and solicitude I'd gotten at AMPAC, I was quite happy tapping on the keys of a Reagan typewriter. I worked hard, as always, and tried to learn as much as I could from the others about the mechanics of running a political campaign. Years later, when I was about to be named Ambassador to Austria, Tom Reed, who had served as Northern California Chairman for Reagan in 1966, told me that my evaluation form that year had described me as "hardworking but limited. No potential in politics." Tom and I roared. "Do you still have it?" I asked. "I'd love to frame it." But he said no, he'd been carrying it with him in his memory waiting for the right moment to tell me.

It's funny, but I can't remember election night 1966. I don't recall if there was a party or celebration of any kind. I suppose I was so intent on the future I simply wasn't focused on anything else. The day after the election, Tom Reed assembled everyone in his office, congratulated us all on a job well done, and mentioned that anyone interested in going on to the statehouse should leave a card in his box. I didn't need any further prompting. In fact, I probably would have camped out on the Governor's lawn in Sacramento if I hadn't been offered something. In the meantime, I was given a job on the transition staff. There were no guarantees, but I grabbed it.

During the transition I began to sense the tension between Tom Reed and Phil Battaglia, the Southern California Chairman. Both were vying for the job of Executive Secretary, the California equivalent of White House Chief of Staff. There were quite a few back-room maneuvers, but in the end Battaglia won out, and we northern Californians dropped down to second place. I was concerned that this might affect my chances of getting a job in the Governor's office.

Meanwhile, on the transition staff, I was no longer typing but sorting mail. The volume was tremendous. Hundreds of letters poured in, not just from California but from all over the country: congratulatory messages, unsolicited advice, job seekers. I sent the important ones on to my boss, Nita Wentner, and answered the rest myself with form letters. Once or twice I got into trouble for failing to recognize a familiar name, but that didn't cause too much fuss. I did, however, commit one whopper of a mistake. I glanced through a letter from a Californian which seemed to me to be complete nonsense. He was going on and on about some issue. I sent him a form response. It turned out that my correspondent was a Democratic state senator in Sacramento, and when he got my form letter he called a press conference and released it. This was a lot worse than dumping cocktails in someone's lap. I was sure they'd fire me, but to my surprise they were very kind about the whole thing and simply assigned someone to help me learn the names of important California politicos.

We waited impatiently to learn who Governor Reagan would appoint to key positions. One of the first appointments he announced was William P. Clark as Cabinet Secretary. He was a lawyer who had served as Ventura County chairman in the Reagan for Governor campaign. I had never met Clark during the campaign, but I had heard talk about him. He was rumored to be very smart, very conservative, and very demanding of those who worked for him. It was with special trepidation, therefore, that I threw my hat into the ring for a position as his personal secretary.

When Clark interviewed me, it was almost a reprise of the interview with Lee Ann Elliott. I was just as nervous, and just as weak on paper qualifications—after all, the only thing I knew about politics was what I'd been able to learn in five months during the campaign. But somehow Bill saw something in me he liked. Maybe it was my Austrian heritage. His wife came from Czechoslovakia. But I think it's more likely that he just saw me as an underdog, and like most Americans, Bill can't resist an underdog. I was hired. But not before he had made it clear that he expected complete loyalty and lots of hard work. I gave him both.

Clark's next choice struck me as just as odd as his choice of me. He picked as a deputy a man named Michael K. Deaver. Because he had worked for Governor Reagan's rival in the primary, George Christopher, it seemed a safe assumption that he shared Christopher's moderate views. Besides, his credentials weren't overwhelming either.

But I grew to like him immensely. We became fast friends and spent a lot of our free time together until he fell in love with Carolyn Judy and married her.

When I think back, Mike didn't seem to stand out any more than any other staffer back then. He worked hard, of course, and he was always alert to what his boss might need. He developed the skill so many staffers do: anticipating the needs or desires of his boss. It was caught comically in the character of Radar O'Reilly in the television show *M*A*S*H*. The truth was that though I was personally very fond of Mike, he had a great sense of humor and was a better storyteller than anyone I knew, I didn't see anything exceptional in him. I didn't appreciate that he had a kind of creativity that would one day make him President Reagan's image-maker. But I suppose we often underestimate people. My boss that year had said I had no potential for politics. So no one is clairvoyant.

My first apartment in Sacramento was a furnished one-bedroom on T Street, within walking distance of the Capitol, where the Governor's office was. I still didn't own a car. My starting salary was $450 per month. When Bill Clark raised me to $750 within the first year I was so shocked that I told him I didn't think I could accept it. But he dismissed this and said I'd earned it. He was right. Bill was an extremely demanding boss. He asked a lot and he gave a lot. The arrangement suited me perfectly.

Mike and I were both kept busy by Bill Clark. Only after I had worked with Mike for some time did I notice a certain fickleness on his part. He used to become infatuated with one staffer and then lose interest and move on to another. The first time I saw that pattern was in his treatment of Charles Tyson, Bill Clark's assistant. Charles was the son of a successful developer from San Diego. He was a young and handsome bachelor, more than a little spoiled, and still immature. Sometimes he would simply disappear for hours without a word to anyone and offer no explanations about his absence when he returned. After several such episodes, Bill became exasperated and threatened to fire him. But Mike defended him strenuously and insisted that he was vital. Bill relented. A few weeks later, Mike had found another staffer who he thought walked on water. He lost interest in Charles and even recommended that he be fired for no particular reason.

Mike and I both thought we had reached the pinnacle of our careers. We sometimes talked about what we would do next. I longed for a family. Mike wanted to open a fine kitchenware store in Santa Barbara. Even more than politics, Mike's passion was cooking.

Bill Clark proved to be a great boss. He had a way of making everyone who worked for him feel that they were more to him than just an employee. He made us part of his extended family. Mike Deaver, Charles Tyson, and I were frequent guests at his and Joan's home in Sacramento or at their sprawling ranch in San Luis Obispo County.

Bill was a fifth-generation Californian, and he was a Westerner through and through. One of his hobbies was collecting and restoring nineteenth-century buggies. His style of speech (slow and deliberate), his dress (cowboy hats and boots), even his walk (a slightly rolling gait), all seemed to be right out of central casting. And yet, with Bill, none of it was affected. He was truly at his most relaxed on horseback, and western ways of doing things, from cooking to investing, seemed to Bill the natural order of the universe.

Bill had just received his pilot's license and fancied himself something of a Red Baron. In time he purchased a little Cessna so that he could easily commute between points in San Luis Obispo County, which is quite large. Always a daredevil, he insisted on landing on the dirt road in the canyon leading to his home. One day, his wife, Joan, was watching through the kitchen window as Bill's plane came in for a landing, caught a crosswind just before touchdown, flipped upside down, and skidded to a halt on its roof. All five Clark children were aboard. Amazingly, no one was hurt, but Joan put her foot down after that. Bill was to fly alone in the future.

In his professional life, Bill was an extremely resourceful lawyer. Much has been made in the press about the fact that he didn't finish law school and only passed the bar on the second try. But I admired his canniness and cleverness. When he wasn't accepted at one of the major law firms, he hung out a shingle and made it on his own through sheer persistence, hard work, and intelligence.

Bill was also very much concerned with what went on in the wider world. Later, that fact would be important to the Reagan presidency.

I thought I had worked hard in the past, but Bill Clark gave new meaning to the term. Our office was on the ground floor of the Capitol, located in downtown Sacramento in the middle of a wonderful park. The Governor's offices were a bit shabby when we first moved in, but Mrs. Reagan set about redecorating right away. She got new carpets and spruced up the walls with some handsome prints.

Bill was a bit of a slave driver (I once threatened to buy him a whip when I had to stay until eleven o'clock two nights running). I answered the telephone, sorted the mail, took dictation, kept track of Bill's appointment calendar, made his travel reservations, and typed all of his work. Bill was responsible for Cabinet meetings, so he took me along to take notes. That was a window into the world of government that I would never have gotten any other way. I saw a great deal while my head was bowed over my notepad.

Bill wanted my notes to be verbatim. My shorthand was pretty good, but not good enough. Each week, he would call me into his office and tell me that the notes were too "fuzzy."

"I'll try harder," I promised. And I did, scribbling as furiously as I was able. But the following day he would still tell me they weren't good enough. I finally became so frustrated that I burst into tears and said, "You'll have to find a robot. I'm only human and can't possibly catch every single word." He never criticized my note taking again.

Though I disappointed Bill as a note taker, I was determined to make myself indispensable to him in every other way. I knew that this job, with its incredible excitement and importance, was the greatest thing that had ever happened to me. I was actually seeing the memos and sitting in at the meetings with the men (there weren't any women then) who were governing the largest state in the United States. My political education was proceeding very rapidly. I used my access to ask questions, especially of Bill, who was usually delighted to instruct me—if he wasn't in one of his sullen moods, which I also came to know well.

Other secretaries simply worked their hours, typed their letters, and never thought much about what they were doing. But I wanted to soak up every piece of information that came my way. I learned about how budgets are prepared and submitted, and about how the politics of the legislative branch affects the calculations of the Governor. On substance I heard the pros and cons on busing, abortion, school prayer, welfare, student loans, and even the proper role of the National Guard.

I also learned a lot in informal settings, particularly when Bill used to entertain on weekends at his ranch in San Luis Obispo County. There was no house there at the time, just an army tent that slept twelve. (Bill later built a house on the land with a special garage to house not just two cars but his Piper Super Cub as well. It was parked with a car under each wing.) We'd bring sleeping bags, steaks, potatoes, Gallo wine, and some heavy sweaters for the evening. I brought along my revolver and practiced target shooting. We'd barbecue the steaks and talk long into the night. The setting was so beautiful. When it got dark, the stars were so bright and numerous that it felt as if they were falling right out the brilliant sky. I still recall those weekends as among the happiest, most carefree times of my life.

During the week, I found myself keeping longer and longer hours. I didn't want Bill to be disappointed in me. For the first few months, I would bring my supper—usually a sandwich—in a brown bag. But after a while I realized that as Bill's secretary I had access to the endless number of statehouse receptions that always seemed to going on around 6 P.M. I started making it a habit to drop by and fill up on hors d'oeuvres. The food was a lot better than my homemade sandwiches.

I was so determined to make myself indispensable to my boss that I sometimes got myself into trouble. Bill not only restored old buggies, he also loved old cars. One of his favorites was a classic 1950s Porsche. It was a beautiful silver two-door that hugged the road and drew stares wherever he drove it. Anyway, just after Bill had had it completely restored I got the bright idea to pick him up at the airport in it. I pictured how surprised he'd be to see his shiny new car waiting to whisk him home. What I forgot to calculate is that driving has never been my strong suit.

I set out for the airport in the early morning. The day was overcast and foggy as only northern California can get in the autumn. The freeway was almost impenetrable, but I almost made it to the airport. At the last intersection before the off ramp a teenager suddenly pulled out of nowhere and crossed the freeway in front of me. We crashed. I remember screaming as the Porsche careened hopelessly into the boy's car. I seemed to be alive, and so was the driver of the other car. There were two very shaken boys, but no one was hurt. I then turned my attention to the Porsche. I nearly fainted. The entire front end of Bill's lovingly restored car was crushed beyond recognition. This time I cried a wail of true despair.

When the police came to tow the car I started explaining the whole thing to them and begged them to take me to the proper gate to pick up Bill. His plane would have landed by now, I remember thinking. The policeman looked at me and said, "Lady, I think you need to get to an emergency room." I reached up and felt that my head was bleeding. Good, I thought, at least maybe if Bill sees me like this he won't be able to show his anger over the car! I wasn't really badly hurt, but I wondered if I could arrange to be carried on a stretcher to the gate.

When Bill came off the plane I immediately told him about the car. He looked so stricken. But my ploy had worked. I looked worse and he just couldn't yell at me.

It turned out that I had more injuries than I felt at first: a broken knee and a head wound requiring ten stitches.

There was nothing I could do about the car, but I felt so guilty that I bought the shattered hulk of the Porsche from Bill and had to shop around for spare parts for months to make the thing run. I wound up combining the parts from that car with the parts from another Porsche. The two were welded together to form one car. Bill inscribed a picture of the repaired car afterward (much afterward!) with the words: "Congratulations on the first Porsche transplant." It was my very first car.

———

Bill Clark was a key man in Governor Reagan's office from the beginning. He decided how tasks would be staffed out. He decided on the agenda. And he helped the Governor to make all of the important decisions. They worked well together because Bill seemed to know instinctively what Ronald Reagan needed. He realized early on that you cannot bury him in paperwork. He hated bureaucratic writing and would quickly get bored and pick up a copy of *National Review* or *Time* instead. Understanding this pattern of Reagan's, Bill instituted the "mini-memo," a one-page summary of an issue with a requested decision box at the bottom of the page.

To those Cabinet members who complained that they couldn't adequately present an issue in one page, Bill would quote Mark Twain, who once wrote at the bottom of a letter to a friend, "Sorry it's so long. I didn't have the time to make it shorter." Governor Reagan appreciated the mini-memos. When he wanted more information, he asked for it when the memo came up for discussion in Cabinet meetings.

Clark also knew that Ronald Reagan thrived on the give-and-take of ideas. He therefore encouraged him to use Cabinet meetings as an opportunity to float ideas. I was always present taking notes and I remember how polite the Governor was in listening to each person's views. Sometimes he would express his own opinion, sometimes not. If the discussion became heated between Cabinet officers with differing views, he would always dispel the tension with a joke or a self-deprecating remark.

I was completely enthralled by Ronald Reagan. The man who had so stirred my emotions and my intellect with that speech back in Chicago was even more impressive in person. What struck me more than anything during those first few months was his commitment to principles, his deep-seated convictions, and his amazing lack of vanity. He was truly fascinated by ideas, but he was always ready to acknowledge when he was wrong. Nor would he attempt to find scapegoats for his own mistakes. Even then I remember thinking that he was a rarity among men with power—in fact, among men in general. He really lived up to the plaque on his desk, a gift from Barry Goldwater: "There's no limit to what a man can accomplish if he doesn't mind who gets the credit."

It was during those early years in the Reagan governorship that I made the friends who would remain close for the next twenty years.

One of my instant favorites on the Reagan team was press secretary Lyn Nofziger. The first time he heard my pronounced German accent he dubbed me "the Nazi," and teased me endlessly about it ever after. I didn't mind. Lyn was kind of a free spirit. It was unusual to find him in a sports jacket. A tie signified real formality. Alone among all of the staffers, he called Ronald Reagan "Ron" instead of "Governor" (a practice he maintained even after Ron became "Mr. President" to the rest of us). Lyn had a wonderfully wry yet playful sense of humor which served him well in his dealings with the press corps.

I didn't immediately form a friendship with Nancy Reynolds, Lyn's assistant—I didn't know quite what to make of her —but I admired her and eventually we became very good friends. Nancy's sense of humor was a match for Lyn's and I always had the feeling when I was around the two of them that I was at the center of everything. They were both so quick, so on top of news and gossip, that their office was like news and entertainment central for the Reagan Administration. When Lyn resigned after the first year, Nancy moved over to become Nancy Reagan's personal assistant—helping her answer mail, serving as informal press secretary and travel companion.

Nancy Reynolds had been born into politics. Her father had been a United States senator from Idaho. She had worked as a local television hostess and then as a homemaker in Boise. I admired her independent spirit. After her divorce, she moved with three young sons to San Francisco. Though she had little television experience, she relied on a combination of persistence and optimism to land a job as anchor of the six o'clock news on station KPIX.

Like me, she was converted into a Reaganite after just one meeting during the 1966 campaign (though, unlike mine, her meeting had been one on one). She joined the Administration when we moved to Sacramento. Nancy has always been one of the most generous people I've ever known. She was always ready to offer help when someone asked her—even if it was a stranger. I can't count the times I've heard her end phone conversations with "Okay, well, if there's anything else I can do to help, please don't hesitate to call." I knew she could be talking to anyone from a colleague to a high school girl working on a report. Nor was her generosity limited to giving of her time. While I am sure she would not want to be known as such, she truly was a hostess-with-the-mostest. Her parties were always gatherings of interesting new people, lively conversations, and lots of laughter.

I met Caspar (Cap) Weinberger too when he was named chairman of the so-called Little Hoover Commission, a group the Governor had charged with reorganizing the California state government. Cap had convened a meeting of the commis-

sion at the Sutter Club in Sacramento. He asked Bill Clark to
send someone to take notes, and Bill, overcoming his distaste
for my note-taking technique, sent me. When I arrived I introduced myself to Cap and he graciously introduced me to the
commission members. Cap was such a gentleman. He would
never dream of not introducing someone just because she was
a lowly secretary. But then we ran into unexpected difficulties.
The manager informed Cap in no uncertain terms that the
Sutter Club was for men only. "Oh, I see," Cap said. Then he
turned to the rest of us and announced loudly, "Sorry for the
inconvenience, but we'll have to go somewhere else." The
manager let us in.

Cap Weinberger was a rarity in public life. He truly
served his country rather than his own private aggrandize-
ment. Countless times during his long and successful career,
Cap gave up lucrative positions in the private sector to take
much-lower-paying government jobs. Once in a job, he threw
himself into the work with everything he had: intelligence,
tact, guts, conviction. But he never stooped to nest feathering
or backbiting. I believe Cap would have made a fine President
of the United States.

After that first meeting at the Sutter Club, we became
friendly. Cap took a personal interest in my development and
made it a point to invite me to meetings and lunches when he
could. When my brother came to visit me from Austria, Cap
invited us to dinner at his home in Hillsborough, a suburb of
San Francisco. His wife, Jane, was obviously devoted to him. I
was amazed by his personal library. I'd never seen such a vast
private collection of books in my life.

Cap was not, at that stage, a core member of the Reagan
team. He'd supported Nelson Rockefeller against Barry Goldwater in 1964 and San Francisco mayor George Christopher
against Ronald Reagan in the Republican gubernatorial primary in 1966. But after the Governor's first finance director
quit, Cap was asked to join the Administration. When he did,
he gave his full loyalty to Ronald Reagan and it remained
unwavering for the next twenty years.

For the first year of the Reagan term, Phil Battaglia served as Executive Secretary. Clark was more or less second to him.

So when Battaglia had to resign unexpectedly for personal reasons, the Governor naturally turned to Bill Clark for his successor. We packed up our things and moved to an office down the hall—directly across from the Governor's inner sanctum. My work underwent a change as well. I no longer took minutes at Cabinet meetings, which was a great loss since I had been able to learn so much by listening. Now, I had less exposure to issues.

On the other hand, Bill had more and more confidence in me to handle substantive matters. He expected me to draft the responses (in final form) to pretty much all of his mail. And they had to sound exactly the way they would if he had written them himself. I had to redo endless numbers of letters for that reason. It sometimes got demoralizing. But then Bill would pick me up with a compliment and I'd be okay again. On the other hand, I also had to put up with my share of "what do you think I'm paying you for?" questions.

Bill's new job also added substantially to his travel requirements. He had always been inclined to change travel plans on short notice but now he was even worse. It got to the point where I simply refused to pick up a ticket until he was literally on his way to the airport.

Bill remained in the post of Executive Secretary one year and a half. But as Ronald Reagan knew, his true ambition was to be a judge, and when an opening presented itself on the Superior Court, Governor Reagan appointed Bill.

At the time I was devastated to be losing my job with Bill Clark. But as my mother might have said to me when I was young, "When one door closes, another opens."

About the time Bill's appointment to the court was announced, news spread that Governor Reagan's secretary was pregnant. Speculation about her replacement buzzed through the statehouse. Her very young helper was being groomed as her replacement. But I had my suspicions that that might not work out. I could only hope.

Meanwhile, there was still a great deal to do to help Bill prepare to switch jobs. He kept me busy right up to the last minute. He had become so much more than just a boss to me. I valued Bill's advice more than anyone's. Where once I would have turned to Marvin Lowe when I needed advice, I now always turned to Bill. I suppose psychologists would say that I was in continuing need of a surrogate father figure. But if so, why not? I don't think there's anything wrong with loving and respecting someone in that way.

I recall those early years in Sacramento with special fondness. I was in my late twenties and was blossoming in so many ways. The rigid workaholic of Chicago days had given way to a better-rounded person. My social skills improved and I learned to appreciate my own abilities for the first time in my life.

Though I had lived for the first year in a humble furnished apartment, by the second year I was able to move into a new apartment complex complete with a swimming pool. I can remember every inch of it even today. It was only a studio, but a bright, sunny bachelorette pad with a full eat-in kitchen, a modern bathroom, a large living room which doubled as my bedroom, and even a little garden with a swing and a camellia bush. I bought a white wicker armchair and got into the habit of relaxing in the garden with a cocktail before dinner on the nights when I got home at a decent hour. It was such luxury.

One of my closest girlfriends during that period was Heide Kingsbury, a friend of the Clarks whose husband had died in Vietnam a few days before the end of his tour of duty. Heide had an interesting history. Her father had worked with Wernher von Braun to develop the V-1 rocket in Germany during World War II. He was one of the scientists the Americans had been so eager to snatch from the clutches of the Soviets after the war.

Heide and I shared a love for the outdoors and for adventure. We teamed up for skiing expeditions, hiking in the mountains, and white-water rafting. Every spring, we joined the Jeepers Jamboree, a jeep race sponsored by the California legislature. Hundreds of jeeps from across the country would meet in Georgetown in the gold country, where the first gold was discovered, and then hightail it over arduous terrain in the High Sierras until reaching a camp in Rubicon Springs. There were prizes for the winners. For the rest there was a huge barbecue cookout, volleyball, and endless war stories about broken axles, flat tires, and hair-raising turns. I often thought, on those bumpy escapades, of Bill Clark's poor Porsche.

Heide's house was on the Sacramento River and had a big backyard. Since we were both German (well, more or less), we used to throw Oktoberfest parties for our friends. We chose to do it in July so our friends could enjoy water sports as well. We served good beer, sausages, cheese, and thick, chewy bread. We played volleyball, and we sang. It was hilarious to listen to the Americans struggling with the German words. Such fun to tease them after the years of teasing I'd taken about my accent and my malapropisms with the English language.

I saw lots of men. I dated young lobbyists and journalists, legislative staffers and others. Among my favorites were the free-spirited Roger Boyette and Sacramento TV newscaster Solon Gray. The late sixties, at least in the conservative part of California I was living in, was a time when gentlemen didn't expect more than a good-night kiss after dinner and a movie. It was possible to "keep company" with several fellows at once and not be considered fickle or flighty. But I never minded the evenings when I didn't have dates. I had lots of girlfriends to enjoy myself with. Maryann Urban, one of the researchers in our office, whom we lovingly referred to as the teenybopper, Kathy Osborne, my assistant after I became Governor Reagan's secretary in the statehouse, and I used to play tennis together. I got a taste of the cultural life of San Francisco with Lynn Wood, a Los Angeles widow who had joined the Governor's staff after working successfully to pass Proposition One, a measure to limit property taxes. I discovered the opera and chamber music thanks to Lynn.

And I even had bridge night. Once a week Pat Gayman, the Governor's scheduling secretary, Lorraine Johnson, an assemblyman's secretary, Helen Kruger, Nancy Reynolds's secretary, and I would bid our hearts out.

———

By the time Bill Clark left, it became official that Governor Reagan's personal secretary was pregnant and would be leaving. Kathy Davis's helper of nineteen or twenty was indeed brought in as a replacement. She was a friendly California girl. But while greeting people in the outer office and answering phone calls were right up her alley, it soon became apparent that she had trouble with the more substantive parts of the job.

Knowing that she needed help, but not wanting to seem overly pushy, I volunteered to help out with the shorthand and paperwork, and in effect became an administrative aide to the Governor. That was when I first got to know Ronald Reagan on a one-to-one basis. Slowly, over a period of weeks, I gained his confidence and he asked me to handle more and more. My big break came one lunch hour when the young secretary was away from her desk and the Governor asked me to find a piece of correspondence. I hunted and hunted for it everywhere, but it wasn't in her "in" box, on her desk, or in her files. I was losing patience and turned to the closet behind her desk. When I opened the door I was nearly buried by an avalanche of mail. For three months, she had just been stuffing most of the incoming mail into the closet, on the theory that she'd get to it later. The job was mine.

On the first day that I took over, Governor Reagan joked that people were going to be confused when they called the Governor's office and heard such a strong German accent on the other end of the phone. I reminded him of how hard I'd had to struggle just to get a dumb job on the campaign. At that point he got sentimental for a moment, and told me how proud he was of me. "You know, you symbolize the American dream, Helene," he said. "So don't try to lose that accent. It's just fine with me."

I was delighted to be taking dictation, running the office, handling correspondence, and generally performing the tasks of a secretary. But I was also determined to make more out of my job than just a secretarial position. I made it my business to prepare memos for the Governor on each meeting he would be attending, whether it was just a supporter making a courtesy call, a legislator with a beef, or a fellow Governor discussing legislation. I got used to what he needed and preparing the memos had the added benefit of keeping me up on things as well.

Getting to know Ronald Reagan proved to be an elusive goal. He was always incredibly kind to me, as he was to everyone. In all of the years I knew him I never once saw him lose his temper with an aide. Sure, he got angry over political battles with the Democrats, and I have to admit I've seen him throw a pencil or his glasses across the desk once or twice. But that was the whole extent of his anger. It was slow to kindle and very short-lived. I admired his skill with people—he seemed to have an uncanny knack of bringing out the best in those who worked for him. He inspired fierce loyalty among us.

And yet, he was fundamentally a very difficult man to know. I suspect he is a much more complex individual than he would have us believe. There was always a wall beyond which you couldn't penetrate. There's an inner Ronald Reagan that no one ever gets to see, with the possible exception of Nancy, but even then, I wonder. If he keeps part of himself aloof from even his best friends (and through the years I got to know them all and we talked about Ronald Reagan all the time), is he able to reveal that inner self to anyone? Even his much beloved wife? I tend to think that people are the way they are. If someone is open with his friends, he's open with a spouse. If he's closed with even his closest friends, it's hard to imagine him undergoing a complete personality change with his spouse. I believe that his inability and/or lack of desire to forge intimate bonds was part of the explanation for his willingness to allow longtime associates and aides to depart. It may also account for the way he permitted Jim Baker and Donald Regan to change jobs in 1984.

Whatever Ronald Reagan's innermost thoughts—I doubt anyone was ever privy to them. I wasn't either. I just sensed there was a great deal of hidden depth, strength, and wisdom, anchored in an abiding and unshakable faith in God which his mother had instilled in him. There was a touch of an interest and belief in the supernatural, but his religion would not have permitted him to become engrossed in it. Watching Ronald Reagan in public, though, was always an amazing experience. He could defuse a tense press conference with a self-deprecating joke that would disarm even his most vocal opponents. And though he was a very gentle man, he could deploy a sharp wit. I recall one day during the Vietnam protests of the late sixties. A bunch of hippie demonstrators had camped outside on the statehouse lawn in a gesture of protest. At an impromptu news conference, the Governor was asked what he thought of the hippies' slogan "Make love, not war." He smiled and said, "Well, I got a look at them and I'm not too sure they're capable of either."

When I took over as Governor Reagan's secretary, I began to piece together the history of his race for the governorship. He had been touring the country as an after-dinner speaker, serving as host for the *General Electric Theater,* and writing. He had reached the attention of California political leaders with a speech he had given on Goldwater's behalf in 1964, but he himself hadn't thought very seriously about running for office. It was a group of California businessmen, who later became known as the kitchen cabinet, who persuaded him to run.

The original members were Henry Salvatori, an oil developer; Cy Rubel, the former president of Union Oil; Taft Schreiber, an MCA executive; and Holmes Tuttle, owner of Ford dealerships. Later, friends joined. Bill Wilson was a cattle rancher and the Governor's financial adviser. William French Smith, a senior partner of Gibson, Dunn, & Crutcher, was the Governor's lawyer. Al Bloomingdale was the founder of Diners Club (his wife, Betsy, was also one of Mrs. R's closest friends). Earle Jorgensen had made his fortune in steel (and his wife, Marion, was also a close friend of Nancy's). Justin Dart was the chairman of Rexall Drugs and came into the Reagan circle after marrying Jane Bryan, a former co-star from Ronald Reagan's movie days. Another marry-in was oil developer Jack Wrather, whose wife, Bonita Granville, had been a starlet in Hollywood.

I always liked Holmes Tuttle the best, but I don't think it's just my personal prejudice to say that he was the prime mover behind the effort to make Ronald Reagan Governor. It was Holmes who put people in touch with one another to the point where he could in honesty call Ronald Reagan on the phone and announce that a Citizens for Reagan committee had been formed. It sounded so much better than simply asking someone to think about running. The kitchen cabinet raised money for the campaign, hired professional campaigners like Stu Spencer, and later helped Governor Reagan choose a team to help him govern. I don't think it's an exaggeration to say that without the kitchen cabinet, Ronald Reagan would not have become Governor and eventually President.

Throughout Ronald Reagan's term as Governor the kitchen cabinet continued to play an influential role. For the most part, they played their parts very well, never asking for inappropriate favors or pushing their influence too far. Occasionally, someone's nose would get out of joint if the Governor didn't take his advice, but that passed quickly.

One of the things I liked so much about Holmes was that he was such a gentleman. He was always available if the Governor asked for his advice, but he rarely offered it unsolicited. Moreover, he never demanded favors—though he would certainly have been entitled to them. By the time Governor Reagan ran for President, Holmes was a sick man and though he dearly wanted to participate—it was the fruition of his dream

—his wife, Virginia, insisted that he guard his health. And I'm glad she did, because I came to rely on him as a trusted friend for many, many years.

It was through getting to know the kitchen cabinet that I got my first glimpse of wealth. There were so many rules of behavior that I had simply never known about: the difference between "black tie" and "white tie," what kind of jewelry was considered appropriate for a weekend visit, what kinds of drinks were drunk at brunch or before dinner, why you sniff a cork on a bottle of wine, and many more details. I knew I'd never live that way myself, but I did try to look around and pick up some pointers when I visited these homes which had been designed by decorators. How else do you develop good taste?

Being Ronald Reagan's secretary meant being able to meet interesting people from several walks of life. There were his business friends, his Hollywood crowd, and now that he was Governor, other politicians.

In 1968, the National Governors' Conference was held in Palm Springs and the Governor asked me if I'd like to go. "Like it?" I asked. "I'd be crushed if you left me home." It was quite a production. The Walt Disney studio masterminded the weekend. They issued each Governor a car with a personalized license plate. The entertainment, including a manufactured "afternoon on the range" complete with cowboy hats and chaps for the men and bonnets and umbrellas for the women, and a western barbecue made getting any work done pretty challenging. I had a fantastic time. And I also managed to slip away for a little while to admire the beautiful houses Palm Springs is famous for. That trip was important for Reagan as well. It was where his friendship with then Governor of Nevada (later Senator) Paul Laxalt began.

———

When the Governor was traveling, he was very heedless of security. This worried me since we had seen so many political leaders shot in the 1960s. And Governor Reagan was not exactly uncontroversial. It was the same in Sacramento. He couldn't believe anyone would try to hurt him. I tried to run interference for him in his outer office, carefully screening people who showed up without appointments. But one instance in particular stands out in my mind because it happened just after our return from Palm Springs.

In order to get to the inner sanctum, it was necessary to pass my desk. That morning, Governor Reagan and some of his aides had gone out to the steps of the Capitol so that the Governor could address the Berkeley student protesters. When the Governor and his entourage returned they were all engaged in animated discussion about the speech and some of the back-and-forth which followed. But I noticed that there was someone there who looked a bit strange. I had never seen him before and he didn't seem to be talking to anyone. As they passed my desk on the way into the Cabinet room, he followed right in step.

I called security. The next thing I knew, the man was being led out with a security guard holding each arm. No one knew him. Each had assumed that he was an aide to one of the others. It turned out that he was just a harmless nut who hadn't intended any harm, thank God. They sent him to a hospital for a psychiatric workup. But I was the heroine of the hour. Everyone agreed that my eagle eye could have saved the Governor from someone dangerous.

The next day Governor Reagan held a mock ceremony at which he presented me with a billy club and a sergeant's star. I still have that star in my jewelry box. The billy club was lost in one of my many moves, which upset me very much. Every gift Ronald Reagan has given me is precious to me.

———

Ronald Reagan had campaigned on cutting taxes. When he took office, however, he discovered that the previous Democratic Administration had kept a secret: there was a sizable budget deficit. The Governor's aides were beside themselves at the idea of raising taxes so soon after the election. But the Governor said that the people of California would understand that he hadn't known about the deficit until after he was sworn in—and they did.

Next the Governor turned his attention to the swollen welfare rolls, which had been largely responsible for the big deficit. There were so many loopholes in the law and other opportunities for cheating that Governor Reagan set out to reform the system so that the truly needy would get the help they needed but those who didn't deserve welfare would not be able to cheat the taxpayers. The Democrats screamed and howled that Governor Reagan was against widows and orphans. But he embarked on a vigorous campaign, explaining the situation to the people of California and encouraging them to write their legislators. It must have worked, because I remember the day the leader of the Democrats in the Assembly came rushing into our office, arms thrown up in the air, saying, "Okay, okay, you win. But stop those damn letters and post cards."

While Governor Reagan did bow to necessity with a tax increase, he was still anti-tax at heart. When a system of withholding was proposed for state taxes, he was totally opposed. He knew it would make tax collection easier for the government, but he also knew that it was a sneakier and less noticeable way for the government to take people's money. "It's less painful when you collect taxes by withholding," urged one aide. "I know," Reagan replied. "But taxes should be painful. People should be keeping close tabs on how much the state takes from them." He wouldn't hear further arguments. "My feet are set in concrete on this," he declared. About a year and half later, the state government was in the midst of a severe cash-flow problem. The Governor's advisers were unanimous in recommending withholding as the only answer. Governor Reagan finally agreed. When he was asked at a press confer-ence about his change in position he didn't attempt to talk around the issue. "The sound you hear," he said, laughing, "is the sound of concrete cracking around my feet." The press later presented him with a pair of shoes in a slab of concrete.

But though Governor Reagan was capable of changing his stand on something like taxes or spending, there were some issues which were articles of faith for him. For example, when the self-styled Symbionese Liberation Army kidnapped Patty Hearst, they issued a demand that the Governor distribute one million dollars' worth of free food to the poor. I could see that Ronald Reagan was deeply upset. His usual sense of humor was gone and he looked almost as grim as during the days of the kidnapping. "I can't do as they demand," he said. "Free food for the poor is fine, but not at the price of a young girl's life. If I do this, every kook with a grievance will view it as an invitation to kidnapping." In the end, Patty's father, William Randolph Hearst, met the SLA demands. But his daughter was not released.

Ronald Reagan was also firmly committed to capital punishment. But when he got to be Governor he had to have the courage of his convictions and it was agonizing for him. His predecessor, "Pat" Brown, had commuted so many death sentences that San Quentin's death row was overflowing. Early on in his first term, a robber who had killed a policeman and was sentenced to death appealed his sentence to the Governor. Ronald Reagan has a soft spot for individuals in trouble, but he just couldn't find any extenuating circumstances upon which to commute the sentence. After a lot of soul-searching and with great sadness, he turned down the appeal and the man was executed.

Governor Reagan's philosophy of government was much more philosophically based than that of other politicians. He read a great deal and tried his best to be consistent. Most politicians don't really believe in much beyond getting reelected. Ronald Reagan was always a breed apart. His conservative, slightly libertarian view of government led him to oppose a measure that would have required motorcyclists to wear helmets. I just couldn't understand how he could take such a position. It was so small a thing and could protect so many lives. "It's the principle," he said. "I believe in wearing helmets. I'd never get onto a bike without one. But I just don't think the government should coerce someone to take good care of himself. If he wants to feel the breeze on his ears and is willing to risk his life in the process, that's up to him."

Yet not wanting the government to infringe on people's freedom is not the same thing as being insensitive or callous. That charge has followed Reagan throughout his political career and it's so unjust I could just tear my hair whenever I hear it. Ronald Reagan made everyone who worked for him into an ad hoc social service agency. I was responsible for seeing to it that anyone who came to see him as a last resort was not turned away. He frequently sent small checks to people who wrote to him about their problems. One man wrote and explained that he was getting married but didn't have enough money to buy a suit. He noted that the Governor and he were about the same size and inquired whether he might have an old one he'd be willing to lend for the occasion. Ronald Reagan sent him a suit—to keep. A little boy wrote saying that his mother's welfare check had been cut in half for no apparent reason. By return mail the boy received a new check and a Christmas visit by Frank Sinatra! And I recall the two sisters who wrote saying that their retarded brother wanted a rocking chair more than anything in the world. Ronald Reagan sent his own.

He never checked up on these people to make sure they were legitimate. He basically liked and trusted people. Also, I think he would agree with me that when you give charity to someone—even to a beggar who is standing outside of a liquor store and you know he's only going to buy booze—you do it because you feel sad that they have fallen upon hard times or by the wayside. It doesn't matter if it was the result of weakness or bad luck or both. I think that was part of the secret of Ronald Reagan's political success. People sensed that he liked them and so they liked him back. You can't manufacture that quality. No media wizard can create the illusion of it. It has to be there. It's altogether a different thing, though, when the government takes money from its citizens and forces them to give it to others.

I remember with special fondness a letter he received from a kindergarten teacher. She wrote: "I was briefing my class on a field trip we were going to take the following day. One of the places scheduled was the Governor's mansion. I asked the class, 'Does anyone know who is the Governor of California?' There was complete silence. 'Oh, come on, children,' I said, 'you know his name. Ronald . . .' Instantly, twenty-three voices shouted triumphantly, 'RONALD McDONALD!' "

That schoolteacher had to know that Ronald Reagan was the kind of man who would laugh and enjoy that story or she would never have written to him. She was right. He laughed uproariously and told everyone he saw that day how popular he was with California five-year-olds.

When Bill Clark left his post as Executive Secretary to become a judge (he later rose to become a judge on the California Supreme Court), his replacement was a man Governor Reagan had admired, Ed Meese. I got to know him and liked him very much.

Meese had come to the Governor's attention when he had served as Oakland district attorney. His strict handling of the Berkeley "free speech" demonstrations gained him Governor Reagan's respect. Actually, it was I, as Clark's secretary, who had been the first Reagan person to speak to Meese. Clark was inviting him to Sacramento to discuss taking the job of Clemency and Extradition Secretary. He did take that job and then was promoted to Executive Secretary. Ed joked for years about how confused he had been to be invited to Sacramento by a woman with such a strong German accent.

I never got to know Ed Meese as well as I did Bill Clark. We didn't work together directly until many years later. But I came to see in him some of the qualities which attracted the Governor. Ed Meese, like Ronald Reagan, had an unfailingly cheerful manner. He never gossiped about other people in the Administration, and he never suspected that people were talking about him. He operated as if the whole world was populated by principled straight shooters like himself. He knew, of course, that people disagreed with him, but he was so honest and had so much integrity that duplicity on the part of his opponents never seemed to occur to him.

Meese had an instant rapport with Governor Reagan. They were philosophically in complete accord, and they enjoyed discussing ideas together.

We all worked hard, but perhaps Ed more than anyone else. I heard that he used to stay in the office until 3 A.M. some nights. I admired Ed tremendously, but I must say in all honesty that I think it was unnecessary for Ed to work such hours. Maybe it's my German background, but I think if you're organized and use your staff well, you can get all your work done in a normal span of hours. But delegation was not Ed's strong suit. Still, if that's the way he chose to do things and if it worked (it definitely did), I suppose I shouldn't criticize. There were just times when I would have loved to send an efficiency expert into Meese's office to get things into order . . . oh well.

Ed Meese wore his allegiances proudly. In his home and car he kept a police radio, and behind his desk he hung three hats: a hard hat, a Cattleman's Association cowboy hat, and a cap from the USS *California,* a nuclear-powered frigate. He also decorated his office with several porcelain pigs—a reminder of what some of the "kids" were calling the police back in those unhappy days of the late sixties and early seventies.

———

I will never forget the first time I met Mrs. Reagan (or Mrs. R, as everyone called her). It was when Bill Clark became Executive Secretary and we moved to offices adjacent to the Governor's. Mrs. R came in to meet her husband because they were proceeding together to some dinner or reception. I'd seen her from afar many times, of course, and even shook hands and said hello a few times during our first year in Sacramento, but this was the first time we were formally introduced and she took note of me. I was struck by her beauty, those large eyes and that lovely skin. She took terrific care of herself and dressed impeccably, of course, but nature had been very generous to her as well. She smiled at me but her smile was without warmth.

I got to know her slowly. It wasn't until much later, when I became the Governor's secretary, that we would really have much to do with one another. I was eager to make a good impression because I thought it was entirely possible that the wife of the Governor might not want a heavily accented person answering his phone and greeting his visitors. Or, I thought, she might have wanted to give the job to someone she knew personally and trusted. But she never seemed to raise any objections to me and for that I was, and still am, grateful.

Mrs. R didn't have the skill with people that her husband had. In fact, where he always gave people the impression that he liked them, she, probably without knowing it, gave the opposite impression. Everyone tensed when she came into the office. I have to admit that when I heard her voice on the other end of the phone I'd always stiffen a little bit in anticipation of some criticism or other. Mrs. R was goal-oriented with people. If you were someone she thought important enough to befriend, she could pour on the charm. And she usually got the friendships she wanted. Similarly, if you worked for her or her husband, she wanted things done a certain way and would make constant demands until she was satisfied. In both cases, it seemed to me that she saw people, potential friends or employees, as means to an end, not as ends in themselves.

I dealt with Mrs. R over the telephone for the most part. I had done this to a limited extent when I worked for Bill Clark and noticed then that she was an extremely persistent person. If she called when Bill was in a meeting, I knew that she'd call back in half an hour. If Bill's meetings ran long enough to provoke a third call from Mrs. R, I'd call Mike Deaver and ask him to talk to her rather than have to tell her that Bill was still unavailable. I believe that was the beginning of their friendship.

Mrs. R did take an interest in the office. She redecorated the Governor's mansion and her husband's office. She had very good taste in everything from upholstery to clothes—but as a working secretary I would sometimes sigh when I saw her coming. I understood her concern with appearances, but she would frequently scold if there were papers piled up on a desk or if a chair was in the wrong place or an ashtray was dirty. I grumbled to another secretary, "This is a working office, not a showplace."

Still, she was known as demanding and I think she scared lots of people, including me, so I kept quiet. I thought it would be impolitic to contradict the Governor's wife on anything. It was a matter of propriety, for one thing. I was his secretary. She was his wife. To put it bluntly, she outranked me. But I could never get over the gap in perceptions between Ronald Reagan and the rest of the world when it came to Nancy. We all thought of her as a demanding and somewhat aloof person. But in his adoring eyes she was the sweetest, gentlest, most wonderful person in the world. It wasn't just that he loved her. Lots of people love their spouses without seeing them in a fundamentally different light from the way everyone else sees them. They just put a different interpretation on the same qualities. What some would call stinginess, for example, a loving spouse might call thrift. But Ronald Reagan didn't even seem to see the same person the rest of us saw. When an aggrieved staffer once approached the Governor about something Mrs. R had done, Governor Reagan was so utterly incredulous and completely unbelieving ("You must be wrong. My Nancy wouldn't do that") that no one ever tried to talk to him about her again. Naturally, some of us did a good deal of speculating as to why this was so. Our best theory was that Ronald Reagan intended to make this marriage work no matter what. Although he never said so, we sensed that the breakup of his first marriage was one of the great disappointments of his life. It appeared he had made up his mind that this would never happen to him again and as a consequence he gave in to Nancy more than he might have otherwise. He was infinitely patient with her and only on the rarest of occasions would blow up at her—but then it could be in front of a staffer. Only once was I witness to it in the White House. She was relentlessly pursuing the ouster of a person and badgering the President mercilessly. I don't remember who it was—it might have been Ray Donovan. RR blew his stack and laid down the rule once and for all: he would no longer tolerate her debating any controversial member of the Administration. The rule stuck for some time. Of course, this didn't mean she wasn't discussing such matters with Mike Deaver and others.

All of this changed when her father, Dr. Loyal Davis, died in the summer of 1982, which was a severe blow to Mrs. Reagan. After her father's death, the President found it difficult to say no to Mrs. R and she began interfering more and more in daily White House activities and staff problems.

Her interests were not restricted to redecorating—not even in the Governor's office. She was always concerned about her husband's image and success. We all knew that she had strong opinions, but in the early days she showed more prudence than later in confiding these only selectively to her friends and associates of the Governor. The kitchen cabinet members I was forming independent relationships with told me that she was quite vocal with them and her husband about individual members of his staff. She always claimed that her interest was only in "people," not in policy. It would be many years later, in Washington, before I understood that there really isn't any difference—especially with someone like Ronald Reagan who attracts people who believe in certain policies.

Mrs. R's biggest concern back then was that her husband not be overscheduled. She was right. If he was left to his own devices he could never say no to anyone and would be left with absolutely no free time.

Nancy's role, though important, was nowhere near the level of influence she came to exert in the White House. I didn't see it at the time in California, but in some ways her ambition was stronger than his. She went on to become an extremely influential First Lady.

HAPPY DAYS

I LOVED BEING RONALD REAGAN'S SECRETARY. BUT I had ambitions of my own which were starting to rattle around in my head asking for attention. I certainly had nothing to complain about in my working environment—Ronald Reagan made every day a pleasure—or in my financial situation. When Governor Reagan took me on as his secretary he said, "How much were you earning with Bill?" I started to open my mouth to reply but he suddenly interrupted me and said, "Never mind, we'll start you at $1,200 a month if that's okay." It was far, far more than I had ever expected. I felt rich.

All the same, there was a certain restlessness in my soul. One evening, as I sat in my garden having a gin and tonic before dinner in the lovely California dusk, I got out a yellow legal pad and made notes on what was missing from my life. I came up with two things: education and a family. This was 1970, so I didn't think of doing both at the same time. I decided that a family would have to come first. I was dating several eligible men at the time and I thought: Helene, you're thirty-two. You don't have forever. Pick one.

I picked Christian von Damm, a German of Prussian descent I'd met a few months before. He hadn't asked me to marry him, but I could tell from the way our relationship was progressing that he would soon enough. He was handsome, intelligent, and charming. I thought our common backgrounds would make the match a success, remembering the unhappy experience with Charles McDonald, with whom I'd had nothing in common. But there were a couple of problems. He was living in Mexico, just starting to rebuild his life after a divorce. If I married him, I thought, I'd have to leave Governor Reagan and move to another country. It would be hard, but I was in love with him and wanted very much to have children. So when he proposed I accepted immediately.

The first person I wanted to tell my wonderful news to was Bill Clark. I sauntered into his office and showed him my engagement ring. His face broke into a broad grin. "Who's the lucky guy?" I told him. But when I added that we'd be moving to Mexico permanently, Bill became concerned.

"You're out of your mind," Bill said. "You ought to think this through again. Chris is just getting started in business. And there are problems in Mexico. You've made a great life here. If you've got to get married, bring him here."

I had never thought of that. When I raised the subject with Chris the following evening, he didn't agree immediately but seemed open to the idea. Luckily, he was accepted very quickly as a Bank of America trainee. It meant starting from the bottom for Chris (he literally had to raise the flag in front of the building every morning) but he was eager. He went to night school to work on his English and he insisted that we speak only English to one another, even when we were alone.

We were married at Easter 1970 in Las Vegas. Chris's best friend from Mexico came up to act as best man. Along with a girlfriend of mine, we spent the weekend there. Senator Laxalt very kindly helped out with the arrangements. I wore a light, summery mini-dress. The civil ceremony was held in the morn-

ing and we had a lovely champagne brunch afterward. When
we returned to Sacramento, Mike Deaver threw a reception
for us. Everyone was there, including the Governor.

I was absolutely sure this marriage was going to work.
Together we built a duplex in the Greenhaven section of Sacramento. We lived in one half and rented out the other. I
threw myself into the task of being the perfect housewife.
Chris liked to have his dinner on the table at 6 P.M. without
fail. Since I rarely got home before 5:30 and couldn't cook
much in half an hour, I made casseroles in the evening, refrig-
erated them, and then reheated them while I set the table and
made the other preparations when I got home from work. I set
up a schedule for myself which rivaled my rigid schedule of
Chicago days. Monday evenings were for laundry. Tuesday
evenings were for ironing. Food shopping after work. House
cleaning on Wednesday evenings.

Things went well at first. I was very happy and fulfilled. I
enjoyed showing Chris all of my favorite places in California.
We went wine tasting in the Napa Valley and visited the Gold
Rush territory in the foothills of the Sierras. As we wandered I
told him about my images of this part of the world which I'd
cherished as a child in Ulmerfeld. He laughed when I told him
that if I could have chosen any period of history to live in it
would have been the taming of the Wild West. "What would
you have done?" he asked. "Be a madam, I guess," I answered.

Our life was full of activity. We rented a cabin at Lake
Tahoe with several other couples and went skiing there almost
every weekend during the winter. After a time, we also joined
with Janet and Gary Raugh to buy a cabin cruiser. In the sum-
mertime we cruised the Sacramento delta or the San Francisco
Bay.

In fact, one of our most harrowing experiences took place
on that boat. I've always had an adventuresome streak in me
and I'm not the kind of person to heed warnings of danger.
Janet and Gary and Chris and I had got it into our heads that
we would take the boat down to Mexico and cruise around the

Sea of Cortez. I told my friend Bill Bennet, who was head of the Navigation Department in California, about our plans. He was aghast. "You can't take the little boat into those waters," he warned. "The sea of Cortez is treacherous." It seemed there were no recent maps or charts of the Mexican coastline in that area. "And don't forget," he continued, "if you get into trouble down there, there's no good ol' U.S. Coast Guard to come and rescue you." But I laughed off his warnings and told him to stop being such an old lady. "We'll be just fine." Still, I did accept from Bill a hand-drawn map a friend of his had made on a recent trip.

That little map probably saved our lives on more than one occasion. We put the boat on a trailer and drove down to Guaymas where we provisioned the twenty-seven-foot cabin cruiser with all of the food, water, medical supplies, kerosene and other necessities for the ten-hour crossing of the gulf to Mulege. We departed as scheduled despite thunderstorm warnings and the darkest, most-fierce-looking skies. The waves were gigantic and tossed the boat around like a matchbook. The lightning was ferocious and I remembered how vulnerable a boat on water is to fire. I had heard somewhere that fire causes more deaths at sea than drownings. Somehow, we weathered the storm and the heavy seas and tried to get our bearings with the makeshift map as we approached the other shore. We all were a bit green around the gills and not exactly feeling like newlyweds. We tried to figure out our position by looking for landmarks in shore but we cruised for hours without seeing another boat or anything closely resembling the entry of the harbor of Mulege. Dusk was setting in and the gas needle approached empty. It was the loneliest feeling I've ever experienced. We were so close to home and civilization and yet it was perfectly possible for us to vanish without a trace and no one would ever know what became of us. Our radio calls were not answered. Bill had been so right. We really missed the U.S. Coast Guard! How I'll never know, but we managed to arrive at night safe and sound in Mulege. We had gotten so frightfully off-course through the heavy sea.

We had to get used to living with daily new hazards. It was par for the course. Our experiences included nearly getting capsized by a whale, getting beached, running out of gas, cruising through a school of sharks, and being stung by a jellyfish. If we were lucky enough to find a sheltered little harbor for the night, we had to prepare for the thunderstorms, which were sure to arrive by midnight. We got down to a drill, dropping anchor and taking turns staying awake to make sure our only anchor line didn't snap in the heavy waves, washing our boat against the rocks. Of course, neither of us slept much offwatch either, not with the boat pitching around like an amusement park ride. We were spooked by manta rays, which jumped out of the water after dusk, spreading their huge fins, which looked like bat wings, and their long tails that looked like rat tails, and then disappearing into the black water.

And yet, despite all the horrors, I'll never forget the unbounded joy we all experienced when we cruised right into a school of porpoises. All around us and almost as far as the eye could see, these fantastic graceful mammals cavorted and leaped around us. We were so excited that we screeched with delight and dashed around the boat like Keystone Kops looking for the camera.

We returned to Sacramento considerably lighter (fear turned out to be the best diet) and wiser. It was 1973. Watergate was in full swing and Republicans everywhere were feeling dispirited and disillusioned. Even in our cheery office the atmosphere was subdued.

It was the same in my home life. I was disappointed that I hadn't gotten pregnant and doctors told me it was unlikely I would.

Professionally, things were changing.

After Governor Reagan finished his second term as Governor in 1974, he decided to stay involved in public life through a syndicated newspaper column, a radio program, and speaking engagements. It was by this point widely acknowledged that Governor Reagan could be the next President, so it wasn't at all difficult for him to command lecture fees of $10,000 or more. He obviously didn't need the kind of staff he'd had as Governor, but he did ask some of us to come to Los Angeles, his new home base. Mike Deaver and Peter Hannaford, who had been the Governor's speechwriter and public affairs officer in Sacramento, teamed up to form a public relations firm, Deaver and Hannaford. Governor Reagan would be their first and most important client.

The arrangement suited Governor Reagan perfectly. Instead of having to form his own organization and run it, being responsible for payroll and loans and equipment and so forth, he could be a client and have all of that taken care of. He was left free to do his thing while Deaver and Hannaford provided all of the backup he would require. There were basically four of us who divided up the labor. Mike handled public relations and political matters, Pete helped out with speechwriting, columns, radio broadcasts, Nancy Reynolds did all of the advance work, and I did everything else.

I was happy that Chris had agreed to move with me to Los Angeles. He was able to get a transfer. While I still thought of myself first and foremost as a housewife, the absence of children slowly made me think of my career as the principal source of meaning in my life.

I did basically what I had done in Sacramento, except that now I had to handle all of Governor Reagan's travel arrangements as well because we no longer enjoyed the luxury of a scheduling secretary. I didn't mind, though, because he allowed me great discretion. I did more than book flights, reserve hotel rooms, and rent cars. I evaluated and recommended which invitations to accept and which to reject and I virtually handled all correspondence without assistance or supervision. It was a measure of his belief in my political judgment that Reagan allowed me to make those decisions. I had certainly come a long way from the callow young girl who sent a form letter to a California assemblyman.

My new responsibilities also introduced me (frequently just over the phone though eventually I came to meet them all in person) to the whole Reagan network which was springing up around the country. I even acquired pen pals, like the irrepressible boy from Pennsylvania, Marc Holtzman, a high-school boy utterly mad for Ronald Reagan. He wrote again and again to express his willingness to go anywhere and do anything for Ronald Reagan. I liked Marc immediately and kept answering his letters faithfully.

As an extra little project of love, I undertook to put together a book of Governor Reagan's personal correspondence during his two terms as Governor. There was so much warmth, humor, and intelligence in his letters to both the famous and the ordinary. I wanted the world to know what a wonderful, thoughtful, concerned human being he was. I excerpted some of the letters and provided background information for others. With Lyn Nofziger's help, *Sincerely, Ronald Reagan* was published in time for the 1976 presidential campaign.

Even before Governor Reagan left Sacramento, the nucleus of the Reagan team had been split. In 1969, President Nixon had asked Cap Weinberger to come to Washington as chairman of the Federal Trade Commission. He had gone on to become director of the Office of Management and Budget, where his zealous cost-cutting won him the nickname "Cap the Knife."

Bill Clark had been promoted first to the California Court of Appeals and then to the California Supreme Court. We were particularly glad Bill was there when we watched Governor Reagan's successor, Jerry Brown, appoint one liberal after another, including Chief Judge Rose Bird, who was later removed by the voters.

Ed Meese had returned to the private practice of law. He also taught criminal law at the University of San Diego and took a job as general counsel at Rohr Industries. Charles Tyson, who had settled down in Sacramento and married the beautiful Missy Heldridge, joined his father's real estate development business in San Diego.

Though scattered, we all kept in touch, knowing that our attachment to Ronald Reagan made our bond special. We shared a belief in his specialness—he was unlike other politicians and loyalty to him was deeper than to ordinary men. Fundamentally, we believed that he would be a great President of the United States and that the country needed him very badly.

The possibility of a Reagan presidency had been floated as early as 1968. By 1974, when he left the Governor's job, the air almost tingled with the feeling of possibilities. There were unanticipated problems, though. Before Watergate, we'd naturally assumed that there would be no Republican incumbent in 1976. But when President Nixon resigned and Ford became President, and after President Ford made it clear that he would be seeking the nomination in his own right, it was a whole new ball game. Ed Meese, ever the play-by-the-rules type, didn't think Governor Reagan should challenge a Republican incumbent. But there were political pros who were now part of the decision-making process.

Mike Deaver had been impressed by John Sears when Sears had worked as President Nixon's convention manager in 1968. Sears was invited out to California, informally at first, later as a paid adviser. He thought President Ford was beatable and urged Governor Reagan to run.

Ronald Reagan took some time to decide. It wasn't easy for him. He had strong party loyalties and he liked Jerry Ford personally, but the grass-roots pressure (we were getting letters and phone calls from Republicans across the country begging him to run) couldn't fail to make an impact. Ultimately, he decided it was fair to challenge President Ford as long as they both observed the so-called Eleventh Commandment: thou shalt speak no ill of a fellow Republican.

He hired John Sears as his campaign manager since Stu Spencer, who had run his gubernatorial races, had already signed on with Ford.

I was thrilled that he was running, but knew that without any national political experience, I'd have to carve out a position for myself. I asked the Governor if I could campaign independently for him and he was more than happy to agree.

So I booked speaking engagements at women's clubs and local Republican events to talk about the subject I was expert on: Ronald Reagan.

I was nervous at first. Public speaking is one of the most terrifying experiences in the world for a novice. No doubt my first couple of speeches sounded wooden and uninteresting. But after I overcame my stage fright, I found that I was a much better speaker when I threw away the prepared text and just talked naturally to a group as I would to my friends. *Sincerely, Ronald Reagan* was selling well in the stores, so with the proceeds I made sure to buy up extra copies from the publisher to distribute on my speaking trips.

The only problem with being on the road so much was that I didn't feel quite at the center of things in the campaign. I tried to glean as much as I could from friends about what was going on.

Apparently, Sears's strategy was to pick three early primary states for a show of Ronald Reagan's strength. The campaign simply didn't have the money to compete with President Ford throughout the whole primary season. Sears wanted to focus therefore on New Hampshire, Florida, and Illinois.

We lost all three.

It was so painful. I could not believe the voters didn't sense what a fantastic President Ronald Reagan would be. There were long faces at the campaign headquarters in Los Angeles. But Sears, to his credit, was not a quitter. Though we were $2 million in debt, he decided to push for a national advertising campaign. It must have worked, because our luck changed. Governor Reagan won North Carolina (thanks in large measure to Jesse Helms), Texas, and California.

The convention that year was held in Kansas City. We arrived knowing that we didn't have enough delegates to win. But it was close. There hadn't been a brokered convention in many years but everyone was saying anything could happen. I sensed very strongly that Ronald Reagan was the sentimental, grass-roots favorite. Everywhere we went he was greeted by shouts and cheers and shining faces. I was so proud to be part of his campaign—even if he was the underdog.

The maneuvering was fierce. Sears knew that our only chance to win the nomination would be to persuade the delegation from some large state to come over to us. Sears thought it would be a great coup if we could get Pennsylvania. He convinced Ronald Reagan to do something unprecedented (so far as I knew): to name his choice for Vice President in advance. Sears figured that Senator Richard Schweiker of Pennsylvania could carry his large delegation over to Governor Reagan if he was put on the ticket.

There was an emergency meeting of Governor Reagan's closest advisers. The kitchen cabinet was unenthusiastic. Schweiker was a liberal Republican and they thought it would hurt Ronald Reagan's reputation for philosophical integrity to make such a choice. But Paul Laxalt, then a United States senator and colleague of Schweiker's, stuck up for him. Laxalt was campaign chairman, and his voice carried great weight. Governor Reagan agreed to meet with Schweiker.

The two men sat in a hotel room while down on the floor people in crazy hats and wild costumes were cheering for one speech after another. But the atmosphere in that room was quiet and contemplative. They discussed their respective political philosophies and it turned out to be as Laxalt promised. Schweiker didn't seem so bad. He favored a strong national defense, opposed gun control, opposed abortion on demand, and had even introduced a constitutional amendment to restore prayer and Bible reading in public schools. They shook hands. It was done.

Well, the announcement caused a huge fuss in the media. There were endless discussions of the meaning of this move by the likes of Walter Cronkite and John Chancellor. But the gambit didn't work. The head of the Pennsylvania delegation was Drew Lewis, and he refused to bolt from President Ford. I was bitterly disappointed at the time, but I did respect Lewis's loyalty. I remembered that four years later when we were looking for a Transportation Secretary.

President Ford was nominated on the first ballot. I cried so hard that I had to take big gulps of air between sobs. Ronald Reagan took it like the gentleman he was, of course. He phoned President Ford to congratulate him and was extremely gracious.

Then he tended to his flock. We were all gathered in his hotel. Our faces were blotchy and our eyes red. He saw this and decided it was his job to cheer us up. He had some wonderful jokes ready, and he urged us to feel proud of the job we'd done. "It wasn't meant to be," he said simply. But then he reminded us that we all had a job to do: seeing to it that Jerry Ford won the general election.

But while Ronald Reagan was fatalistic, others were looking for scapegoats. Lyn Nofziger, who had led a revolt during the primaries to replace John Sears, vowed that Sears would never again be part of a Reagan campaign. Together with Ed Meese, who as a friend of Governor Reagan had been present at the convention though he hadn't played a role in the campaign, Lyn took control of the remaining campaign funds and with the approval of Governor Reagan, Deaver, and Hannaford formed Citizens for the Republic, Ronald Reagan's political action committee. Lyn Nofziger became chairman.

I returned to California and to my studies and my work for Governor Reagan. Deaver and Hannaford got back into gear, and now there was also Citizens for the Republic as a platform for him.

As for my personal life, there was some urgent sorting out that had to be done.

Chris and I were not as well suited to one another as I had originally thought. Maybe all of my years in the United States had made me more of an American than I realized. But Chris's Prussian way of doing things began to strike me as extreme.

I was always a good housekeeper. Being neat and organized comes naturally to me. But I wasn't up to Christian's standards. I remember the leaves around the swimming pool of our Los Angeles house as emblematic of our marriage. The pool was kidney-shaped with a large brick patio around it. The surrounding trees would drop leaves every day and they'd gather on the bricks and sometimes in the pool too. It was a chore to dispose of them, but I figured we'd sweep the pool daily and the bricks twice a week. That wasn't what Chris had in mind. He wanted the bricks kept clean at all times and he expected me to help him do it. I couldn't believe my ears and was tempted to ask him why he didn't just post himself out there all day with a butterfly net and catch the leaves before they could touch the precious bricks. It became a bone of contention between us. I wanted to go play tennis, he wanted to sweep the bricks. I wanted to go to a friend's for bridge, he wanted to sweep the bricks. And he would get very angry with me if I defied him. It was awful.

As our marriage began to deteriorate, I found myself spending more and more time at the office. I was looking for more things to do just so I wouldn't have to go home and face Chris's constant criticism and disapproval. I took classes in public relations and management at UCLA at night—more excuses to be away from home. Ever since my experience with Chris I've always had an eagle eye for marriages on the rocks. When a man or a woman finds a million excuses to be away from home, it's almost always a sign of a bad marriage. If you want to badly enough, you can always find the time to be with your spouse.

I was hurting inside. I felt like a freak. Other people had happy romances in their early twenties, fell in love, got married, and lived happily ever after (or at least that's the way it looked to me then). I had failed at my first marriage and was now failing in a second. I was sure that I was a deeply flawed person. Yet when I asked Chris to go with me to a marriage counselor, he refused.

I lay awake nights thinking about our relationship. I tried so hard to make him understand that since I couldn't grow into motherhood, I needed to grow in other directions, like continuing my education and pursuing my career. But I couldn't really get through.

I now know that what happened to me was happening to thousands of other women caught in failing marriages around that time. The women's movement was just blossoming. At first I couldn't imagine leaving. But slowly I began to feel that being on my own wasn't such a terrible thing. It wasn't necessarily a failure of my soul that I couldn't stay in a marriage which was stifling me.

When Governor Reagan decided to run for President in 1976, I was incredibly relieved. It would mean a renewed purpose for my life, not to mention plenty of opportunities for travel. I was sent to Washington for several months to work at our national headquarters. I hoped the separation would "make the heart grow fonder." But in our case it had the opposite result. I was so relieved to be away from him that I knew divorce was the only answer.

———

I postponed my final decision until after the convention. The time had come. Before talking to Chris I wanted to clear my head. So I signed up for a mountaineering course with the Sierra Club. It was an Outward Bound kind of experience, complete with rope climbing, rappelling, winter snow camping high in the Sierras, and survival in the desert. It was quite challenging physically, and more than a little frightening, but the effect was tremendous. I found that my feelings of self-confidence were much enhanced. When you've conquered a mountain, the rest of life seems much more manageable. Also the beauty and solitude of the mountains did my heart good.

I got support and succor not just from inanimate objects, though. My friends came through for me as well. I will never forget the gesture from Mrs. Reagan. She knew about how things were going with Christian, and I was truly touched when she invited me to spend Christmas Eve at their house. I was tempted. I knew their home would be full of light and life and laughter, whereas mine would be grim. But I didn't feel I had the right to intrude on such a family occasion, so I declined. But I was filled with gratitude to her for offering and

I've told and retold that story in the years since when people (myself included) have criticized her coldness.

After returning from my mountain retreat, I told Chris that I'd be leaving him permanently. His reaction was totally unexpected. Suddenly he seemed prepared to do anything to save the marriage. But tragically, it was too late. My heart had been hardened against him after all the hurtful things that had passed between us. And in my heart I didn't believe he was trying to save the marriage out of love for me but rather to save his own pride. I may have been very wrong about that, but personal relationships are frequently nine-tenths emotion and one-tenth logic. The marriage had lasted for seven years.

I stuck to my resolution and moved out. My friend Lynn Wood had offered me her Hollywood apartment since she was then living in Palm Springs. It was an apartment building with a history. Cecil B. De Mille had built it to house the Broadway actors and actresses he brought West to make films. I had asked if it would be all right if I stayed two weeks. "Of course," said Lynn, "stay as long as you need to." I stayed two years.

I kept my studies going and deepened my friendships. I saw a lot of Nancy Reynolds, Dottie Dellinger, Deaver and Hannaford's bookkeeper, Elaine Crispen (the new office manager for Deaver and Hannaford—later Nancy Reagan's personal secretary and then press secretary), Kittie Baier, Elaine's assistant, and Claire Dorrell and Leslie Ohland, both full-time volunteers on Reagan's 1976 presidential bid.

Since my marriage was over, I was more ready than ever to pour myself into work. But after the high excitement of the campaign, things seemed a bit dull.

To make matters worse, Nancy Reynolds announced that she was leaving to accept a position with Boise Cascade Company in Washington, D.C. I would miss her very much. But we did concoct a little scheme together before she left. Over lunch we discussed the possibility of my taking over Nancy's job, advance work, in addition to my own. It would be an opportunity for me to grow—and I really needed the change.

I made an appointment to see Mike Deaver and explained how great it would be for Deaver and Hannaford not to have to hire a new advance person. I'd do both jobs for the same salary! Mike frowned. He obviously didn't think I could handle it. But I was a bulldog. I explained that I had my other responsibilities so organized that it scarcely took up half my day to do all my work. "Besides," I reminded him, "the Governor isn't traveling as much as he used to and some of my work—like the correspondence—can be done on the road." Mike shrugged and agreed to let me try.

6

SEARCHING

PEOPLE OUTSIDE OF POLITICS MAY NOT UNDERSTAND what an advance person does. But within that world, advance work is highly valued. It's not uncommon to see, if a political rally is going poorly, someone standing at the back of the room, shaking his head, and saying, "Poor advance work."

Basically the advance person handles all of the logistical details for a candidate's or public figure's appearance. The advance person travels a few weeks ahead of time to the spot the candidate will visit. He ensures that the motorcade is paid for and will be at its appointed place. He makes all hotel arrangements and flight reservations. He hooks up extra phone lines in a hotel room to be used as a traveling business office. He examines the room where the speech will be held, checks the height of the podium and of the microphone, looks over the exits, the lighting, and the acoustics. He also plans whether the audience will ask questions, and how long the candidate will spend with VIPs before and after the event.

But despite the best-laid plans, advance work is really a catalogue of unanticipated disasters. You need a cast-iron stomach for that kind of work. I recall a speech Governor Reagan was supposed to deliver in Westchester, a suburb north of New York City. I had checked everything from the invited guests to the length of the speech to the lighting. I had neglected only one thing: directions from the airport. Well, I consoled myself, we were going to be met by a police convoy when our private jet landed at Teterboro Airport in New Jersey and they would surely know the way. No such luck.

With fingers crossed we started across the George Washington Bridge thinking we'd then head north into the Bronx and beyond. But we must have taken a wrong turn and soon found ourselves in the heart of Harlem. We looked out of the windows at the crumbling buildings and the street gangs and tried to find a known landmark. The motorcade seemed to be picking up speed. Mike Deaver was furious. "What do you suggest we do now, Helene?" he demanded tartly. I was mortified.

But Governor Reagan, as always, was his cheerful self. "Let's look at the street numbers," he suggested, "it looks like they're getting smaller." He was right. We were heading south. Westchester was north, so we turned the whole motorcade around and just kept going north until we saw signs pointing to Yonkers. We were home free. We were only a few minutes late, as it turned out. And Ronald Reagan was not upset with me at all.

Despite the inevitable screw-ups, I liked advance work. It was basically a man's world back then, but I thought I did a very creditable job. Governor Reagan seemed to think so too, because he complimented me on several occasions.

It therefore came as a total shock when Mike Deaver called one afternoon, after a particularly successful speaking trip which had gone without a hitch, to say that I was no longer to travel with the Governor. Mrs. R's orders.

"But why?" I asked, knowing full well that protest would be futile.

"She doesn't think it looks good to have a woman traveling with her husband," Mike explained.

"But when Nancy Reynolds had this job she always traveled with him," I persisted.

Mike didn't answer. He merely shrugged his shoulders.

For the first time in my life, I began to wonder whether women really did get a raw deal in life. I had always conducted myself with total propriety: I'd never spent time with Ronald Reagan alone in his hotel rooms, I'd never eaten breakfast with him on the road, and I'd never traveled in a private plane alone with him. It goes without saying that his behavior was beyond reproach. But my sex alone was now denying me a job I enjoyed and was good at.

Suddenly, I took a more jaundiced view of the whole system. As a grateful immigrant, I was for a very long time reluctant to question any aspect of American life or society. But now I looked around and noticed that the women at Deaver and Hannaford were in the less substantive jobs (Nancy Reynolds had been an exception in her day). None of the women on the staff—and that included Nancy—had an office with a window. Dave Fischer, the new advance man, was earning more money than I had for the same job.

Well, there was no point sitting around just licking my wounds. I kept as busy as I could with the usual tasks of a secretary and the months chugged slowly by. But I needed to find something else to fill the gap. My salvation came in the form of a new account executive at Deaver and Hannaford, Craig Fuller. (Craig had a bright future. He went on to become Cabinet Secretary in the White House and later Chief of Staff to George Bush.) He took me under his wing and introduced me to the Coro Foundation, a public affairs leadership training program. Craig suggested that I apply for their three-month training program for women. It seemed perfect. I worked on my application for hours and got friends to check for any incorrect idiomatic expressions which might have sneaked into my essay (I was famous for those). For admission, I had to undergo a full day of verbal tests. For these, we were divided up into teams and given a series of tests and riddles to work out—all while being observed by silent testers. It was nerve-racking. To my delight, I was accepted and offered a scholarship.

I asked Governor Reagan for a three-month leave of absence. He agreed readily but it pained me to think that he probably had no idea why I was no longer doing his advance work. Since it was his wife who had made the decision, I had to bite my tongue.

The Coro Foundation was located in downtown Los Angeles. It was an exhilarating three months, though not easy.

Our first assignment was to prepare a comprehensive report on one of the incorporated cities just outside Los Angeles. We had to master everything from the form of government to cultural attractions, the budget, recreational facilities, tax base, and population makeup. Everything had to be learned in three days, at which time we had to present our findings to the town's mayor and city council. It was intense, but I think our group did a fine job.

It was a very enriching three months and I was sorry to see it end. It had done as much for my professional self-confidence as mountaineering had done for my personal sense of self-worth.

I returned to the office and resumed my old activities. Everyone was wonderfully gracious and I got taken out to lunch every day my first week back. Though I worked pretty independently by now—using my own judgment in the selection of Governor Reagan's speaking engagements—the job hadn't changed and the routine included handling mail, supervising the office, answering the phone, and such. The Coro experience had raised my expectations about what was possible. I started to believe that I could do far more than be a secretary or assistant. Again, time weighed heavily on me. It was now two years since the 1976 campaign and I was almost parched for stimulation of some kind.

I began to consider leaving Deaver and Hannaford.

After my limited experience in the 1976 race, I thought

perhaps campaign work was my calling. I looked around and decided I could wangle a place at the Republican National Committee's school for campaign management. It would mean a trip to Washington, D.C., but there was nothing holding me in L.A.

Campaign school was fun. For a week, we all sat around in the proverbial smoke-filled room and plotted strategies for different kinds of races. I was convinced that my mythical candidate was going to win by a landslide, but when the pros decreed the results, I lost.

Still, the week was special because I got a chance to renew some old friendships, and to see Byron. Since my divorce from Chris I had dated casually but no one had really impressed me. Perhaps it was because ever since 1963 I had been carrying a secret.

———

I was married to Charles then. My trip with my mother to New York City and Niagara Falls was really the first time I'd had since my wedding to move about freely. One day, when we were in New York, I sneaked off to a telephone to make a call. I remembered that Byron Leeds, my first love, had lived in New Jersey. I couldn't quite remember the city he lived in, but I remembered where he said the family business was located. I called there and a kindly voice explained that the Leedses had long since moved away. But when I explained my situation, she was kind enough to give me a forwarding number. I called Byron, and his wife, Marsha, answered. She seemed to know all about me and explained that Byron was out but she'd give him the message. I left a number where I could be reached in New York. The next day, Byron called. He told me he had dropped the pizzas he'd been carrying when Marsha told him who had called. He called me that night and we met the next afternoon.

He looked wonderful, handsome as ever, though a bit more manly. All of the feelings I had had for him as an eighteen-year-old came flooding back. I knew that he was still my one and only love. And I sensed that he felt the same about

me. But his life was full now. He was married (though, I de-
tected, not altogether happily) and he had two small sons. I
told him I was leaving Charles. And that was that. We promised to keep in touch. But I never sent him my forwarding
address in Chicago. I was sure our lives were pulling in opposite directions. Byron told me years later that he had called
Detroit, discovered that I'd moved to Chicago, and spent an
entire evening dialing every McDonald in Chicago searching
for me. He never found me because I wasn't listed. I was
living in a residential hotel.

Only later, when I went to California and became the
Governor's secretary, did I decide on a lark to send him a
postcard. He wrote back immediately, ecstatic to have found
me at last. We kept in touch on an irregular basis after that but
another thirteen years passed before I saw him again. It was in
1976 when I worked at the Reagan for President headquarters
in Washington for a few months. By then I had difficulty recog-
nizing him, as his hair had turned a premature silver-gray—but
he hadn't lost the sparkle in his eyes.

When I knew I was going to be in Washington again, I
called him to let him know. Byron owned a business in New
Jersey but said he'd happily come down to D.C. to see me. I
felt a rush of girlish glee. "Of course," I said. "Come. Come."

It was fantastic to see him again. He was divorced now
and his sons were almost grown. Our romance was rekindled.

The evening after my mythical candidate had been declared a loser and I was feeling dispirited, Byron picked me
up. We were supposed to have dinner at Claire Dorrell's house
(she had recently moved from Los Angeles to the D.C. area).
"Let's have a drink," I suggested. "I need to drown my sorrows." Byron hesitated.

"I don't think we'll have time. It's six now, and we need
to get changed, and"—he paused—"you might want to wash
your hair." I was startled. It wasn't like Byron to make comments like that. It was true that it was totally out of character
for me to show myself in public with dirty hair, and I had only
done so now because of my punishing schedule, but I didn't

think that was necessary just for dinner at Claire's. A wave of stubbornness came over me. I was in a grumpy mood anyway and it didn't take much to push me even further. I agreed to change clothes but I drew the line at hair washing. Byron shrugged, and we hailed a cab.

As we walked into Claire's charming townhouse in Old Town Alexandria, a roomful of people, a mixture of friends of Byron's and campaign workers from the 1976 Reagan for President team, leaped out of the darkness to shout, "Surprise!" It was my fortieth birthday. I had completely forgotten. I was touched but couldn't help wishing I had a paper bag to put over my head all evening. Moral of the story: if Byron says wash your hair, trust him.

The week was over all too quickly. When I returned to California, only one thing about my future had been settled in my own mind. Politics was fun but campaign school had taught me that I was not a political groupie who could move from campaign to campaign changing loyalties as easily as bumper stickers. I loved politics only when the candidate was Ronald Reagan. Once again, I returned to my old job and kept looking for ways to use my mind.

I started to think of other options. Could I be happy in business? I didn't have much experience. I talked to Nancy Reynolds about it. She had left Boise Cascade for Bendix Corporation. She told me that William Agee, the chairman of Bendix, was looking for an executive assistant. Nancy told him about me and I flew out to Detroit to meet him. We hit it off immediately but didn't make any final decisions. When I returned to California, Mike told me it was a pretty sure thing that Ronald Reagan would run for President in 1980. That settled it. I would stay typing letters and whatever for as long as it took the campaign to get into gear. I even took it in stride when I had to give up Lynn Wood's lovely apartment because she needed it back. It was late 1978 and I figured the campaign would start soon. Mike Deaver had promised to assign me to the East (where I could be closer to Byron), so I moved into the closest apartment I could find to Deaver and Hannaford without even checking it out before plunking down a deposit. What a mistake! It was a dark and dingy hole in the wall with thick brown shag carpeting. I had nightmares about that carpet, imagining that it contained every bacterium known to man. I never stepped on it barefooted. This was my home for over six months. I still shudder at the memory of it.

As I look back, though the years between Ronald Reagan's governorship and the presidency were difficult and frustrating, I think they played an important role in propelling me from a secretary to a professional.

The only role model I had in California was Nancy Reynolds (though Lee Ann Elliott had been important when I was in Chicago). But Nancy had a full life with her husband and children. She worked for fun and money, not to build a sense of identity. It was different for me. There was a hungry need in my soul to be involved in something big. It had propelled me ever since my childhood in Austria. I was happiest when I was passionately involved in something. That need made me open to lots of possibilities. I wasn't rigidly tied to any one career path, but imitated Nancy's serendipitous approach. Seize opportunities as they present themselves. Don't be afraid to take risks. And I wasn't. I had come from nothing, so I guess I never really felt I had that much to lose.

Moreover, I was grateful for everything I got. Years later when I was one of the twelve Assistants to the President of the United States, I was constantly being asked by the press about the "secret" to my success. I realized then that there was a subtle interplay between my gender and my attitude which helped me. Yes, I was very focused and a great organizer willing to outstay and outwork anyone. But I was also competing in a world dominated by men in which highly skilled, aggressive-seeming women were pounding on the door and demanding their due. I think the men were intimidated by those women. But since the prevailing climate required that they place women in positions of responsibility, it was perhaps easier to appoint someone like me, who always seemed so grateful, and unthreatening, and who could do the job. Some of my detractors thought my gratitude was an act. It wasn't. I never altogether overcame the immigrant's awe at being able to rise above the station of her birth. I really was grateful. Though that didn't mean I was a pushover.

Now that we knew the campaign for President was going to be a reality, I wondered where I'd fit in. Campaign school and 1976 experience notwithstanding, I still expected to be someone's assistant—not a line officer myself. Besides, Governor Reagan was gathering the smartest political operatives around. I chewed on a few pencils figuring out where I could provide unique help. Another independent speaking tour didn't appeal to me. I wanted to be where the action was this time around. It occurred to me that Governor Reagan did not yet have a nationwide finance operation. The kitchen cabinet had been extremely successful raising funds in California, but their influence in the rest of the country was limited.

This is where I'll make my mark, I thought. No one knows Ronald Reagan better than I and I can sell him. I asked for a finance position in the East (Byron and I had been calling and writing and I wanted to be near him). They agreed, but until a Washington office opened I had to make do with Los Angeles.

A MISSION

I WATCHED THE BATTLES WITH FASCINATION. THE FIRST concerned who would serve as campaign manager. Sears was the obvious first choice since he'd done the 1976 race. But his detractors, including especially Lyn Nofziger from among Ronald Reagan's closest advisers, were still steaming over what they saw as his betrayal in the Schweiker affair. (They should have given him some credit; after Senator Schweiker met Governor Reagan his voting record became much more conservative.) But Mike Deaver still thought Sears was the smartest and the best. He lobbied hard for Sears and finally prevailed.

I watched as the inevitable factions formed within the campaign. Deaver and Sears were clearly a team. They brought in Jim Lake to serve as press secretary and thus alienated Lyn Nofziger, who had held that job in every previous Reagan campaign. Of course, Lyn should have expected it after the bad blood between him and Sears in 1976. However hurt he might have been, he accepted his fate like a trooper and settled for directing the finance operation.

No one quite knew how difficult Nofziger's job was going to be. Financial circles were different from political circles and among the wealthy donors Ronald Reagan was considered something of a political cowboy. Neither Sears nor the kitchen cabinet had succeeded in finding a well-connected Fortune 500 CEO to head up the effort, as is customary in presidential races.

Some of Governor Reagan's critics came to think of him later as the darling of big business. What they're forgetting is that in 1980 the man who went through corporate America like a vacuum cleaner was not the cowboy named Ronald Reagan, but the cowboy named John Connally.

Without big business connections, Lyn Nofziger and the handful of us who'd been assigned to finance muddled through as best we could. The operation was quite amateurish at first. We were just wildly dialing around the country looking for support. The network I had developed of Reagan supporters across the country came in handy at that time, but all too often my network people were passionate but not rich. It was that simple. A presidential campaign can't run on love alone.

The top people in the campaign recognized that as well. After just a few months, Sears and Deaver decided to replace Nofziger. They told him he'd be responsible from now on for the campaign in Texas. It was about the broadest hint they could have delivered. Lyn resigned.

Mike took over the finance operation, and Mike Wallace, a friend of Bill Clark's, was hired as executive director. By now everyone, including Governor and Mrs. Reagan, knew that the campaign couldn't keep going without a top-notch national finance chairman. They found Dan Terra, chairman of Lawter Chemicals. Though not a household name, Dan was respected and his company was listed on the New York Stock Exchange. Besides, everyone else had said no. Dan told me years later that he too had hesitated. It wasn't that he didn't believe in Ronald Reagan but he doubted whether he'd do the job justice. "It was Mrs. R's charm," he confided, "which finally did the trick."

Dan Terra and Mike Wallace drew a map, dividing the country into six regions with dollar targets for each. There would be six regional finance directors—I will be Northeast director with a target amount of $3.5 million—and we in turn, with Dan's help, would recruit state chairmen. Mike Wallace, from campaign headquarters in Los Angeles, would handle overall administration of the finance effort.

I was very gratified with my new responsibility. This would allow me to be on the inside instead of being on the outside looking in. I was also excited about the prospect of being close to Byron, who was then living in New Jersey. But as the day for my departure approached, I realized just how many things I hadn't yet planned for. I had no place to live and knew that with campaign finances as tight as they were, there was no chance that the campaign would pay for my housing in Washington, D.C. It would be unseemly at this stage of my life to live in a residential hotel, yet on my salary I really couldn't afford to rent a nice apartment.

Once again, Nancy Reynolds came through for me. We had kept in touch, and when I told her I'd be in her part of the world as Northeast finance director, she immediately invited me to stay with her and her son Mike in their town house just outside Washington in Old Town Alexandria. I told her she had saved my life and moved in in August 1979. Nancy did everything to make me feel utterly comfortable and welcome. And I was again struck by what an extraordinarily competent woman she was—juggling family and career, and making and maintaining contacts, and all of it in an utterly cheerful and enthusiastic manner. Nancy was also a compulsive shopper and an incredibly generous giver. I recall when she once returned from a trip to Kenya. She had bought twenty necklaces to give as gifts. She showed them all to me and urged me to pick the one I liked best. I did so. But she wasn't finished. She picked out another and said, "Oh, take this one too. It's a great color on you." By the end of twenty minutes, she had given me all twenty.

Nancy was interested in more subjects than I think I could name. She loved primitive art, travel, anthropology, the American West, Native American culture, and so much more. I didn't know how she had time to keep expanding her knowledge, considering all of her other activities, but then, living with her during those months of the 1980 campaign, I discovered her secret. She doesn't sleep. I'd frequently find her light on at three o'clock in the morning. Sometimes I'd knock softly on her door and she'd invite me in, snuggled in bed with a book and her big glasses sliding off the bottom of her nose. She never seemed tired.

Nothing scared Nancy Reynolds. I recall that she was invited by the Harvard Business School to participate in a seminar. "Won't you be nervous?" I asked. "Why should I?" she replied. "It should be great fun." And it was. She was a hit at Harvard, as I should have anticipated. Nancy has a rare combination of chutzpah, creativity, and style. She's quite a lady.

Her town house was very comfortable and was located in a nice neighborhood. Unfortunately, the Reagan for President offices weren't in such a terrific section of town. I wasn't nervous arriving in the morning, but leaving late at night sometimes made me uneasy. My car had been burglarized just outside our window in the middle of the afternoon. It was especially heart-wrenching because my car had been filled with the wedding-shower gifts my secretary had received that very day from all of us.

I dove into the work with gusto. The fund-raising effort was divided into two parts: direct mail, which was aimed at getting small contributions from large lists of Republicans and which was subcontracted out to a private firm; and direct solicitation for larger amounts, from $500 to $1,000 (the maximum permitted by law) from individuals.

I thought that Governor Reagan would be an easy product to sell—but I didn't anticipate what a different world the

East Coast is. No one knew of his record as Governor, but everyone seemed to know that he had "co-starred" with a monkey in *Bedtime for Bonzo*. Besides, corporate America was for John Connally and George Bush. Big business was very uneasy about Governor Reagan's deregulation talk. Government preferences and regulations kept them fat and happy—remember how the airlines howled when President Carter deregulated them? (One of the few good things President Carter ever did.) Reagan's true constituency was not big business but small business; entrepreneurs to whom more government paperwork was a burden and who bore the brunt of minimum-wage laws and other governmental tinkering.

Be that as it may, my first priority was to find prominent businessmen to act as state chairmen in each of the thirteen states I was responsible for. With the Connally juggernaut and the Bush establishment bandwagon moving along, I wasn't sure if I'd even be able to fill all of the positions. I felt like the beggar at the feast.

Still, I had to start somewhere. New York was the richest state in my region so I decided to start there. I had three names in my pocket: William E. Simon, former Treasury Secretary; William Casey, lawyer and conservative activist; and Maxwell Rabb, a lawyer and former Cabinet Secretary in the Eisenhower years who could be a conduit to the Jewish community as well.

I made appointments with each of them. Simon was first. He listened to my pitch and told me that while Governor Reagan was his choice for 1980, he had a firm policy against getting involved in campaigns before the candidate announced. We weren't planning to announce until November, I explained. He shrugged, wished me luck, and said to keep in touch.

I struck his name off the list.

Casey was more helpful. He had been a longtime admirer of Ronald Reagan's and (I knew) had often written to him after he left the governorship saying that if he ever ran for President, Casey would be glad to help. But he sincerely didn't think he was the right man for the finance job. He asked me if I'd had lunch. When I said no, he ordered in sandwiches and coffee and we sat and strategized about who would be a better bet for the job. Casey offered to make a dozen phone calls himself. While I munched on a roast beef sandwich, Casey gestured for me to stay comfortable. He headed for his Rolodex and found the card he needed. It was John Shad, vice chairman of E. F. Hutton. Casey told me about Shad, his fine reputation in the business world, his smarts, and his political views and then raised an eyebrow as if to say: should I call? I nodded. In another minute he had Shad on the phone. Five minutes after that I was talking to Shad myself. Five minutes after that, I had a state chairman.

I was very happy to have recruited Shad. He was an impressive person: a Wall Street heavyweight. But he was new to fund-raising and so he made his share of mistakes in the beginning. For example, he started out by sending solicitation letters to ten thousand wealthy Republicans in the state. Even I could have told him that large contributions never come in the mail.

Since Shad had accepted the post of state chairman, I could approach Max Rabb for more generalized help on the finance effort. He was a joy to work with. Always courteous, always cheerful, Max never made me wait for an appointment and always returned phone calls promptly. He was more than happy to help out with fund-raising and hosted the first luncheon for Reagan with opinion makers in New York City.

Max was also a good recruiter. He got Lee Weil, an investment banker with good connections, to join our campaign. Networking is what fund-raising lives or dies on, and Max Rabb was great at it.

Another of his finds was the controversial Roy Cohn, the lawyer who had first come to national attention when he worked for Joe McCarthy. I knew of Roy's reputation—tough, doesn't like to lose, a little rough around the edges—and so I was pleasantly surprised by how sensitive he proved to be. He knew that it would be better, from a public relations point of view, if he kept out of the limelight and did his work for us behind the scenes. He brought us his partner, Tom Bolan, chairman of the East Side Conservative Club, for the more public roles. Tom was a gem. He worked day and night for us and I can honestly say that he is the most saintly human being I've ever known.

We made slow and humble progress in New York. I had a wonderful assistant in Tony Faillace and he and I raced up and down Manhattan Island, frequently on foot, sometimes by subway (the campaign certainly couldn't afford taxis and I learned every stop between Wall Street and Rockefeller Center), trying to persuade everyone that Ronald Reagan was going to be the next President. For the most part we were met with patronizing looks. Those I valued the most were the ones like Henry Zenzie, Ben Smith, and Preston Long who didn't quite believe Governor Reagan would make it but thought that he should and therefore agreed to help in any way they could.

Our New York headquarters was a tiny two-room office at Madison Avenue and East Twenty-ninth Street. We used the office to make the hundreds of follow-up calls that were always necessary. The office was grimy and cramped. But I did enjoy seeing the young, starry-eyed volunteers who were always floating around looking to be useful.

It's interesting to recall that Don Regan of Merrill Lynch was nowhere to be seen back then. Dan Terra attempted to recruit him several times but without success. Only much later, when Ronald Reagan was clearly going to be the nominee, did Regan begin to return our phone calls, and host a small fundraiser. I got some sense of his authoritarian style when I tried to tell him how a fund-raiser should be run. He informed me in no uncertain terms that he was going to do it his way!

After the New York operation had gotten off the ground, if just barely, I tried my luck in New Jersey and I was fortunate enough to hit it big right away. I had met a New Jersey businessman named Ronald Schiavone years before when Ronald Reagan had come East to give a speech. I called him now to ask if he'd be interested in becoming state chairman for the

Reagan presidential campaign. "I'm not your man," he said, "but I know a better man anyway. Let me put you in touch with my partner, Ray Donovan."

I liked Donovan immediately. He had a very unaffected, down-to-earth quality. I also liked what he had to say. He agreed to be chairman and he promised that if I could get Ronald Reagan to meet with some New Jersey businessmen for half an hour on his next trip to the region, he could get the campaign $50,000.

I thought he was joking. That kind of money was way beyond anything I would dream of raising even at a big dinner. But Ray was serious. And the money was real. His people came through with the fifty grand, and Ray never looked back. He just kept piling up commitments. It was amazing to watch. At one fund-raiser featuring Frank Sinatra and Ronald Reagan we raised $175,000—a record for the pre-announcement days of the campaign.

Though Donovan pretty much operated a one-man show, he did recruit William McCann, another prominent New Jersey businessman, who turned out to have a bit of the Midas touch as well.

But while New York was doing fairly well and New Jersey very well, I was having a much rougher time in the other states. I couldn't find a state chairman for Maine or Rhode Island. Connecticut was so solid for Bush that I didn't even try to put together an organization there, but Allie and Lee Hanley certainly were a one-couple army. We did have a team in Vermont, but they insisted they couldn't charge more than $10 per fund-raising reception. At that rate, Governor Reagan's grandson might have enough money to run for President. And the political directors in Massachusetts and New Hampshire preempted Dan and me totally and absorbed fund-raising into their operations. They sent strong "hands off" signals, and I suffered a huge amount of worry and grief over those two states.

Pennsylvania was iffy. At first I despaired of getting a good team together. My first chairman seemed unwilling to put in the time required to do a good job. I began to look elsewhere. I remembered Drew Lewis and his qualities of loyalty and integrity as they had been demonstrated at the 1976 convention when he stuck with President Ford. I decided to give him a call. He was already committed to Governor Reagan this time around; in fact, he had signed on as Pennsylvania political chairman. But he told me bluntly that he didn't know of anyone good enough for the job of finance chairman who wasn't already committed to Connally or Bush. He heard my despairing tone on the telephone and then he added, "But don't worry. As soon as I get some of this political stuff out of the way, I'll do it for you myself."

I hung up thinking that Pennsylvania was down the drain. It was generous of Drew to offer to handle both jobs. But I didn't want to kid myself. No human being could manage both. So I struggled along with very enthusiastic but inexperienced volunteers.

Reports began to reach us from headquarters in Los Angeles that the campaign was in serious financial trouble. My region was holding its own compared with the others (which I took pride in, considering the uphill battle we had), but still the bottom line was all that counted. I felt frustrated and depressed. I was sure I was letting Ronald Reagan down. I had been at it for six weeks without really striking the ore which existed in such plenty in the rocks of Manhattan.

And then Charlie Wick called. I knew that Charles and Mary Jane Wick were close friends of the Reagans. I had never actually met Charlie and wasn't exactly sure how he had made his money, but I did know that he had a reputation for a mercurial temper. I was a little apprehensive when I returned his call.

To my relief, he was offering his services to help raise money. "Terrific," I said. "Are you coming to New York?"

"What would you think about announcing the candidacy in New York?" he responded.

I couldn't believe my ears. Why announce in New York, where we were barely scraping by, when we could have thousands of delirious supporters at a California rally without any trouble at all?

"That would be wonderful," I told Charlie.

"Great. How much do you think we should charge people to attend the event?"

I almost laughed. Charge? We'd be lucky to drag out a decent crowd in New York for free. In fact, we might have to pay them!

"Well, I'm just wondering," he continued, "whether we should go for five hundred dollars or a thousand."

I thought Charlie needed psychiatric help. But as I was to learn over the coming months, when Charlie Wick gets an idea into his head, he's persistent. The announcement dinner was planned for the New York Hilton on November 13, 1979, in the Grand Ballroom.

I decided that announcing in New York might not be so bizarre an idea after all. It generated excitement for our region and we needed it. California didn't need another Reagan event to solidify its support. Also it didn't hurt that two Northeasterners were rumored to be on Reagan's mind for the vice presidency: Jack Kemp of New York and Bill Simon of New Jersey.

———

The Wicks and their dynamic friend June Walker arrived in New York in September to plan the dinner. They stayed at the Mayfair Regent Hotel. The campaign couldn't afford to put me up in a hotel as well, so I commuted daily from Byron's place in New Jersey into Manhattan. Sometimes, particularly on the late nights when I had to rush past the pimps and pushers on Forty-second Street to get to the Port Authority Bus Terminal, I did feel a twinge of resentment.

The first thing we needed was a small staff to organize the dinner. We were planning on having 1,500 people at $500 per person. I suggested two staffers: Lynn Wood, whose apartment in California had been my home for two years and who was a whiz at administration; and Tad Tharp, a young and very dedicated Washingtonian who had impressed me during the 1976 campaign both for his commitment to Ronald Reagan and for his talent for knowing everybody.

Charlie was the impresario, though. And his gift for gimmicks really paid off. First he lined up a cast of stars to attend. Then he had the invitees divided into groups to make them feel special. I recall that one group was to be called the "ground-floor committee" and was to have a reunion exactly one year later in the Rose Garden. It takes a certain flair to come up with ideas like that. It may be part show biz, but politics always will be that and I admired Charlie for his pizzazz.

The six weeks of preparation were probably the most intense of my life. I lost ten pounds—perhaps out of sheer worry. Charlie presided over daily progress meetings in his hotel suite. Among the regulars were Bill Casey, along with Max Rabb, Ben Smith, John Shad, Preston Long, and Tony Faillace.

At first there was nothing to report. We had to sit there and say that reservations simply weren't coming in. Actual ticket sales were even slower. All of us were working incredibly long hours making follow-up phone calls, but our staff was too small for the job. We tried to rope some of the political people in (the finance people from surrounding states were already helping) but they resisted. There was a firm line of separation between fund-raising and political work in the campaign. The political people thought fund-raising was less glamorous and it was difficult to get their cooperation.

Drew Lewis was an exception. When I called him for some help he said, "I'll tell you what, give me fifty thousand dollars' worth of tickets on credit."

I gulped. "On what?"

"On credit," Drew repeated.

I waxed indignant. "I have never heard of handing out tickets to a fund-raiser on credit." I said the word with all the derision I could muster.

"Look, Helene," said Drew, "as I understand it, you folks are having trouble even filling the room with bodies. I can give you bodies. In a few months you'll get the money. That's all I can offer you right now. Take it or leave it."

Drew had a talent for getting to the heart of the matter. I knew I had to trust him on this one. He was right. I had no choice. "Okay," I sighed, "I'll take it."

It's amazing to me now that a friendship was ever able to blossom between Drew and me when I think of how I plagued him with phone calls asking for that money. I must have called him every week asking when it would be coming in. Drew doesn't ruffle easily, but it was clear he was getting tired of me, to say the least. I could almost feel the heat through the phone cord. "I told you I'll get the money. You're not going to make it come in any faster by calling me every goddamn week!"

I didn't want to offend Drew, but for me the money issue was much more than an accounting detail. I felt that every dollar was going to determine whether Ronald Reagan got to be President or not. As far as I was concerned, the future of the country rested on my doing my job well. Perhaps I could have been more diplomatic about it. Certainly Drew Lewis proved that he deserved my complete trust. He did come through with the money (and more) just as he had promised. In all of our subsequent dealings I have found him to be the same. Drew is a rare find in politics: someone who delivers more than he promises, always plays straight, and always keeps his word (remember his loyalty to President Ford in 1976). He is someone I'm proud to call a friend.

But despite Drew's success, the dinner was still coming up short. We were obliged to hire the Oram Group, a firm which specialized in fund-raising. The Catch-22 was, however, that the Oram Group's fee was so high we now were sure not to earn a penny out of the dinner and would be lucky to break even.

"Relax," Charlie Wick told me when I presented these facts to him. He thought the actual cash return of the dinner wasn't so crucial. Making a splash was. After that, the money would start to come in without our even having to ask for it.

I hoped he was right. But I was getting more worried by

the day. Even with the Oram Group, we were having trouble filling the hall. It would be mortifying to have cameras pan around a half-empty ballroom. Charlie came up with a brilliant idea. He sent mailgrams to everyone who was planning to attend saying that they could bring a guest under the age of twenty-five free for the privilege of witnessing this historic event. Nearly everyone could bring along one of their children. It was a stroke of genius.

I spent the night before the big event until 3 A.M. arranging the seating chart. Charlie had invited a fair number of Hollywood stars and I had carefully spread them around the room so that everyone could go home boasting about having been at or near the table of a celebrity. That turned out to be a mistake. The first star to arrive was Robert Stack. When I escorted his wife and him to their table he just stood there and asked stonily to speak to Charlie. Charlie placed them at a table in the center of the room and then came back to scream at me. We were all under a huge amount of pressure. But when Charlie started screaming at me for not putting all of the stars together in the center, I broke into tears. I had to run to the ladies' room to wash my face and regain my composure. Knowing that tears are considered equal to unprofessional, I was furious at myself on top of it for not being able to hold them back. For the umpteenth time I wondered why women and men aren't allowed to express their emotions differently. Men can swear without being labeled unprofessional, so why can't women cry?

As it turned out, the dinner was a terrific success. We got what we needed: publicity. The news of Ronald Reagan's announcement was on all the front pages the following morning.

THE MAKING OF A PRESIDENT

*T*HE FOLLOWING WEEK WAS THANKSGIVING AND FOR the first time in six weeks I was able to relax. I spent the holiday with Byron at his home in New Jersey.

The respite was short, though. No sooner did I report back to work than I discovered that Mike Deaver had been let go from the campaign by John Sears. At first I thought there must be some mistake. Deaver had been close to both Reagans for many years. Would they allow him to be forced out? And the last I had heard, Deaver and Sears were allies. It was Deaver's advocacy which had gotten Sears the campaign manager's position in the first place. And I have to admit, it did cross my mind that if Mike could be let go, what might happen to me?

The infighting in a presidential campaign is fierce (matched only by the infighting in the White House). Though we'd love to think of it as one happy family all pulling together for a common purpose, it was nothing of the kind. Envies and hatreds proliferated. Fights were loud and bitter. I heard that the Deaver blowup was the result of Sears's dissatisfaction over how the fund-raising was going (Deaver had taken charge after Nofziger). Apparently, after the announcement dinner and two other events failed to bring in the kind of money Sears was hoping for, there was a meeting the weekend after Thanksgiving attended by the Governor and Mrs. Reagan, Deaver, Sears, and his two allies, Charlie Black and Jim Lake. After an acrimonious few hours, Mrs. R turned to her husband and said, "Honey, I think you're going to have to choose." Before Governor Reagan could say anything, Deaver stood up and said, "No, he doesn't have to choose. I'll leave." And they let him.

It was a bitter moment. I phoned Mike to express my sorrow. But I didn't have time to dwell on it. I still had my $3.5 million to raise, and time was getting short. It was December 1979 and the first primaries would be in February.

Charlie Wick's prediction that contributions would flood in after the announcement didn't prove true. The "smart money" was sticking with Connally and Bush.

I knew I had to find new sources. Through the existing committee I was introduced to George and Janice Abbott (he was chairman of Ithaca Industries). George never asked for anything. He only wanted to see the right man in the White House. Meeting him, especially after seeing all of the back-biting going on in the campaign, restored my faith. George seemed to know everyone in New York, and through him I was able to make some respectable progress toward that $3.5 million. He agreed to co-host with Tom Bolan our first private fund-raiser in his wonderful town house in the Seventies off Fifth Avenue where we'd charge $1,000 per person. It was a success, and so was our friendship, which has lasted down to the present day.

Another eager, if unfortunately underappreciated early supporter was Bill Fine, an old friend of the Reagans' and then president of Denny Cosmetics. He made up in enthusiasm what he lacked in clout. His unceasing efforts to persuade anyone who'd listen to support Ronald Reagan were part of our ultimate success in New York. Bill introduced me to Norma Dana, one of New York's famed charity hostesses, who threw a lovely party with Mrs. R as the star attraction.

Though Mrs. R was very fond of permanent bachelor Jerry Zipkin, one of the fixtures of the New York social scene, he played his cards close to the vest. When we sent out invitations to Ronald Reagan's announcement dinner, we asked everyone on our finance committee and everyone else we knew who was supportive to give us lists of names of people to invite. Jerry is one of those people who are always too busy for you. He just couldn't get it together to make up a list. But I knew that Jerry knew everyone, so I had to send Lynn Wood to his apartment to get him to part with some of the names. It took all morning. When Lynn came back she could tell I was irritated by her long absence. "I'm sorry, Helene," she explained, but Jerry bustled from one appointment and address book to another, saying, "Oh, let me see, let me see." His parting words were "Remember, don't use my name!"

While I was mildly disgusted by Zipkin's spineless behavior, I was disturbed to find that Mrs. R showed a similar reluctance to call upon her New York friends for help. All of us were going to our friends to ask for assistance and to lean on them if necessary. It wasn't that I expected Mrs. R herself to approach these people with a tin cup. All I wanted was her permission to approach them myself. But she would never give her consent. I remember getting very annoyed. "What does she think is more important," I recall steaming, "her social network or her husband's chance of being President of the United States?"

She and I were thrown together fairly often during the campaign, though, and I couldn't let my frustration show. Actually, with the exception of the money business and her impatience with unalterable things like weather and traffic, I found her quite willing and eager to help with the campaign.

And I'd be disingenuous if I didn't admit that I enjoyed getting a glimpse of the glamorous life some of the Reagans'

East Coast friends lived. The Annenbergs of Philadelphia, for example, lived on an estate the likes of which I'd seen only in movies. Walter Annenberg had made his fortune as the founder of *TV Guide*. Yet both he and his wife, Lenore, were totally unaffected and very friendly. I liked them instantly. Walter had a terrific sense of humor as well as another quality which is quite rare in the wealthy: gratitude for all his blessings.

I drank in all the details of their magnificent estate and took note of the way they lived. I figured their way must be the right way. That theory was somewhat modified when I noticed how my bed was made. There was a fitted sheet on the bottom. So far, so good. A flat sheet above that. Okay. A thick blanket. And then another sheet! Did the blanket want protection from the bedspread? I wondered. Was the rationale that one might wish to nap on the top sheet in the afternoon without actually unmaking the bed?

Each night our beds were turned down for us and a fresh basket of fruit placed on the table with a pitcher of ice water. As Jean Harlow once said, "Honey, I've been rich and I've been poor and let me tell you—rich is better!"

———

One of my great joys during the campaign was getting to know Dan Terra. He was the loveliest, most generous man I've ever met. Dan's dedication to Governor Reagan and the campaign was total. He never seemed to get tired or grumpy, and treated even disappointing news with an upbeat riposte and a twinkle in his eye. His stamina was all the more amazing for a seventy-year-old man. But age never entered your mind when you were with him. His strength of personality and magnetism simply blotted out biology.

The campaign was rough: personal rivalries and back-biting, frustrations, delays, and disappointments. But I could forget all of that when I was with Dan. He would really make me laugh. We spent so many hours together—on trains, on planes, in cars, and in meetings—that I was able to learn an incredible amount about his life. I teased him once that I probably knew him better than his mother did.

Dan divided his time among all of the regional finance directors, though my region may have required a bit more effort because fund-raising in my area was particularly tough. Compounding that problem were incessant political fights within the campaign. The only saving grace was that it meant I got to see a bit more of Dan.

I loved hearing about his early life. He told me that as a youngster he'd had his heart set on being a song-and-dance man. He was the performing star of his high school. But when he reached Penn State and auditioned for the school play he was turned down. He told me how utterly dejected he felt until one of the senior boys took him aside and explained that everyone thought he was great. The only reason he'd been rejected was that there were so many seniors who'd never get another chance to perform. "Don't worry, Dan, you're a sure bet for next year's lead when we're all gone."

The following year, Dan showed up for auditions with his music under his arm, his lyrics memorized, and his dance steps down pat. He felt on top of the world and decided to watch as the new freshmen came up, one after another, to try out. "I watched, Helene, and my heart dropped like a stone," Dan recalled. "There was a freshman out there who danced like I'd never seen anyone dance before. When he finished his act the entire place gave him a standing ovation. I had to stand up too. His talent was irrefutable. I'll never forget his name, but then, neither will anyone else: Gene Kelly."

Dan never lost his love for the arts. In later life, he acquired one of the finest private art collections of American impressionists. I used to urge him to teach me what he knew (though that would be impossible). Dan opened up whole new worlds for me and he did it with humor and respect and a sense of proportion. Some art lovers, like some wine lovers, seem to forget that there are other things in the world. Not Dan. He is one of the most well-balanced people in the world.

Not everyone was such a joy as Dan to work with. At one point I recall being so disgusted with Jerry Carmen, our New Hampshire political state chairman, that I actually took notes on all of the obstructions he placed in my way. I was sure that people like him were going to cost Ronald Reagan the nomination and I wanted to be prepared to do an article entitled "The Unmaking of a President." Happily, the article never needed to be written.

I was constantly butting heads with Jerry or Keith Bulen, his political counterpart in Massachusetts. They either failed to keep me informed of what was happening or actually attempted to freeze me out of events. I know the presence of a fund-raiser can sometimes get in the way of politics or seem slightly uncouth at a glamorous function, but politics ain't a coming-out party. We needed cash as much as we needed the support of local officials and party leaders—probably more.

Roger Stone, by contrast, was responsible for New Jersey and New York and was a complete professional. We worked together and not at cross-purposes.

I talked to the other regional finance directors and found that they were having similar problems across the country. We were all so tired and so frustrated by February that Dan decided to assemble all of us for a meeting in California. Mike Wallace and Dan presided over what seemed like a college bull session. We certainly weren't shy about expressing our anger. How could we be expected to keep the campaign afloat if the political people continued to treat us like hired help instead of the suppliers of their paychecks?

Dan seemed uncomfortable. He didn't answer our points directly but hinted that there were unspecified "problems" among the top political advisers. What had started as a rift between Sears and Meese had broadened into a seismic fault. Though Ed was the only Californian still formally on the staff, there were many others calling plays from the sidelines. It was becoming clear that another showdown was in the offing.

The worst news was yet to come. Mike Wallace told us that the campaign would be out of money by May 1.

The tumult I felt as I flew back to Washington was almost indescribable. We had the perfect candidate running at the perfect time (the country was fed up with Jimmy Carter) and now, just when we were on the verge of getting what we'd dreamed of, we might be allowing the presidency to slip through our fingers through our own incompetence and in-fighting.

The one person (other than Byron) whom I felt I could talk to when I got back East was Ray Donovan. I told him everything I'd seen and heard in California. He was appalled. It wasn't much consolation to see his reaction, but it was sooth-ing in a way. Misery loves company and all that. But after we got over the shock, we put our heads together to come up with a solution.

Ray had not known Sears until this campaign, but his East Coast background gave him a different perspective from mine. He argued that Sears was the best political strategist in the business (if not exactly the most likable). It would be a mistake to let him go, said Ray. It would be a disaster to fire him before New Hampshire. I tended to agree with him, so I sug-gested that a co-manager, someone from Governor Reagan's old California team, be named to serve with Sears.

"Would that satisfy the Californians?" he asked me.

"It would if it was Bill Clark."

Ray called Sears to float the idea and Sears was receptive. Being in Washington, I was never actually sure why the plan fizzled, but I gathered later that Clark and Governor Reagan had both felt that Clark's position on the court was too impor-tant to sacrifice at that point. After all, Ronald Reagan hadn't even won his first primary yet.

The Iowa caucuses were held early in February. It would be the very first test of the candidates' appeal to voters. Ed Meese wanted Governor Reagan to participate in a debate with the six other candidates which had been scheduled for the night before the voting. Sears felt that Governor Reagan should stay away. He thought Ronald Reagan's stature as front-runner would be damaged by appearing as just one of seven.

When George Bush won the caucus we were pretty sure that Sears would be history. But it wasn't quite over. Another couple of weeks of maneuvering and deal-making followed which would have required a playbook to sort out. If you believed the stories the Californians were circulating, Sears attempted to consolidate his position by asking Mrs. R and Dick Wirthlin, Governor Reagan's pollster, to force Meese out. They also believed Sears called for Dick Allen's resignation (Dick had been working closely with Meese). But Dick phoned the Governor and asked point-blank, "Do you want me in the campaign or not?" Ronald Reagan assured him that he did want him to stay.

"Well, Sears is moving against Meese," Allen added.

Of course, things looked quite different from the Sears camp. They were disgusted with Meese for failing to provide the candidate with accurate briefings as they traveled together and frustrated by the overall quality of issue papers. They were embarrassed when Governor Reagan made statements which later had to be retracted, such as the one where he asserted that there were more oil reserves in Alaska than in Saudi Arabia. Sears and his allies didn't blame Meese for Governor Reagan's error but they were impatient with the way he handled the press afterward. Instead of cleanly disposing of the question, they claimed, Meese sidestepped and attempted to fudge the answer.

Sears, knowing that Meese and his allies were gunning for him, attempted to get cover by bringing Bill Casey on board as co-manager. He floated his name with Governor Reagan after the Clark idea didn't materialize.

The pot continued to boil in the days that followed. The other campaigns were gleeful at the seeming disarray of the Reagan team. (It's funny to think that one of those who must have been popping a champagne cork or two was James A. Baker 3rd.) I heard that at one meeting where Sears seemed to be forcing Governor Reagan to choose between himself and

Meese, Ronald Reagan became so angry that he almost hit Sears. I don't really believe that story because I've never seen Ronald Reagan lose his temper in that fashion. But the campaign was such a tense time, it might be true.

About a week later, Ronald Reagan won the New Hampshire primary. Sears was fired that day, and Mike Deaver and Lyn Nofziger were invited back. Ed Meese was named chief of staff; Marty Anderson, Governor Reagan's domestic adviser from California, who had withdrawn from the campaign earlier, was soon on a plane East; and my friend Bill Casey, the New Yorker with the thick glasses, became campaign manager.

I was not in the thick of all the events surrounding Sears's departure, but it did seem to me that he and Charlie Black and Jim Lake all handled themselves with grace. They walked away from the campaign and never said a bad word about Ronald Reagan or the Californians.

———

After New Hampshire, we could see the promised land. As always with a winner, supporters suddenly came out of the woodwork. Big-name money types began to offer their services. I was relieved that we were at last rolling along toward our goal and that it finally seemed within reach, but I was also dismayed by some of the changes Casey wanted to make.

With prominent people now coming forward to help with fund-raising, Casey actually suggested that the finance team, Dan Terra and the paid regional finance directors, be let go. It wasn't that Dan drew a salary from the campaign but rather that the "big boys" wanted to freeze him out now that everything was rolling. I couldn't believe my ears. Casey couldn't possibly be so insensitive to the importance of rewarding loyalty in politics! I went to Casey and told him he was crazy to cut people off that way. "As for me," I said, "I'll continue to work as a volunteer. It won't be the first time. But you cannot do this to Dan when he has been sweating in the trenches for all these months without getting a dime."

Casey agreed to let all of us stay on staff, though our

salaries were cut. My views about Bill were changing. With power he suddenly seemed opportunistic; ready to let ends justify means. I was reminded of his background and wondered if he learned this at the knee of Wild Bill Donovan, wartime leader of the OSS. But I think he knew that when he tried to ease out Dan Terra, I was ready to go to Governor Reagan about it. "Listen, Bill," I said, "the money is pouring in now. You can't justify this on financial grounds. And remember, you can't buy loyalty like Dan's!"

Casey backed down. But I found that there's a price for victory as well as for defeat.

The rest of the primaries confirmed Governor Reagan's popularity. I recall an item in *National Review,* which noted the low esteem in which Ronald Reagan had been held by the opinion-making elite and then remarked: "It seems no one likes him . . . except the voters."

The convention in July didn't run quite as smoothly as I was expecting. The sudden idea of a Reagan-Ford ticket, with President Ford getting certain prerogatives ceded to him in advance, threw the place into an uproar for a couple of days. But the conclusion was just as I'd imagined it so many times: the hall filled with exuberant Reaganites and a warm, inspiring, and hopeful speech from the candidate.

———

After the convention, I went to stay with Byron at his place on the Jersey shore for some much-needed rest. We ate clams and lobsters, swam in the warm ocean (I noticed that the Atlantic seemed greener than the Pacific and Byron said it was just more algae), and talked about the future. I think both of us knew by then that we'd probably be getting married at some point. But we weren't eighteen anymore and there was no rush.

I considered what my future would hold. Of course, there wasn't any question that I'd be offered a post in the Administration if we won the general election, but I wondered whether I'd get the level of responsibility I'd had during the campaign. It was a nice surprise therefore to get a call from Ed

Meese asking me to work on what he called the "pre-transition" team.

"What's that?" I asked.

He told me campaigns usually see only one or two days ahead. He wanted our campaign to begin thinking about how we'd staff the government if we won.

"But, Helene," he cautioned, "be discreet. If it gets into the press that we're so cocky about victory that we're already picking a Cabinet, it's gonna look awful."

I promised. The new job would mean going back to Washington.

I was delighted that my usefulness was being acknowledged by this new assignment and also, from a personal point of view, I was glad to be close to Byron again.

And then it dawned on me. I was being asked to help pick the Cabinet of the President of the United States. I'd be in the market for Secretaries of State, Defense, Treasury, Commerce, and all of the others. It was a stunning realization.

To test out how it felt, I cuddled up to Byron the night after I'd received the call from Meese and whispered, "Byron darling, would you like to be Secretary of Commerce?"

"No," he said, without skipping a beat. "I'm holding out for Emperor for Life."

Meese had recruited his friend Pendleton (Pen) James, who had his own executive search firm in Los Angeles, Dan Terra, and me. I was to be Pen's full-time assistant.

Whatever thoughts I may have had about our assignment being premature gave way when I saw the kind of paperwork we were going to be faced with. Ours would be the first Administration subject to the post-Watergate disclosure laws. These included 250 pages of conflict-of-interest rules and comprehensive and exhaustive financial disclosure forms the nominee and his or her family would have to complete. On top of those were the usual requests to examine tax records, detailed personal histories, and some highly personal questions.

Pen and I set up shop in Alexandria, Virginia, just south of Washington, in mid-August. With a small black-and-white television set keeping us abreast of the Democratic convention, we began the laborious and yet exhilarating process of forming a new government.

Pen was a pleasure to work with. His experience in headhunting (corporate, not jungle) had given him an eagle eye for talent. And he complemented that with a willingness to hear his opinions challenged or even contradicted. He respected Dan's and my political acumen and frequently deferred to our judgment about someone's philosophical suitability for the Administration.

We were hamstrung by the secrecy requirement, though. Pen shook his head after he received yet another call from Ed Meese stressing that we keep our activities strictly confidential. He knew that a headhunter who can't reveal the nature of the job he's offering is not really a headhunter at all, more like a eunuch.

Still, we did what we could. I knew that we wouldn't be requiring a large staff and yet there were articles to sift through and disclosure forms to familiarize ourselves with, and criteria to systematize. There was enough for a small staff to do, and recalling how much it had meant to me to work on Ronald Reagan's first campaign, I brought some young people on board. I hired Lee Weil's daughter Cary, Patrice Malone, Marc Brazil, and Chris Schiavone, Ronnie's son.

We drew up a list of the 100 most important policy jobs in the Administration. We then listed the criteria, in order of importance, that would be considered in any nominee: (1) commitment to Ronald Reagan's philosophy and objectives; (2) integrity; (3) competence; (4) team work; and (5) toughness (ability to withstand pressure).

But without the ability to discuss real jobs with any of the candidates we came up with, our efforts were reduced to not much more than batting different names around among ourselves.

Things at the campaign had changed dramatically since the nomination. Now the entire apparatus of the Republican

Party was behind Ronald Reagan, and the key political advisers from the other campaigns, particularly Bush's campaign manager, James Baker, were now on board with us.

A series of debates to include President Carter, John Anderson, and Ronald Reagan were planned for the autumn. But President Carter, arguing that Anderson did not represent a party, declined to participate. The League of Women Voters, the sponsoring group, asked Governor Reagan and Anderson if they'd go ahead without the President and both agreed.

Jim Baker took charge of preparing the candidate. Knowing of Ronald Reagan's acting background, he figured a dress rehearsal would be the best preparation. He signed on George Will to play the press, Jeane Kirkpatrick to play the Democrats, and one of John Anderson's recent supporters, Congressman David Stockman, to play Anderson.

Stockman played Anderson perfectly and received everyone's acclaim for his performance. But I felt uncomfortable. Why shouldn't he know exactly what his former boss would say and do? Couldn't any staffer do as much? Besides, I value loyalty. I acknowledged that Stockman was bright and energetic, but the man he had pledged himself to, the man who had been his mentor, Anderson, was still in the race and yet here he was with the Reagan people, winning applause by coaching Governor Reagan on how to beat Anderson. I don't like opportunists.

In the end, of course, President Carter was the big loser of the Reagan-Anderson debate, because he seemed to be hiding in the Rose Garden (a strategy which had also served him poorly during the primary season, when he lost several big states to Teddy Kennedy).

And so, reluctantly, Jimmy Carter agreed to debate Ronald Reagan one on one. I wasn't at the debate but watched at the home of friends in Washington, along with millions of other Americans. When Governor Reagan looked over at President Carter and said, "Now there you go again," I knew we had won. Ronald Reagan had proved to the country the one thing they needed reassurance about: that he was not some sort of trigger-happy demon. After that, we could almost coast to the election.

Charlie and Mary Jane Wick invited Byron and me to spend election day with them at their beautiful Los Angeles home on Sunset Boulevard. I was delighted to accept. I wanted to be back in California when the votes were finally counted. We arrived the night before and spent a long and luxurious evening swapping campaign stories (we'd become close friends since the New York announcement dinner). Now, with victory in sight, the travails of the campaign suddenly seemed funny instead of fatal. We went to bed late.

The following morning at nine (noon Eastern time), Ray Donovan called to tell me he had just sent a bouquet of roses in the shape of New Jersey to Governor Reagan.

"Isn't that a bit premature?" I said, laughing.

Ray said it wasn't. He'd been on the phone all morning to polling experts and news organizations and the signs were all pointing toward a landslide. I didn't believe that but decided to humor Ray. "Gee, that's terrific. Keep me posted."

Charlie, Mary Jane, Byron, and I spent the afternoon glued to the television. We were all so giddy about the accumulating signs of a great victory that we seemed drunk even though we were only drinking Coke.

Toward evening the Wicks headed over to the dinner which was being hosted by the Jorgensens for the Reagans. Byron and I went to the Century Plaza, where Pen and Betty James were hosting a dinner for us and Cap and Jane Weinberger, Drew and Marilyn Lewis, Dan and Adeline Terra, and Verne and Joann Orr. We had a private room equipped with a large television so that we could follow the returns as we ate.

We had drinks at six-thirty. The television maps of the United States showing Carter victories in red and Reagan in blue were already as blue as the Pacific. By the time we sat down for our meal, we were startled to see President Carter standing at a podium in Atlanta and conceding defeat. I just sat there with my fork suspended in midair, a piece of romaine lettuce dangling helplessly. Was it over? So fast? The polls were still open in California. We all looked at one another. Someone asked Cap if it was legal for Carter to concede with the West Coast still voting. He said it didn't matter. Even if the entire West went for Carter (and everyone knew it was solid for Ronald Reagan) he didn't have the electoral votes to win. "I think it was rather gracious of him to concede early," someone said. "Many politicians don't have the grace to admit when they've been beaten."

We quickly finished our dinner, but with the outcome known, some of the fun had gone out of the meal. We were now all eager to be where the action was—the Century Plaza ballroom where Ronald Reagan would celebrate the victory.

The hotel was teeming with celebrants and with Secret Service agents. We decided the best way to get downstairs would be to take the staff elevator down to the kitchen and make our way through it to the ballroom. Entering the room, we saw that the Reagans and their four children, along with the Bushes had already assembled on the stage. We made our way quickly to the special roped-off section for VIPs. President-elect Reagan approached the microphone. The crowd was delirious. Suddenly, I felt a tremor of emotion shake my whole body. I couldn't stay to hear his speech. I ran out of the room. Tears were streaming down my cheeks and I couldn't stop shaking. It was so overwhelming. To work toward something with every fiber of your being for fifteen years and then see it happen. I was overcome.

The applause and shouting went on and on. Then suddenly I realized that the Reagans and the Bushes would be leaving the hall via the same door I had. Mrs. R was the first out. She looked at me, but seemed to look through me. She was hot from the TV lights and seemed drawn and tired. Ronald Reagan was right behind her. He saw me crying and stopped, saying, "Nancy, look who's here," and then he hugged me. She turned and came over to hug me too.

I spent the rest of the night in a bit of an emotional fog. Byron and I visited all of the VIP suites where celebrations were taking place. Mike Deaver, finally reinstated into the inner circle after all of his problems during the campaign, had brought his children down to the Century Plaza and they were racing from room to room shrieking and giggling.

It was well after midnight when we got back to the Wicks'. Byron went straight to bed because he had an early plane to catch the following morning, but I asked Charlie if I could use the typewriter in his study for a few minutes. He pointed the way and I sat down and wrote a letter.

> Dear Governor and Mrs. Reagan,
>
> While my head is still spinnning from last night's triumph, I wanted to forward a few thoughts to you without delay.
>
> Realizing that our perceptions about people are, to a great extent, colored by the remarks we hear about them by those surrounding us, I hope I may give you my observations about a few individuals whose loyalty, dedication, and talent make them special to you. However, by reason of their selflessness, I am afraid, these same people may be lost in the upcoming confusion and shuffle.

I singled out Ray Donovan, Charlie Wick, Dan Terra, and Drew Lewis. I was afraid that so many people had muscled their way into the Reagan inner circle since the primaries that the truly dedicated might be neglected.

I was a prophetess.

THE WORK BEGINS: THE KITCHEN CABINET AND TRANSITIONS

ALMOST IMMEDIATELY AFTER THE ELECTION, THE great job scramble, also known as the transition, began. The old kitchen cabinet from California days wanted to flex its muscles and asked for a meeting with Pen James, Ed Meese, Dan Terra, and me to discuss Cabinet-level appointments. William French Smith, the appointed head of the kitchen cabinet, invited us all to his law firm to talk things over. I was the only woman in the room. Some of the others were Justin Dart, Holmes Tuttle, Ted Cummings, Bill Wilson, and Jack Wrather of the kitchen cabinet, and Bill Simon, Cap Weinberger, Paul Laxalt, and Charlie Wick.

I had only known about the meeting for a week and I was a bit apprehensive about it. Pen and I hadn't really come up with short lists for each Cabinet post and weren't ready to discuss specifics. We had heard that some key members of the kitchen cabinet had already made decisions about who should get which job. I worried, in the taxi ride to William French

Smith's office, whether the kitchen cabinet thought they were going to play exactly the same role at the national level that they'd played in Sacramento.

When I arrived Pen took me aside and said, "I've just talked to the President-elect. He asked me to get three recommendations for each post." I was relieved. Now it would be clear that we were here to receive recommendations, not marching orders. It turned out to be just the first of three meetings to be held on the selection of the Cabinet.

We all took our places and the name game commenced. We decided to consider the Cabinet posts in alphabetical order. Agriculture was first. Pen and I rolled our eyes at one another. We knew that we hadn't come up with one decent name for that department.

"I nominate Richard Lyng," said Cap. He had been deputy secretary of agriculture in California. I don't know how we overlooked him. His name went to the top of the list. Everyone agreed that he shared the President-elect's philosophy and had a good head on his shoulders.

Someone else suggested Governor Robert Ray of Iowa. A few other names got mumbled around the table, but then Laxalt interrupted to point out that the post should get no further discussion until someone had consulted with Bob Dole, who was the ranking Republican senator from the farm belt.

We next turned to Attorney General. It had been a foregone conclusion that the post would be offered to William French Smith, but out of deference to the formalities, he left the room while we discussed it. It took such a scant few moments to agree that the post was Smith's for the asking that everyone was smiling when he was almost immediately called back into the room. "It wasn't exactly like choosing a pope," someone quipped.

Director of the Central Intelligence Agency was considered next. Someone mentioned Casey. Bill Simon thought Casey was hoping for something higher but would accept this if offered. Charlie Wick didn't think it was appropriate to discuss Casey's fate. He was the campaign manager and surely he would deal directly with the President on which job to take. But there was more discussion. We wound up putting his name on the list for CIA and Commerce.

Now, Pen and I had compiled a very, very long list for Commerce. Perhaps because we spent so much time during the campaign trying to interest business people in fund-raising for Reagan. Anyway there were thirty-three names on our list, though none with Washington experience. Bill Simon suggested James Baker, Bush's former campaign manager, who'd done such a fine job prepping Ronald Reagan for the debates. Names flew around the room so fast I had trouble getting them all down. This was clearly an area where the men in the room felt confident to make selections. The final short list became: Bill Casey, Anne Armstrong, George Scharffenberger, Jim Baker, and Elizabeth Dole.

Defense came next. I wasn't happy with our list, which consisted mostly of the presidents of aerospace companies, but then Pen, Dan, and I had been under orders from Meese not to just "retread" old Republican appointees.

Someone threw out John Connally's name. Someone else floated Bill Clements's name. "Is there anyone tough enough for the job who isn't from Texas?" I asked. Bill Clements was Governor of Texas. Jack Wrather chimed in at that moment to say we'd better think twice before removing a Republican governor of Texas. There were nods and grunts around the table. I drew a line through his name.

Bill Smith asked tentatively, "Can Haig be Secretary of Defense?" It seemed there was some legal technicality that would have to be worked out. We put a question mark next to his name. Someone else suggested Sam Nunn, the moderate-to-conservative Democratic senator from Georgia. That provoked a lively discussion.

"There's a lot to be said for having a Democrat in the Cabinet," said Cap. "He's enormously respected, but I wonder if he'd feel comfortable in this position."

Simon thought he wouldn't and urged the group to find a Republican. Donald Rumsfeld's name came up and was immediately shot down. "He doesn't want anything," explained Cummings.

"What about John Tower?" said Laxalt.

The list of names grew longer and longer and included Shultz and Weinberger before we were finished. Then Shultz was dropped and Haig was added.

We moved on to Education, a Cabinet department President-elect Reagan had talked about eliminating. Simon recommended George Roche, the thoughtful president of Hillsdale College. Simon was also very high on Thomas Sowell, a brilliant black economist. "I'd like to see Sowell serve," he said, "but I don't think he's ready for a Cabinet-level post." Sometime later, when Pen called Sowell to feel him out about coming to Washington, he more or less hung up. He wasn't interested. Pen and I still smile about that.

The next department was Energy, like Education a Carter-created department, and a political problem. It's hard to ask someone to preside over the destruction of his own agency. "Whoever it is will get killed politically," said Laxalt. "If you want to put the agency out of existence."

And indeed we did.

We came up with Wally Hickel, former Secretary of the Interior under Nixon and a champion of the Alaska oil pipeline, and James Rhodes, Governor of Ohio. Cap was skeptical about Hickel's administrative abilities. He strongly urged that Frank Carlucci be considered. That's when Dave Stockman's name was suggested.

By the time we turned to Health and Human Services we were all bone tired. We'd been talking for four hours and my bladder was so full of coffee I thought I was going to die if we didn't take a break. Seeing that no one else was going to take the initiative, I suggested that we break for a half hour for lunch. There was unanimity for the very first time that day.

When we returned, Cap announced that he didn't want to be considered for HHS. "I've been there," he explained.

Anne Armstrong, President Ford's Ambassador to Britain, was mentioned. Laxalt said she had already announced her unwillingness to serve under any circumstances.

"An experienced recruiter ignores Shermanesque statements," Pen said, smiling.

More names flew. Rita Campbell, Frank Carlucci, Ben Fernandez. Then Laxalt thought of Dick Schweiker. Memories of 1976 came flooding back to me. He was my sentimental favorite but I didn't say anything. After much discussion he did wind up at the top of the list, with Armstrong second.

When the Department of Housing and Urban Development was discussed, the fact that we had yet to come up with a black for a Cabinet post was mentioned. "I know one," said Al Bloomingdale. "Sam Pierce."

And so it went. Donovan for Labor. Cap for OMB. To overcome Cap's objections (like HHS, OMB was another post Cap had already served in), Bill Simon said, "I think Cap is the only one who can do the job. But it's currently a second-level Cabinet post. The answer is clear. Let's upgrade it to a first-tier post and leave Cap no choice." Everyone roared.

Perhaps the longest discussion came over Secretary of State. It's considered the plum Cabinet appointment, and since we weren't strong on foreign policy experience it was crucial that we come up with qualified and philosophically correct people. Everyone seemed to have a name: Kenneth Dam, Alexander Haig, Henry Kissinger, Donald Rumsfeld, George Shultz, Cap Weinberger, John Connally, and Howard Baker. We ended up ranking them Shultz, Haig, and then Baker.

"Should we talk about Kissinger?" asked Bloomingdale. Bill Smith said no, "Ron knows about him if he wants him."

Transportation was next. I was disappointed that it went so quickly to Drew Lewis, since I was hoping he'd become Chief of Staff at the White House. Ironically, at that time, everyone assumed the Chief of Staff would be Meese. A surprise was coming.

When Treasury was considered, we asked Bill Simon to leave the room and there was a hell of a row. Justin Dart argued so strenuously for him that Smith couldn't help but tease him with "Does this mean you want him on the list?" "This means I want nobody else on the list," shot Dart right back. "He got on board early," said Charlie Wick. I gave Charlie a startled look. That wasn't quite true and he knew it. It got even more embarrassing after that. Holmes Tuttle said that Simon would have taken the finance job if Terra hadn't.

"No," said Dart, "he turned us down and that bum got it." "Jus, for God's sake, Dan is sitting right here," cried Tuttle.

I don't know if Dart knew that Dan had come into the room after lunch or not, but it was an excruciating moment. Dan pretended not to notice. I suppose, like everyone else, he knew that tough talk was part of Dart's repertoire without meaning to offend, but I wasn't used to it and I wanted to crawl under the table.

The meeting ended soon thereafter, but that was only the beginning. I flew back to Washington and the arguing and shuffling of names continued in the capital. But I had more to do than just argue over lists of names. My job as one of six associate personnel directors for transition administration and control was to coordinate the huge flow of calls and letters we were now getting daily. I wanted to be sure that we kept all of the résumés in some kind of order. Also, seeing a potential appointee through the process: Hill clearance, FBI checks, conflict-of-interest checks, and so on. I was also on the lookout for loyal Reaganites, to help them out. I think I was the only one in personnel who had the institutional memory to do that.

Most of the résumés were standard fare, but some were doozies. Miss Ann Elizabeth Abernethy of Oklahoma City was kind enough to send us a ten-page typeset booklet featuring the Abernethy coat of arms on the front. Several fetching photographs of Miss Abernethy adorned the back cover. It seems she had worked briefly at an advertising agency but would accept "an executive level position in the White House."

Where possible I tried to bring my old comrades from the campaign onto the transition staff. I found slots for Ed Weidenfeld, Art Quinn, Jay Morris, Wayne Roberts, Lynn Wood, and

Tad Tharp. But it was painful to have to turn people away. No one was more concerned than I with making sure that Reaganites and philosophical conservatives got into important posts. But there were some conservatives who seemed to view an Administration appointment as an entitlement. And they had to be firmly turned away. I knew there were many embittered friends, but we were staffing a government, not holding a house party. Experience and ability counted too.

———

Ronald Reagan had put Ed Meese in charge of the transition and by now Meese had put together a team. Besides us, there was Cap Weinberger preparing a report on the budget for the incoming financial team; Bill Casey working on a foreign policy report; Elizabeth Dole writing the report on Health and Human Services. In addition, Drew Lewis headed up the team coordinating state and local liaison. Charlie Wick and Bob Gray, then a senior vice president and head of Hill and Knowlton's Washington office, were planning the grandest Inaugural in history.

There were four hundred policy experts working on fifty different task forces. The transition even had its own zip code.

———

On November 16, I flew back to Los Angeles for the second meeting of the kitchen cabinet on selecting the President's Cabinet. This time I came with three boxes of papers, mostly résumés and background information about the candidates.

The second meeting was more serious and subdued. Perhaps the seriousness of what we were undertaking had sunk in. There was an additional face in the group. Joe Coors, an ardent supporter of Ronald Reagan and of numerous conservative causes, had been invited by the kitchen cabinet to join us.

Again we went through the departments in alphabetical order. We were trying now to hone the lists so that we could give two or three names to the President for each department. When we came to Commerce, Elizabeth Dole's name was first on the list. There was some discomfort that she would be seen as too liberal.

Joe Coors agreed. "I know Bob," he said, "but I don't think she belongs on this list. When I talked to Nixon he said, 'Don't pick her.' I think Ronald Reagan should have a completely Reagan Cabinet."

"She was a Democrat until she married Dole," offered Glenn Campbell.

We scratched her off the list.

Health and Human Services still created tension. Dart was adamant that Dick Schweiker's name be removed from consideration. "This guy is ideologically a bum," he pronounced.

"The New Right is high on him," countered Bill Simon.

"Ron likes him," said Tuttle.

"I dislike him," said Dart.

"That's nothing new," said Tuttle.

The tone was elevated by Cap, who soothed things by saying, "Maybe we should put him in another category. If he is a latent big spender, this is not the post for him. I'm worried about him in this job."

They moved on to OMB.

"Who is the equivalent in private industry?" asked Wick.

"Cap Weinberger," said Simon. Cap, of course, had done that job for President Nixon.

"Oh no," said Cap. "Simon would be great!" (He didn't want it either!)

"I think it's only fair to put Simon on," said Campbell.

I scratched Cap's name off the list, and wrote after it: "asked to be taken off but was overruled."

"What about Carlucci?" suggested Cap.

Carlucci was already on the list for four or five other departments. I put him in category II.

"David Stockman would be perfect," said Simon. "He's young enough."

"It's the call of duty," said Cap to Simon. "How about that?"

Simon left the room.

Cap made a motion to put Simon on the list. "That will teach him to leave early!" he says.

I put Simon on, but later scratched him off too.

"I suggest Dan Terra," says Cap.

Everyone stared.

"Is he interested?" asked Casey.

Dan wasn't there, so everyone looked at me. I was dumbfounded.

I knew that Dan was only interested in being Ambassador to the Court of St. James's. When I mentioned it to Dan later, he smiled wistfully and shrugged his shoulders. "Dan," I said, "What's going on?" Dan still didn't answer. He just kept on smiling—a devilish little smile, I thought, getting frustrated. I now yelled, "Are you playing politics?" Unperturbed he replied, "If I do, I learned it from you!"

The meeting broke up at six in the evening. We agreed to meet again with the President-elect on Saturday, November 22. When they indicated they wanted to continue our meetings to look at sub-Cabinet-level appointments, however, Pen was thunderstruck. As we were leaving, he pulled me aside, looking very concerned. "Do they think they're actually going to *choose* the Cabinet?" he asked. "And the sub-Cabinet? How do they think they can cope with the paperwork?"

"No, no," I assured him. "They're just an advisory group." But the truth was, I wasn't so sure.

———

Because I was so incredibly busy in Washington, I hadn't planned to go to the next kitchen cabinet meeting with the President, in Los Angeles, but Dan Terra had insisted. "It's history in the making," he told me, "and besides, if you don't go to this meeting, you won't be invited the next time." Or to other key political and personnel meetings. He had a point!

Byron was disappointed when I called to tell him, because he had planned to come to Washington that weekend to help me find an apartment.

But Dan was right: I had to go.

I flew to Los Angeles on Friday night.

Again, Bill Smith had reserved a conference room at Gibson, Dunn & Crutcher. The press had found out that the President-elect was coming, and they were there to meet us in the lobby.

There were two new faces at the table: Anne Armstrong and Jim Baker.

Anne I'd expected. She was a key Republican and she had been vice chairman of the Reagan-Bush campaign.

Baker was a different question. At the time I didn't know that he had already been named Chief of Staff, but I knew from the very fact that he had been invited that his star was on the rise.

We chatted among ourselves until President-elect Reagan arrived.

After a five-minute hello, Ed Meese suggested that candidates whom Ronald Reagan knew well and who were present did not need to be discussed. "That way we won't have to have any jumping in and out of the room," he explained.

"That's not fair," interrupted Terra in rather untypical fashion. "Some of his closest friends are sitting around this table. We need to talk about whether they should be in the Cabinet."

Everyone agreed that Dan was right.

"Okay," said Ed. We would talk about everyone.

"I've been enjoying Jackson House," the President-elect began. "I hope that next time I'll be in Blair House but Helmut Schmidt beat me to it." He then recounted how one morning he had been curious as to what was behind a door, so he had kicked it open and surprised a typist, who screamed.

We all laughed.

Then we got down to business. Ronald Reagan's time was too precious to waste.

For some reason we didn't talk about the departments in alphabetical order this time. Instead Smith began with Defense.

Everyone chimed in with praise for Haig and Shultz.

"What about Cap?" asked Dan.

Cap left the room so that the others could talk about him.

"I talked to Bill Clements," said President-elect Reagan. "He thinks Cap is the best choice for Defense." The Defense Secretary would have to oversee a budget of $150 billion and budgets were Cap's forte. He then reminded everyone how effective Cap had been testifying on budget cutting in California, citing page and paragraph.

I knew Ronald Reagan well enough to know that he was really telling us that Cap was his man.

Someone mentioned Simon.

"He's very outspoken," said the President-elect. "And that could be dangerous since the department is armed."

Clearly Simon had been vetoed for Defense.

Someone asked Bill Smith to leave, and everyone clamored to say that Smith was the first choice for Attorney General.

"A President needs a friend somewhere," said Laxalt.

There wasn't any expression of doubt on their faces, but Dan nonetheless proposed Bill Clark. "He's better-qualified than Smith," he said. The argument against Clark had always been that his seat on the California Supreme Court was too valuable to throw away, but Dan said that that was nonsense. "California is important. But not more important than the United States."

I watched Ronald Reagan's face. I didn't think Clark had a chance.

Pen went out to the hallway to get Cap and Bill.

As he walked back to his chair, Cap laughed that Lyn Nofziger had said hello when they were waiting; Lyn, Ronald Reagan's campaign press secretary after Sears had left, had come to handle the reporters in the lobby. "I can't understand why they made you leave the room," Lyn had told them. "I wouldn't hire either one of you."

Next was Agriculture, but Anne Armstrong had seen her name on the Commerce list and she interrupted to make sure we took it off. "The only person more important than the

President is my husband," she said. And she wasn't going to ask him to move to Washington after he'd accompanied her to England.

We didn't have any good names for Agriculture in any case, and Ed Meese suggested that the only way to sell the farmers was to get Bill Clark to come from the Supreme Court. "We need more names," he said. "Why don't we have a sub-committee work with Pen."

Commerce was another problem, and had been even when Anne was on the list.

"If you make it more important," said Laxalt, "if you make it the bridge between the government and private industry, then it would be a good job for someone like Casey."

Casey was at this meeting too, but he didn't comment. He'd already made it clear that he'd take the job if it was offered, although it wasn't his first choice.

Meese wasn't sure that the President-elect knew that. "Bill would prefer the CIA," Ed volunteered. "That would be better than giving him Commerce because Bill could turn the CIA around in two years. It's going to take four years to solve the problems at Commerce. I doubt that Bill will stay that long." (Bill did get CIA and, contrary to Ed's expectations, stayed seven years before he was forced to resign after learning that he had a brain tumor; he died in 1987.)

Next was Labor. That was a tough appointment since, as Meese reminded everyone, we had to choose someone who would be acceptable to the unions and would follow our philosophical direction.

Smith read down the list of names.

Before we could discuss any of them, Ronald Reagan started to talk about Ray Donovan. He told us the story of Ray's life, how the seven Donovan kids had supported each other shining shoes. "I understand that the Teamsters told Bob Gray that they could work with Donovan," he said.

We all knew what that speech meant: Donovan had the job.

"Despite Ray's building the tunnel [in New York], he doesn't have tunnel vision," joked Charlie Wick.

When Smith got to Health and Human Services, Dart took the floor. "Schweiker called me," he said. "Dick heard that I was leading the opposition and he wanted to talk." Half an hour had clearly gone a long way to calming Dart's fears. "I talked to Orrin Hatch about his voting record." Orrin was a leading conservative senator. "I think he's okay."

President-elect Reagan didn't think that merited discussing. "I want Dick Schweiker," he said. "Next."

We still hadn't solved the HUD problem.

"I suggest we form a committee," said Laxalt.

"It would be a good agency for a woman," said Meese.

"Al," said Smith, looking at Bloomingdale, "you want to speak to Sam Black." Meaning Sam Pierce, who, of course, was black. Everyone laughed. Smith was obviously joking.

"Drew Lewis would be great for Transportation," said Dan Terra.

"He's also a graduate of Harvard Business School," said Wick.

"So much for his liabilities," joked Ronald Reagan.

No one seemed just right for Energy, a department that we intended to dismantle.

"Let's put John Connally on the list," said the President-elect. "John told me during the campaign that he's not looking for anything, but he's willing to help. He gave me one of the best briefings I've ever had on his recent trip to the Middle East. He's a superb mind."

Meese had already mentioned Casey for CIA, so there wasn't much to add when Smith pulled out that sheet.

"Goldwater suggests Bobby Inman," Laxalt reminded us.

"I got some input from someone at a comparable agency in Europe," said President-elect Reagan. "They no longer give sensitive information to the CIA because it is so infiltrated."

The last department was OMB. That was up in the air—

everyone teased Cap and Bill Simon again—although Ronald Reagan agreed it should be raised to Cabinet level.

We swore we wouldn't leak any of the names discussed.

This session, I think, showed very clearly that RR makes his own decisions, even though his style is laid-back.

Smith had ordered catered sandwiches for lunch and almost everyone stayed.

Except the President-elect.

He was too busy to have time for a nonworking meal. As soon as we had finished the discussion of OMB, he rushed out to another meeting.

I chatted with Cap. Cap had privately talked to Ronald Reagan about naming Clark Attorney General. He shook his head as he told me it wasn't going to fly. My only consolation was that Cap was as disappointed as I. The fact that Bill apparently wasn't going to end up in Washington at all saddened us both.

Because I had decided so late to go to Los Angeles for the meeting, I hadn't been able to book a direct flight back. The only flights available went through Chicago, so I'd chosen to fly with Dan Terra and spend the night in Chicago. We left for the airport at three in the afternoon, and after a 5 A.M. wake-up call the next morning, I was back in Washington by ten o'clock.

Pen had stayed behind in Los Angeles to meet with President-elect Reagan on Monday at his house in Pacific Palisades to go over the final Cabinet recommendations with Meese, Casey, Deaver, Laxalt, and Nofziger. Pen called me Tuesday morning to say that the President-elect had chosen seven and we needed to prepare the announcement papers. Drew Lewis for Transportation, Casey for CIA, Donovan for Labor, Schweiker for HHS, Smith as Attorney General, Weinberger for Defense, and Baldrige, a Connecticut businessman and close friend of George Bush, for Commerce. The nominations would be announced as soon as the paperwork was ready and the FBI checks came through.

Ronald Reagan had already begun to make his calls. Baldrige, a nationally ranked steer roper, had been out riding when he called to offer him the job. "That's my kind of man," he had told Mrs. Baldrige.

George Shultz had made it known that he was not interested in being named to the Cabinet, although I was not aware he had not been asked. (Someone must have told him he wasn't selected.)

Pen told me that Simon had called the President-elect from Saudi Arabia to withdraw his name for Treasury. Apparently his feelings had been hurt when he wasn't considered for Defense and his idea of an economic czar was coldly rejected.

I must have explained dozens of times to hopeful job seekers that we had to fill the top posts in the Administration first in order to give his Cabinet some flexibility in choosing their own staffs.

Those hectic days were dizzy with excitement. I tried to keep notes of what was happening on a daily basis because I was so filled with a sense of history in the making. I suppose I had a hand in that history myself, though I didn't dwell on that part of it.

I found I was no longer an anonymous staffer. The German and Austrian press had gotten wind of the fact that I was a close Reagan aide and it seemed every time I turned around another reporter from one of those countries was dogging my footsteps. I was flattered, but I couldn't possibly handle the volume of calls and also do my job. So I decided to grant an exclusive to Klaus Emmerich, Washington correspondent of the Austrian Broadcasting Corporation, on condition that he help me screen the rest of the press calls. For a week he followed me everywhere, including to the beauty shop to get my hair cut, to nonconfidential meetings, and even to lunches. I told him he knew more about me than my mother did.

The pace was unrelenting, so I still hadn't gotten an apartment of my own and continued to camp with Nancy Reynolds. That was probably for the best, since I tend to get too serious at times of high stress. She always helped me maintain my perspective, especially since she was always laughing at some

new piece of gossip. She also kept me abreast of how the staffing was going for Mrs. R. Apparently Mrs. R's first press secretary, Robin Orr of the Oakland *Tribune,* was not working out
as expected. At a dinner with "Tish" Baldrige, formerly social
secretary to Jacqueline Kennedy and an etiquette expert, Orr
committed the unforgivable faux pas of continually interrupt-
ing the guest to give her own opinion. But what came next was
even worse. She held a press conference across from the White
House to describe the whole evening. Mrs. R was frantic.
Nancy Reynolds said, "As you can guess, we're in the market
for a new press secretary."

Nancy Reagan eventually found Sheila Tate, a highly respected Washington public relations executive. It was a fine
choice, as Tate was later responsible for turning around the
extremely negative press treatment the First Lady received
during her first year.

It was through Nancy Reynolds that I first heard that I
was being talked about as the President's personal secretary. I
listened without saying anything. It was a ticklish situation for
me. I didn't want to seem ungrateful and there was no doubt
that it would be an honor to be the personal secretary to the
President of the United States. Yet during the campaign I had
performed well in a really substantive job and I was proud of
it. I didn't want to step back down to a secretarial position. So
as Nancy spoke I just bit my cheeks.

It was odd, because while I was being talked about as a
secretary I was also flying back and forth to California for
more meetings on selecting the Cabinet. My role was recognized as substantive at one level—my judgment about personnel was respected—and yet I seemed to be in a kind of suspended animation when it came to being considered for a
substantive position. Perhaps I should have pushed, I don't
know.

———

Byron and I spent Thanksgiving with his mother and his
two sons in New Jersey. I used the long weekend to do my
clothes shopping for the coming year. I've never been the type

who shops for entertainment. I just go through the stores once or twice a year and buy what I think I'll need and get it over with.

Being in New Jersey gave me a chance to catch up with Ray Donovan. Things had been going badly for him. The President-elect had offered him the post of Secretary of Labor, but he was beset by rumors. The FBI, when it conducts a background check, is supposed to listen to rumors. That's one of their methods of getting leads on people. But it can also mean that the clearance is held up. Without FBI clearance the public announcement of his appointment was on hold. It was galling to consider that Don Regan's appointment as Treasury Secretary was in all the papers. Dan and I remembered only too well that Regan (whom I had brought to Pen's attention as a possible Treasury Secretary after Bill Simon turned it down) had been lukewarm toward our campaign until we were sure primary winners. I've even heard a story that Regan contributed $1,000 to both Ronald Reagan and Jimmy Carter—not unusual among CEOs who like to hedge their bets. On the other hand, I think Regan went on to serve the President faithfully. He never had his own agenda.

Meanwhile Ray, who had committed himself to us so early, was being harassed. Someone on the transition team who favored another candidate for the Labor post was passing himself off as an FBI agent and phoning Ray's friends, associates, bankers, and lawyers.

Ray Donovan had never been under any cloud of suspicion in his life. But now rumors flew that he and his partner were somehow involved with the Mafia. It was the start of a nightmare for Ray which pains me so much. He was an innocent and good man caught in a witch-hunt. After many years of accusations, Ray was finally forced to resign his post to defend himself. He was tried and acquitted. But what a price to pay for the honor of being Secretary of Labor.

When I returned to Washington, it dawned on me that some of the key Californians were not yet established in jobs. I had read in Evans and Novak's column that Bill Clark was being considered for the slot of Deputy Secretary of State. But Meese, Deaver, and Nofziger were still unemployed.

Meese was the director of the transition team, but he hadn't yet been offered the obvious White House job for him: Chief of Staff. Nofziger was moving to Washington, but he made it clear he didn't want to be press secretary. And Deaver maintained that he wanted to return to private life in public relations, though he too was moving to Washington.

It was through Mike that I learned who was going to get the Chief of Staff position. Apparently, even before the election, Mike had spoken with Ronald Reagan about Jim Baker. Perhaps there were others who recommended him as well. Mike didn't tell me whether Mrs. R had a hand in that, but I knew that she had been impressed with how competently Baker handled the debate preparation, so it wouldn't surprise me if she backed him too.

The decision was a closely held secret for a time. Mike Deaver told me that he didn't have the heart to tell Meese about it. Consequently, when Meese suggested that Deaver accompany him to a meeting with President-elect Reagan "to discuss the organizational chart," Deaver just went along mutely.

When they arrived at the Reagans' house, the President-elect examined the chart, showing Meese in the Chief of Staff post, and told Meese that he had decided to give the job to Baker. Meese was nonplussed. But he accepted it like a good lieutenant. After they left, Meese turned to Deaver and said, "You knew, didn't you?"

"Yes," said Deaver. "In fact, I suggested it."

When Mike told me that, I was surprised at how brutally blunt he had been. Tact had always been one of his long suits. I wondered if the tension of the campaign and the crushing disappointment he had suffered at Ronald Reagan's hands (he had been let go) made him unsympathetic when other old Reagan staffers were similarly let down.

Bill Clark told me that President-elect Reagan was distressed about the Meese thing and had asked his advice on how to handle things after the Baker decision was known. Clark, ever ingenious, came up with the idea of creating a new post called "Counselor to the President." And that's what Meese became.

Until the middle of December, Mike kept saying that he wasn't going to join the Administration. I was skeptical. Sure enough, the shrinking violet saw his way clear to accepting the third most powerful post in the White House, Deputy Chief of Staff.

I just couldn't believe that Mike had pushed so hard for Baker to become Chief of Staff and then accepted the post as his deputy by accident. Maybe there was no plan. But Mike was smart and knew how to maneuver. It would be insulting to his many skills to suggest that he just landed in the job by serendipity.

Years later I asked Mike why he pushed so hard for Baker, a Republican moderate of the Ford-Bush wing of the party.

"We needed Baker," Mike explained. "We Californians couldn't have governed ourselves."

Perhaps not, but Mike was forgetting that Ronald Reagan hadn't worked so long and hard to become President just to govern, just to preside over the federal bureaucracy. He had come to make a fundamental change in the direction of our country.

The week before Christmas, Pen and I scheduled the first meetings with the newly appointed Cabinet members to begin talking about substaffing.

How differently they all acted. Drew Lewis knew exactly what he wanted and couldn't wait to get started. He quickly signed on two very capable former associates. Predictably, Weinberger was already pushing for Frank Carlucci, his man Friday, as Deputy Secretary of Defense—never mind that neither of them had ever had any experience in the department. Baldrige and Donovan were uncertain, though, almost apprehensive, and Secretary of State Alexander Haig, who didn't yet know who his deputy would be, was silent. In a rare demonstration of presidential authority, the President-elect asked Haig for a concession when offering him the job of Secretary of State. He made it clear that he, not Haig, would name his deputy and it would be a Californian.

During the transition, I had developed great respect for Dr. James Cavanaugh (Deputy Chief of Staff in the Nixon White House), who was brought in by Pen as his deputy. And in keeping with my pattern of going to people I respect for advice about my career, I asked him what I should do if the President-elect asked me to be his secretary.

Jim felt strongly that I had proved myself during the campaign and in the transition and shouldn't accept anything less than a substantive or "line" position. I listened to him and felt ten feet tall. He was right. I had done a great job on the campaign. I would simply ask for something in personnel.

But when the time came, I lost my nerve.

Pen, Mike Deaver, and I had met with President-elect Reagan at Blair House to discuss Cabinet and sub-Cabinet appointments. While we four were chatting about Haig, and Terrel Bell, and Weinberger, Pen suddenly launched into a long tribute to me and what a fine job I'd done over the past few months. Ronald Reagan grinned and said, "You'll understand when I don't express surprise over that." We all laughed and then Mike raised another subject.

Pen told me later that he had intended that compliment to be the opening for him to ask President-elect Reagan to appoint me to his staff. He had been named Assistant to the President for Presidential Personnel, responsible for staffing all of the most important jobs in the federal government. But the moment passed and Pen didn't sense another opportunity to raise the issue.

After the meeting, Mike took me aside and said, "The President-elect wants you to run his office."

I hesitated for a second, and then I said, "I'd be thrilled."

Mike broke into a big grin and hugged me. It may have

been my imagination but he seemed relieved. But after I accepted I added a list of provisos. I told Mike I'd want to be involved in scheduling decisions, appointments, and invitation lists. After all, I was part of Ronald Reagan's institutional memory. Also, Jim Cavanaugh had impressed upon me how important titles and symbols were in the White House, so I asked to be named Special Assistant to the President and also to be allowed to attend staff meetings so that I'd know what was going on.

Mike was sympathetic but said he wasn't really in a position to promise everything I'd asked for. He told me he'd see what he could do. In the end, Mike came through for me. He even went further and secured a few more perks for me, such as access to the White House tennis courts and to the Executive Mess and a parking space just outside the canopy of the White House basement—all usually reserved for higher-ranking officials.

I was pleased and impressed. I hoped the perks and the sheer excitement of the White House would compensate for the lack of a more substantive job. I was resolved, in any event, to make as much as I possibly could out of being the personal secretary to the President.

———

To my amazement, the kitchen cabinet suddenly demanded an all-hands meeting in Washington on Saturday, December 27. I was staying in the city for Christmas anyhow, because I planned to spend both Christmas Eve and Boxing Day working, but the other people in personnel were upset that they had to break their vacations with their families to come to a meeting that promised to be pointless and possibly unpleasant. Pen flew in from Los Angeles. Jim Cavanaugh came from the ski slopes in Vail.

The meeting dragged on.

Bill Smith had dropped out of the group since being nominated for Attorney General, and Bill Wilson had replaced him as kitchen cabinet chairman.

The complaints were simple, and at least partially true.

We did not take their recommendations as commands. We had not given them the feedback they wanted. Now we were not including them in the selection of the sub-Cabinet.

Henry Salvatori wistfully recalled the days when Ronald Reagan was Governor and they were accorded the status they deserved. "Some of us literally moved to Sacramento," he said.

I guess we had asked for trouble. Instead of trying to accommodate the group, we had largely ignored them. We had scheduled the sub-Cabinet meetings and hoped they wouldn't notice or would forget.

No, they had not. They said they had a mandate from the President.

It wasn't that we were unwilling to be cooperative with Ronald Reagan's best friends, who wanted to help, but we didn't have the time. The pressures on us were enormous.

"I'm going to move to Washington to help with the staffing," said Wilson. He wanted to talk to the Cabinet officers himself and attend our meetings with them to get a better feel for what was needed.

Pen, already exhausted and tired from all the pressure and long hours, had had it. For weeks, he had tried to get Ed Meese to tell the kitchen cabinet that they wouldn't be able to continue their activities once the Cabinet was chosen. He was adamant that we would never get our job done if we had to cater to the kitchen cabinet. "I quit," he said. "I'm flying home." He stormed to the Jefferson Hotel to pack.

I followed along, trying to coax him to change his mind. Nothing I said seemed to do any good. He finally calmed down as he drove to the airport, although he would not turn around.

By the time I got back to Washington after watching him board the plane, Dan Terra had talked the matter over with Wilson, and Bill had agreed not to move to Washington after all. Dan had suggested that the best way to improve communications was for us to choose someone like Wendy Borcherdt, my fund-raising counterpart in California during the campaign, to be liaison to the kitchen cabinet, and Bill had agreed to try.

As soon as I got to the office on Monday, I alerted Ed Meese to what had happened. I called again two days later to be sure that Ed had done something about it—he hadn't—and to say that Pen was needed back in Washington. Again, Ed promised.

Meanwhile the situation was deteriorating.

Bill Wilson wasn't taking Dan's advice. Rather than stepping back, he was getting more aggressive. When he got back to California, he formed a kitchen cabinet subcommittee and called Cap Weinberger to say that the subcommittee didn't want Frank Carlucci to be Deputy Secretary of Defense.

"I need a schedule of your meetings with Cabinet officers," Wilson told Pen on the telephone. "I'm going to schedule separate meetings of my own too. I'll be in Washington tomorrow."

Pen was almost incoherent when he called me.

I called Ed Meese again.

Ed still hadn't talked to Pen or the kitchen cabinet, but "the President-elect knows what's going on," he assured me. "We're trying to resolve the problem."

Maybe they were, but nothing happened, except that Pen was finally persuaded to return to Washington.

The day after the Inauguration, Wilson had lunch with Jesse Helms to complain that the recommendations of the kitchen cabinet were being ignored by both Ed Meese and Pen James. Helms wrote an angry letter to the President-elect demanding that the kitchen cabinet be restored to the rank it had had when he was Governor and that it be given veto power over appointments approved by Pen and Ed.

To my knowledge, President-elect Reagan never responded to the letter, and he never talked to the kitchen cabinet about the problem.

Instead, the group self-destructed.

The day of the Helms lunch, Wilson had gotten White House credentials and an office in Suite 180 of the Executive

Office Building, across an alley from the White House. There he quickly got on the wrong side of almost everyone, but refused to leave until late February, when Fred Fielding, White House counsel, told him that he, and anyone else who wanted to work in the White House, would have to pass an FBI investigation in order to stay.

———

Christmas Day was awful. Because I was going to have to work the next day, Byron had flown down from New Jersey to be with me at the small apartment I'd finally rented in the Foggy Bottom section of Washington. But it was a cold Christmas. For one thing, Byron was sick with a cold, and I'd been so busy that I hadn't had time to cook anything. We thought we'd go out but absolutely everything, including supermarkets, was closed. Despairing, I looked in the freezer and found two lasagna TV dinners. That was our Christmas meal.

But New Year's Day was much better. Nancy Reynolds was away on vacation in Idaho and she offered me her house to use for a New Year's party. I accepted happily and planned a party with Missy Tyson and Carol Laxalt (Paul's wife). I had to smile to myself when I surveyed our guest list. It looked like the standard Washington power party. The names included Mr. and Mrs. Don Regan, Mr. and Mrs. Caspar Weinberger, Senator and Mrs. Dick Schweiker, Mr. and Mrs. Charles Wick, Senator and Mrs. Mark Hatfield (she was a real estate salesperson in her spare time and had helped me find my apartment), Bob Gray, Mr. and Mrs. Richard Allen, and many more. We had much to celebrate and the affair was a fabulous success. I would not see all of those people that relaxed ever again.

———

There were a few official functions I was invited to attend before the Inauguration. One was a luncheon President-elect Reagan hosted for female members of Congress. His reputation among women was a bit weak, and this was one of his attempts to prove his critics wrong. He wanted to show that he did take women seriously.

I was fascinated to meet Shirley Chisholm, the black congresswoman from Brooklyn, who had run for President. And I was immediately charmed by Millicent Fenwick, the pipe-smoking patrician from New Jersey. Though the outspoken lady was already in her seventies, her bearing seemed more like a fashion model's than an elderly lady's. She was the Katharine Hepburn of politics.

I was also flattered to be invited to attend the very first meeting President-elect Reagan held with his Cabinet on January 8, 1981. After an incredible amount of fighting, bitterness, worry, and sweat, all of the posts had finally been filled. Some of the members of Ronald Reagan's old kitchen cabinet in California had been offended when they didn't get final say, and lots of feelings were bruised, but it was finally done. The strangest incident I recall from that time was a telephone call that the President-elect made to Frank Sinatra explaining that he had chosen Bill Wilson as his envoy to the Vatican and he hoped Frank would understand. To this date, I wonder what this was all about. Did Frank have a personal interest in that post or did he have his own candidate?

But the days of deliberation on the Administration's top posts were finally behind us and the President-elect stressed now how much he was going to rely on his Cabinet. He urged all of them to participate in policy discussions whether it bore directly on their area of responsibility or not. And he reminded them that he never wanted to hear a discussion of the political consequences of any particular policy around his Cabinet table.

He congratulated them all, wished them good luck, and closed by reminding them that "when we start to talk about government as 'we' instead of 'them,' we've been here too long." Everyone roared, even the Californians who had heard the line so many times before. You become funnier when you're the Commander in Chief.

We had just ten days before the Inauguration and I was swamped with paperwork trying to push through as many as possible of the appointments of deputy secretaries for the various departments. During one harried afternoon, Pen stuck his head into my office looking grim. "Got a minute?"

"Of course," I said. "Come in."

Pen sat down, sighed, and explained that he'd just found out that Dan Terra was not going to get the job he'd been dreaming of: Ambassador to Great Britain. It seemed the post had been promised, the previous weekend, to John J. Louis, Jr., heir to the Johnson Wax fortune and a friend of Walter Annenberg's.

"Are you sure?" I asked. There was no reason for President-elect Reagan to offer an ambassadorship this early and it didn't sound like him. He hadn't discussed it with any of his aides.

Pen said he was certain. I was crestfallen. There was only one person who could be responsible. The Wicks knew that Dan had his eye on the Court of St. James's and Mary Jane might logically have mentioned it to Mrs. R. Mrs. R was aware of how much her husband thought of Dan and knew that his chances for the job were good once Ronald Reagan was informed. But she probably didn't think Dan had the right cachet for that post and therefore headed him off at the pass by getting her husband to offer it to Louis. I heard later from a member of the kitchen cabinet that Louis had been at the Annenbergs' with the Reagans on New Year's Eve and that they had all toasted the appointment at 2 A.M.

I was heartsick. Dan Terra absolutely embodied all of the qualities a political candidate needs to succeed: unselfish devotion, intelligence, tact, a capacity for hard work, and persistence. They say no good deed goes unpunished. Dan wasn't even allowed to compete openly and fairly for the job he wanted. I was so angry and disappointed that I did something unusual for me. I picked up the phone and called President-elect Reagan. I reminded him that Dan had been with us in the trenches long before almost all of the others. He listened sympathetically, but pointed out, correctly of course, that he couldn't withdraw his offer to Louis now. (For the record, Louis was recalled later during the Falklands crisis and I took some grim satisfaction in that.) I knew that was true and if I hadn't been so upset I would have thought of it myself. But I wasn't sorry I'd made the call. Someone had to stand up for Dan.

After the call, I decided I needed some air. It was evening and a light snow was dusting the city. I set out walking toward the White House, my tears stinging my face in the cold. I walked around the gate at the bottom of the South Lawn and looked up at the majestic columns of the portico. The lights were on inside and the snow, heavy now, framed the scene like a postcard. I gazed up at the beautiful little mansion and wondered: how many more dreams will shatter against those lovely white columns?

A NEW BEGINNING: THE INAUGURATION AND THE FIRST DAYS AT THE WHITE HOUSE

As INAUGURATION DAY 1981 DREW CLOSER, THE EXcitement became palpable. After the backbreaking labor of the campaign, this was the moment to savor victory and the tingling sensation of a new beginning. It was more than personal. The whole country seemed to share my anticipation of the dawning new era. The yellow ribbons reminding us of the hostages held by Iran were finally coming down. We were going to replace those symbols of helplessness and despair with symbols of renewed strength and resolve.

It was a rare moment of exhilaration, but also of confusion, chaos, and mixed signals. I was suddenly deluged with requests for tickets from scores of people. Everyone I'd ever dealt with seemed to be calling and writing. There was little I could do for any of them (tickets were not in my sphere), and yet I owed it to most of them to try and it was draining to keep dialing the ever-busy line to the Inaugural Office in hopes of catching one of the principals and convincing them of the need to get tickets for so-and-so.

Byron's sons, Warren and Michael, came down to Washington with their girlfriends, Wendy Schier and Debra Perskie, for the weekend, and I did manage to get them tickets for some events. It was such a whirlwind weekend. A huge frustration for me was that, because of protocol, Byron wasn't invited to all of the same events that I was. This caused me no end of anxiety and posed logistical nightmares—about where to meet and at what time, never knowing when events were actually over and uncertain about the availability of cabs or access to certain areas of town.

The festivities began with an elegant dinner at the State Department on Saturday, January 17. The Diplomatic Reception Room, probably the most beautiful in the building, afforded a lovely view of the Lincoln Memorial and of the fireworks over the Potomac which began the celebration.

The following day, Byron and I attended a brunch hosted by Senator and Mrs. Mark Hatfield at their wonderful old sprawling home in Georgetown. It was a fabulous combination of Hollywood and Washington stars: everyone from Elizabeth Taylor to Henry Kissinger was there. And in the evening there was a candlelight dinner at the Kennedy Center. There I felt as if I were floating in a sea of Reaganites—all the friends and contacts I'd made over the years were there and I was constantly exclaiming over one long-lost pal or other.

Monday was spent packing up my last remaining papers at transition headquarters (I didn't want anyone else to get their hands on them) and transporting them over to the White House. In the evening we headed out to the Capital Center, a sports arena, where the Inaugural Gala was being held. Frank Sinatra was the emcee and the show also included Bob Hope, Johnny Carson, Marie Osmond, and many others. We had great seats and just felt high as kites. Struggling through the awful traffic to get back into town was draining, though. When we got home we fell into bed. The next day was Inauguration Day.

I didn't sleep well that night. When morning came at last, I was disappointed by the clouds. But nature, as she so often has in the past, cooperated with Ronald Reagan. When he and Nancy stepped onto the platform erected in front of the Capitol, the sun emerged.

I was seated on the platform with the Reagan staff and family. Byron, unfortunately, wasn't allowed to sit with me and attempting to find him in the crowd was impossible. I hated being separated from him.

After the swearing-in ceremony, Byron and I found each other in the Capitol building. We had lunch together and then I made my way through the crowds to get to the White House before the new President, who by tradition lunched with congressional leaders in Statuary Hall after the Inauguration. I wanted some quiet moments to survey my new surroundings.

My office was directly outside the Oval Office with French doors opening onto the Rose Garden. It was far smaller than I had expected (everything in the White House is actually smaller than we are led to believe by movies and spy novels), but I didn't mind. In the beginning, even breathing the air in the White House was thrilling.

Though the actual office space for the President's secretary was quite small, the telephone banks left little doubt about the importance of the office next door. There were lines to the White House operators (an extremely friendly, intelligent, and skilled staff who handled the huge volume of calls to the White House every day), secure lines which sent scrambled messages anywhere in the world (though there is no "red phone"), direct lines to the Pentagon and the CIA, and private lines for the President's use.

The President returned from the Capitol and took a few minutes to try out his new surroundings in the Oval Office before changing clothes for the Inaugural Ball. He had brought with him from California the chair he had used (and loved) as Governor. Unfortunately, the chair was too high. The new President found that his knees wouldn't fit under the desk. But his love for the chair overcame the discomfort. For several months, he sat at the desk in the Oval Office sideways. Visitors may have found this strange. Finally, when he was away for a few days, a bunch of us got together and had a riser installed on the bottom of the desk so that he could work comfortably. He was really touched when he returned.

While I was getting to know the White House phone system, Ed Meese, Jim Baker, and Mike Deaver had gathered in Meese's office down the hall. There were smiles all around about the news that the hostages in Iran had been released and were on their way home. The conversation drifted to the ceremonies just completed and the revelries still to come. I was surprised when Al Haig arrived accompanied by Cap Weinberger. Only later did I discover, through the gossip network of secretaries who worked for the top Administration aides, that this was the so-called Haig power play, in which he presented Meese with a document for the President's signature which would have given him sole authority over all foreign policy matters. It didn't work. Power in the Reagan White House was acquired gradually and subtly, not by a stroke of a pen.

Late in the afternoon, I hurried back to my apartment to prepare for the Inaugural Ball. I had chosen a long black taffeta skirt and a red ruffled blouse. As I rushed to meet Byron at the Washington Hilton, I was giddy. We had the time of our lives. Pure celebration. No clouds on the horizon. Byron shared my delight. We danced almost until dawn.

———

Slightly bleary-eyed from the previous night's celebration, I arrived at the White House the following morning for the first real day of the Reagan Administration.

We wanted to do everything at once. Time is the most precious commodity in the White House. In addition to whatever substantive goals the President wishes to pursue, he must always take time for his ceremonial responsibilities as head of state. In other democracies that role is filled by a constitutional monarch or by a ceremonial president, but the U.S. President is both head of government and head of state. So while we were taking the first steps toward implementing our political agenda, there were calls to place to foreign dignitaries, a luncheon with leading mayors, a Salute to Congress dinner, and an official welcome home to the former Iranian hostages and their families as well as the families of the marines who had died trying to rescue them.

We wanted to use every minute to its fullest. Partly, I suppose, because any Administration would do the same. But we were also influenced by a study Dave Gergen, the new communications director, had prepared. He compared the first one hundred days of every Administration since Roosevelt's and found that only those Presidents who established key themes early in their tenure were able to accomplish anything.

Everyone knew where we stood. Our priorities were to revitalize the economy and to restore our defenses. Even before he left the Capitol on Inauguration Day, the President had signed an executive order freezing federal hiring. Within days he had also issued orders cutting the use of government consultants by 5 percent and trimming travel expenses by 15 percent.

On the first day, the President also chaired a meeting of the National Security Council. El Salvador was then in the grip of a bloody civil war. Armed Communists and rightist militias were exacting horrible tolls on one another. The President was determined to support the democratic center, and asked the Congress for $25 million for that purpose.

Another of his first official acts was to fulfill a campaign promise to lift the grain embargo President Carter had imposed on the Soviets after they'd invaded Afghanistan. The President felt that since the Soviets were merely buying the wheat from other sources (some of whom got their wheat from us), the embargo had hurt the American farmers and not the Soviets.

Meanwhile, over in the Executive Office Building, David Stockman and his number crunchers were huddling to figure out ways to cut the budget. They had begun what would become a six-month marathon of negotiations with the Cabinet and Congress. At the same time, Max Friedersdorf, Congressional Liaison, and his deputy, Ken Duberstein, were working out the details of the Kemp-Roth tax cut.

The pace was incredible. In the first two months of the Administration, the President met with four hundred legislators.

But as hard as he worked to persuade members of Congress, the President always understood that his greatest strength was in speaking directly to the American people. When speaking of Congress he would frequently say, "If you can't make them see the light, you can make them feel the heat." The heat could only come from their constituents.

Mike Deaver and Dave Gergen made preparations for a televised speech to the nation about the economy. We were all hoping for something as powerful as Franklin Roosevelt's first fireside chat. We knew our man could do it.

But when the President came into the office on the morning of the speech, he was visibly upset. He said he'd spent the previous evening going over the draft prepared by the speech-writers, and it just wasn't good enough. Throughout his career, Ronald Reagan has made thousands of speeches. But he never regarded them as routine. He worried about each one, and, time permitting, he wrote them himself. Indeed, before becoming President, he had written most of his speeches. In the White House, he didn't have time to undertake such a massive work load—but he always reworked the important ones carefully. In fact, he later told me when I was going to give a speech myself that my nervousness was a good thing. He thought anyone who wasn't a little nervous wouldn't give their all.

I canceled all of his morning appointments and held all calls. He needed silence and time to work that Reagan magic. I peeked inside the office once or twice to see him scribbling on a yellow legal pad. He looked up, shook his head, and said, "I woke up in the middle of the night with an idea. It was so strong I was sure I'd remember it without writing it down, but now I don't." I told him I was sure that if it was as good as he thought, it would probably surface, and if not, maybe it wasn't worth remembering.

After several hours, he strode into my office smiling. The speech was finished and he was pleased. He even prepared his own cue cards, written in big block letters.

George Bush happened to be standing in my office and they chatted about the prayer breakfast both had attended that morning.

Late in the afternoon, the technicians descended. All three networks sent crews to light and wire the Oval Office. Unfortunately, my little office wasn't spared. I had to step over thick cables and try not to pull any plugs as I attempted to keep the office running. The President didn't mind the turmoil. I can't say the same for myself. The White House may be a bully pulpit, but it's also a workplace. The two sometimes clash.

The countdown to the speech was filled with suspense. I decided to stay at the White House and watch from the press-room. The screen filled with the presidential seal, and then he began. "It's time to recognize that we've come to a turning point," he said. "We're threatened with an economic calamity of tremendous proportions, and the old business as usual treatment can't save us. Together we must chart a different course." From that moment on, and for many years to come, Americans were happy to let President Reagan be the navigator.

The Reagan Revolution had begun.

———

It took weeks to learn the ropes at the White House. The security measures aren't glamorous. Quite honestly, I found them to be a pain in the neck. If you forgot your White House pass, you sometimes had to wait outside the gates in the cold while they identified you. All sorts of areas within the compound were off-limits. During the first weeks, two staffers got hauled in for walking across the lawn to the tennis courts without permission.

My biggest headache was classified documents. The first time you see a folder marked "Top Secret," a little thrill runs down your spine. It passes. But the endless security procedures don't.

Every night before leaving, I would clear the President's desk, but I frequently left a stack of letters and memos on my own. Little did I know that the Secret Service sent agents around after hours to check all the desk tops for classified documents left out in the open. Soon I was arriving in the morning to find big violation notices staring me in the face. I was embarrassed. Would national security crumble because of me? I phoned the number listed on the notice and explained that I left papers on my desk only because I had nowhere else to put them.

That was a mistake. Two hours later, the Secret Service arrived wheeling a horrible, difficult-to-operate, complicated, sure-to-induce-ulcers safe. I have a terrible time with ordinary combination locks. But the Secret Service lock seemed to be devised by Houdini. I was constantly struggling with it. Half the time it wouldn't open and the other half it wouldn't close. I wound up hiding the classified material in piles on my desk. They always found me out, though, and I accumulated violation notices the way some Boston drivers acquire traffic tickets.

The President, God bless him, had a sense of humor about his mechanically inept secretary. After I'd received two notices in a single week, he whispered to me, "I'd be getting them if you didn't," which was both gracious and true. And when I thought the Secret Service had really lost patience with me and might be planning a trip to Allenwood, the President winked and promised "to visit every Thursday."

I wasn't the only one who got into trouble with the security folks. Mike Deaver's office was the room Jimmy Carter had used as a private study. Mike claimed he got that office because nothing else was left when he belatedly decided to join the staff. I was skeptical, to say the least. Though smaller than some other West Wing offices, Mike's was the only one with a private door entering directly into the Oval Office. Anyway, Mike was still finding his way around the place on his third day at work. He noticed a button on the wall and pushed. Pandemonium. Sirens wailed, doors flew open, and the Secret Service went flying into the Oval Office. It turned out that the former private study hadn't yet been rewired from President Carter's time. The button on the wall was for the President to use in an emergency.

When they burst into the Oval Office they found the President conducting an interview with George Will. Ronald Reagan, sunny as ever, was amused. George Will looked totally bewildered. Mike learned to ask questions first and push buttons later.

I understood from friends who worked at a greater distance from the Oval Office that the White House could frequently be cruel. All of the little advantages I enjoyed because of my closeness to the President were sometimes arbitrarily denied to others.

Perks were the coin of the realm in the White House and they were withheld even from high-ranking officials at the pleasure of the senior staff. When Haig was feuding with the White House, for example, he was assigned to sit at the back of Air Force One instead of up front with the senior staff. Lower-ranking officials suffered other indignities—such as losing a parking space or being denied a seat in a motorcade.

But I'd be a liar if I didn't admit that the perks were wonderful—especially at first. All I had to do to get my office redecorated was lift the phone. We got the best furniture and the finest paintings in the White House collection. When the President wasn't using it, I could use his box at the Kennedy Center free of charge.

"The box" is one of the best perks in Washington. Usually, when I go to the theater, I choose seats somewhere in the orchestra, always mindful of the prices. A box seat is a level of luxury I don't even think about. And the presidential box is in a category all by itself. You relax in a private sitting room complete with rest room, closet, and refrigerator stocked with champagne, wine, and soft drinks. When the lights dim you emerge into the very center of the theater, the best seats in the house. It's the perfect place to take guests. I liked to take longtime supporters of the President with me. It was a unique treat for them. The feeling of being special and pampered is unparalleled in ordinary life.

White House staffers with presidential commissions— those who are Special Assistants to the President and above— also have access to White House cars for official and sometimes not entirely official business. Whenever my new status required me to attend a cocktail party or reception outside of the building, I was assigned a car (with a telephone) and a driver. No special markings indicated that the car was part of the White House fleet, but Washington is such a status-conscious town that everyone knew what those dark blue Chrysler Le-Barons were.

Perhaps the most prized and envied White House perk was access to the mess. Again, mess privileges were assigned by rank, but exceptions were made, leading to the most brutal competition among staffers. I had the top prize: a place in the Executive Mess along with the other top people in the West Wing, Ed Meese, Jim Baker, Mike Deaver, and others, including the Vice President and Cabinet members when they chose to attend.

It's funny that so much fuss was made over the mess. The room was small and windowless with low ceilings. The food was only fair; there were far better restaurants within a block's walk, such as Maison Blanche. The atmosphere was strained. Everyone whispered. Maybe they were discussing sensitive security matters, but I tend to think they were just caught up in the paranoia which afflicts everyone in the West Wing. You don't want to be overheard because your political rival—or worse, someone who is secretly allied with your political rival —may be sitting at the next table. Still, the mess was always where visitors wanted to be taken, and it made me happy to be able to offer that treat to the President's political supporters when they were in town.

But all of the privileges and status and perks, as lovely as they were, could not compensate for the underlying restlessness I was feeling. During the campaign I had been one of six regional finance directors for the Reagan campaign. My work was substantive and challenging. I missed that. And in retrospect I think I concentrated on the perks to compensate for the essential emptiness of my job. Now I was simply sorting through paperwork for the President. When he wasn't in meetings (rare), he went over his papers in private. He didn't dictate to me but preferred to speak into a recording machine. Not only that, but he was so undemanding he never even asked me to sharpen a pencil for him or get him a cup of coffee. He did those things for himself. Henry Kissinger once said, "Never take a job without an 'in' box." That was exactly my problem as Ronald Reagan's secretary. My "in" box wasn't for me. Later, that knowledge would propel me forward.

But in the meantime there was the great barbershop dispute to settle. For as long as anyone could remember, the White House men had been served by one old-fashioned male barber in the basement. But the women's movement had changed the complexion of the staff, and during President Carter's time the old barber was fired and a young couple specializing in unisex haircuts had been brought on board. Someone in our crowd decided that the old barber should have the place back again and let it be known that the couple were going to be fired.

The women were outraged. Mike Deaver proposed a Solomonic solution: the old barber would work three days a week and the young couple two days a week.

But the old barber wasn't exactly a team player. As soon as he returned he began to make life as unpleasant as possible for the couple, whom he regarded as usurpers in his clipper kingdom. He complained. They complained. Both went to Mike. This time Mike abandoned Solomon and leaned more toward Herod. He fired the couple.

The response was almost as electric as when he pushed the security buzzer in his office. The women were up in arms. They attempted to end-run Mike by seeing Jim Baker about the problem, but he refused to overrule Mike. Then the ladies came to see me.

I was reluctant to get involved in such a seemingly petty issue, but I didn't want the women on the staff to think I was getting high and mighty. I promised to raise the issue with the President at the next opportunity.

He's such a softie. I shouldn't have been surprised by his response. Like the gentleman he is, he sided with the women. In fact, he called the old barber and made it quite clear that if he couldn't get along with the young couple, the White House wouldn't be requiring his services. The barber capitulated. The women were jubilant. I asked Byron, who was in the graphic arts business, to design a card which read "Happiness is a President who appreciates beauty" and we all signed it.

A couple of months later (the press is much slower to pick things up than one might think) the *Washington Star* carried a story about the male chauvinists in the White House. But because of his valiant defense of women's equality in the barbershop, Ronald Reagan was cited as the one exception.

The President loved the article and couldn't resist ribbing the fellas about his superior status. While he was enjoying their embarrassment I got a few deadly glances from the guys. I knew they suspected that I had purposely brought the *Star* article to his attention. When they were out of earshot, I asked the President to cover for me. He chuckled and promised to tell them he'd noticed the article on his own. But Mike Deaver was not convinced. On his way out the door he turned and asked sarcastically, "Are you on a campaign again?"

———

The relationships among the Californians inevitably changed in Washington, though. We were all so busy that we mostly just waved to each other at parties. There was almost no time for individual entertaining at home the way we had so comfortably in Sacramento.

But our working together ran smoothly because we knew so well how to read one another.

I had fought and played and strategized with the Californians for so many years that they were like family. I knew their strengths and weaknesses, as they knew mine. For example, if

Ed Meese said he'd get back to me, I knew I'd better have a fallback plan, because as often as not he wouldn't. If I approached Bill Clark with a friendly greeting and saw his "Don't bother me, I'm carrying the weight of the world on my shoulders" look, I'd steer clear. I knew that if Lyn Nofziger was muttering that someone or other was a son of a bitch, chances were good that Lyn respected him. And when Mike Deaver told me I had too many plants in my office and that I ought to get rid of some, I didn't argue with him. I was probably receiving an indirect directive from Mrs. R.

Though I was feeling somewhat stymied by my role as secretary, it did give me a unique vantage point from which to evaluate the many new faces surrounding President Reagan.

Like most new Administrations, the Reagan team had grown to include many of the people I had traditionally mistrusted. George Bush, for example, had not endeared himself to me during the campaign. I didn't dislike him personally, but I was irritated at his claims of "Big Mo" and the insinuation that Ronald Reagan was an extremist. But as I got to know him on a day-to-day basis in the White House, I was impressed.

For some reason the newspapers and other media are stuck on the image of George Bush as a wimp. I don't understand it. Bush had strong opinions which he did not hesitate to argue forcefully in staff or Cabinet meetings. He was not afraid to disagree openly with the President. But when a decision had been reached, he closed ranks and supported the President. George Bush regarded loyalty and discretion as virtues at any time, but especially in a Vice President. It's worth remembering that he was one of the very few senior officials who was never, even in office scuttlebutt, accused of leaking to the press. He's an honorable man. I also appreciated his sense of humor, which, like President Reagan, he used to defuse tense situations.

As skeptical as we Reaganites had been of George Bush, we were downright leery of Jim Baker. We hadn't forgotten that as Bush's campaign manager he had coined the term "voodoo economics," and we thought it was something of a betrayal to appoint to one of the most powerful positions in the Administration a man who was neither a Reaganite nor part of the conservative movement in the Republican Party.

I often wondered what course the Reagan Administration would have taken if Drew Lewis had been appointed Chief of Staff instead of Baker. Drew had all of Baker's strengths: organization, political acumen, and managerial experience. But in addition, he was more readily accepted by the Reaganites. Forgotten was Ford and 1976. What they remembered was that Ronald Reagan was his first choice in 1980. Besides, Drew was able to forge a relationship of trust with all the Californians.

But I came to like and admire Jim Baker and I now believe that without him many of the first-term triumphs wouldn't have been possible. He was a superb administrator, dynamic and decisive—a pleasure to work with. His keen attention to detail never let anything slip through the cracks. He understood Washington in ways Ed Meese, his chief rival for influence, never would.

Baker was certainly no liberal, but I sympathized with conservatives who felt betrayed by his appointment. The Administration was becoming divided between "us," the Reaganites, and "them," the moderates. Making one of them first among equals was a blow to conservatives. It wasn't so much a commentary on the Bush crowd—after all, we had married them—as it was a cry of frustration because we had waited so long and worked so hard to get a true conservative into the presidency.

Conservatives never trusted Baker and blamed him for all of the missteps of the first term. It was certainly true that Baker was cool to the social agenda of the right—school prayer, abortion, tuition tax credits, and more—but the truth is that the rest of the Administration also had other priorities. The President was focused primarily on economic reform and rebuilding the military. Since the conservatives couldn't whip Reagan, Baker became the scapegoat for all their disappointments.

Sometimes he deserved it, most often not. Years later, during the second term, Paul Weyrich, a prominent New Right leader, broke ranks with many other conservatives and directly criticized Ronald Reagan. "We've all played this game of 'blame the Chief of Staff' too long," he said.

On the other hand, I think the conservatives were absolutely justified in their outrage at the tax hike of 1982. After the Administration worked so hard to achieve the first Kemp-Roth tax cut, which was central to the President's plan to strengthen the economy, Jim Baker persuaded the President to reverse his position and support a tax hike which wiped out many of the gains so dearly won the previous year. Baker promised that if the President approved the tax increase, the Congress would cut $3 in spending for every $1 in new revenue. The tax was signed into law. We're still waiting for those budget cuts. Reagan said later that the "compromise" was the greatest sham he'd ever seen. Conservatives remember it as the perfect illustration of Baker's willingness to sacrifice substance in the name of legislative victories.

But Baker's skill with people allowed him to bounce back from setbacks like the tax hike. He knew that dignity is more prized in Washington than gold, and he made sure that he gave people their due. He never left the office at night without returning calls from the press and members of Congress.

But Baker also understood how to take advantage of people's weaknesses. Ed Meese was a devoted and intelligent Reaganite. But his work habits were slow and deliberate. He was a poor delegator of authority. The papers on his desk would frequently pile so high that no wood was visible, and when there was no more room on the desk, the papers would settle happily on the floor. Baker's desk, by contrast, was always immaculate. He was a terrific delegator. We all suspected that he quickly took advantage of this by burying Meese with paper when he wanted to thwart him on something. By the time Meese had gotten to the paperwork, the decision would already have been made.

Moreover, Ed was a straight shooter. He didn't know

how to use the press and wouldn't have been comfortable doing so. Baker had the field to himself. He was able to shape policy decisions by leaking to the press and drawing criticism for the "hard-liners." He could then truthfully tell the President that if he chose the more conservative option, he'd be doing something "controversial." Meese could easily have played the same game, leaking to Evans and Novak or Pat Buchanan in advance of a decision, drawing criticism of the "moderates," and then telling the President that to choose the pragmatic approach would be "controversial." It might have been a very different four years if he had. Though I was inclined personally to Meese's straightforward methods, I do think it would have been better for the conservative agenda if the conservatives had played the Washington power game as successfully as the pragmatists did.

———

Meese and his staff, which consisted mostly of conservative Reagan people with limited Washington experience, were no match for Baker and his team, who were seasoned Washington hands.

If left to themselves, the Big Three would, I am sure, have worked together with less friction and distrust of each other. Their staffs did a lot to influence the atmosphere, though. It stands to reason. If their boss looked good, so did they; if their boss got more power, so did they. Most of the leaks undoubtedly came from them, and not the top, although both Baker and Deaver were experts in manipulating the press corps too. That they were the press's best sources can be deduced alone from the fact that they were seldom the victims of attacks. The press may be free, but too smart to dry up their sources.

I'm speaking here about Baker vs. Meese because Deaver became part of the Baker team.

As far as I could observe, they worked differently from Meese with the President too. Meese, an instinctive team player, was more inclined to wait to present a policy recommendation to the President in Cabinet meetings. Baker and

Deaver often beat him to the punch by talking to him beforehand and thus having a leg up.

Despite the inroads the moderates were making, there
were still plenty of Californians in key posts. Charles Tyson,
who had worked for Bill Clark in Sacramento, was now on the
National Security Council staff. Craig Fuller had left Deaver
and Hannaford to become Cabinet Secretary under Ed Meese.
My old chum Elaine Crispen became Nancy Reagan's personal
secretary. And Dave Fischer, who had handled advance work
in California and during the campaign, was given the title Special Assistant to the President. His duties consisted mostly of
ushering people in and out of the Oval Office.

In a brilliant political move, Jim Baker appointed another
Californian, Lyn Nofziger, to head the political liaison office.
Now Baker had to be granted some grudging approval by the
Reaganites while at the same time guaranteeing that President
Reagan's traditional constituency would be kept happy. Lyn
knew everyone—all of the people who had helped put Reagan
where he was. And they trusted him. If Baker said something
couldn't be done, they were suspicious. If Lyn said it couldn't
be done, they were disappointed, but satisfied.

Washington brought Bill Clark and me back together.
We'd never stopped being friends, but we'd been separated
for so many years, he in San Francisco, I in Sacramento, Los
Angeles, or New York, that we'd lost touch somewhat. Bill
was quite a character on the Washington scene. Unlike so
many who came with the Reagan Administration and immediately wanted to fit in with the city's ways, Bill remained his
unique self. While he wore dark pin-striped suits, he sported
cowboy boots and a large silver belt buckle, just as he had in
Sacramento. Nor did he adopt the standard Washington briefcase. He carried his papers in a leather shoulder bag which
doubled as a suitcase when necessary. I was delighted to have
him back, and we quickly resumed our old friendship.

Bill is not the sort of person to admit that he's worried,
but in those early days, I sensed that he was edgy about his

upcoming confirmation hearings. The Senate Democrats were feeling somewhat bitter after the Reagan landslide of 1980, particularly since the Senate was now in majority Republican hands. Confirmation hearings on Reagan appointees were one place where the minority could vent their frustration.

Bill was not appointed as Deputy Secretary of State because he was a foreign affairs specialist, but rather because the President respected his judgment and shared his instincts. Bill understood that Communist regimes are inherently expansionist, something that many of the foreign policy specialists have yet to grasp. Still, he knew the senators were going to grill him on specifics and was doing his best to study. Larry Eagleburger, Assistant Secretary of State for European Affairs at the time, was very helpful.

But it did turn out as Bill had feared.

With the help of eager staffers feeding the senators questions, Bill was given an international civics test. He was asked everything from the name of the Prime Minister of Zimbabwe to the reasons behind the split in the British Labour Party. It was rough going. At length, he was confirmed, but by one of the smallest majorities of any Administration appointee.

The Senate also enjoyed a little infield practice with others. When Al Haig marched up to the Hill for confirmation hearings, he was bombarded with accusations about his conduct as President Nixon's Chief of Staff. Bill Casey was pilloried for misreading the directions on his financial disclosure forms. William French Smith was grilled for hours about his investments in an aggressive but legal tax shelter. Tiring of the abuse, he voluntarily pulled his money out and paid the taxes he had not legally owed.

Washington is a tough town.

LEARNING THE ROPES: LIFE IN WASHINGTON

*T*HOUGH I WAS NOW THE PRESIDENT'S SECRETARY, I was involved with personnel decisions. When the old-time supporters of the President wanted a job, they would naturally go first to someone they knew. Very often, I was that person and I was therefore constantly in touch with Pen James, now director of personnel.

There were so many federal jobs to fill and the office of Presidential Personnel was falling behind. It was a huge task complicated by several factors. The Reagan Administration was the first truly conservative presidency in anyone's memory, and we were eager to place philosophically sympathetic people in important positions. On the other hand, we had to balance the need for experience. Further slowing progress on personnel were the painstaking FBI checks and financial disclosure process. The President's rule was that no appointments would be announced until the candidate had cleared those hurdles, and that could take as long as six months. Though Pen

James and I had begun looking for people back in September 1980, many of the top positions were still not filled in the spring of 1981.

Being selected for a presidential appointment is a great honor, but in the days of post-Watergate morality it can also be a curse. Judge Douglas Ginzburg wasn't the first to have his career damaged by being chosen for high office. I remember ruefully our experience with the selection for Ambassador to Ireland. It was a case where we broke our rule against announcing nominees in advance of clearance, and we lived to regret it.

William McCann was an insurance company executive who, together with Ray Donovan, had given our campaign a needed shot in the arm financially when many others were still holding back. The President announced him as Ambassador to Ireland when he took him along to the celebration of St. Patrick's Day at the Irish Embassy before the clearances were complete. At President Reagan's urging, Bill took a bow. Later he took a tumble.

As soon as his selection was announced, Bill had leased his home in New Jersey, notified his company's board that he was leaving, and enrolled his children in Dublin schools.

Later, the media fanned rumors that Bill's insurance company had been mentioned in a Teamsters Union corruption case several years before. Bill himself was not implicated. When the unsubstantiated report became public, he pleaded for the opportunity to prove his innocence and to protect his own and his family's reputation. But the consensus at the White House was that the appearance of scandal would hurt the Administration. Bill's name would have to be withdrawn.

It was awful. Bill felt so betrayed. "I stuck with you guys through the tough days," he reproached us. And he was right. We were letting him down. I bled for him, but there was nothing I could do. It was a shared view among top White House officials: the integrity of the presidency had to take precedence over personal considerations, and sometimes even over fairness. Bill McCann was later cleared of any cloud, but I'm sure he was very bitter about the whole episode. Later, as I came to know Washington better, I saw that it was not so simple. Character assassination is a blood sport in the nation's capital. And if people are fired just on the basis of accusations—or the appearance of impropriety—the integrity of the democratic process is threatened.

———

Pen James appreciated my input on personnel. He thought it was important in vetting candidates, to have someone who had an institutional memory with President Reagan and who could look out for loyal supporters. Pen also kept one eye on the Reagan agenda at all times, although the conservatives didn't always give him credit for it. Because he had worked for the Nixon Administration they didn't totally trust him. And besides, he was the person who often had to say no to their hopes for particular jobs. But it's worth remembering that Pen suspected that Baker would one day aim for a high Cabinet post. Accordingly, he paid a visit to William French Smith and said, "Bill, I've heard rumors that you're not planning to stay very long. If that's true, I hope that when you submit your resignation to the President, you'll recommend Ed Meese as your successor." A seed well sown. Knowledge is power.

Fitting the person to the job was like a jigsaw puzzle. Some fits, like Charlie Wick for the United States Information Agency and John Shad for chairman of the SEC just seemed to fall into place. Others didn't.

My wonderful friend Dan Terra had been so hopeful of becoming Ambassador to Great Britain. But it was not to be. Dan was so hurt by the way he'd been treated that he asked me to give the President a letter withdrawing his name from consideration for any Administration post. I did not cooperate. I felt his disappointment almost as acutely as he did, but I was determined that something worthwhile be found for him.

Bill Clark and I huddled over sandwiches one evening and considered what could be done. Bill, ever inventive, came up with the perfect idea: Ambassador-at-Large for Cultural Affairs. It was ideal. In addition to his boundless generosity, good humor, and dedication, Dan was also a great aficionado of the arts. He had just opened the Terra museum in Evanston, Illinois, and was planning another on the Miracle Mile in downtown Chicago. In his hands, cultural affairs would be a substantive job, not just a sinecure.

The following afternoon, Bill mentioned the idea to the President. To say he approved would be an understatement. "God is with us," he said, glancing toward the heavens. At that moment I sensed that President Reagan too had been feeling badly about Dan's disappointment and was glad to be able to make it up to him.

When the painful period was over, and Dan was happily settled into his new position, Bill and I used to tease him about his official car. For some reason only the bureaucrats in Washington understood, Dan was driven around in a Plymouth instead of a limousine. We asked him if they provided beer instead of champagne for his toasts. Dan was a great sport about it all—partly because that's the kind of person he is and partly because he truly loved his work. In the eight years of the Reagan Administration, I never saw anyone work as enthusiastically as Dan Terra.

Another priority of mine was trying to find the right slots for women in the Administration. But there were difficulties in attracting qualified conservative women. The case of Marilyn Lewis illustrated the problem.

I had been urging Marilyn Lewis, Drew's wife, to consider the job of chief of protocol. She was a professional who had served in the Pennsylvania legislature and had all of the personal traits which I thought were necessary for the job. But Marilyn turned it down. She was worried that with her husband already committed to a demanding job as Secretary of Transportation, their happy marriage might suffer if she too were to undertake a demanding position.

Marilyn's personal values matched her political philosophy. She typified the Reaganite woman: conservative about family roles as well as defense policy. Under the circumstances, I take a certain pride in the fact that we were able to match the number of women appointees the Carter Administration had hired.

As deputy chief of protocol, Mrs. Reagan and Mike Deaver had selected Morgan Mason (James Mason's son). Morgan is a delightful person—savvy, witty, and charming—who became and has remained a good friend. Unfortunately, after only one month on the job, Morgan found that he wasn't clicking with the new chief of protocol, Lee Annenberg, so he resigned. I admired Morgan's style. So many people who found themselves in similar situations would cling or whine or gossip. Morgan simply moved over to a deputy position in Lyn Nofziger's shop and expressed his gratitude to Lyn and Mike Deaver for the wonderful opportunity they were affording him. What aplomb!

———

During those early months, I acquired a reputation for being able to make things happen. But I couldn't perform miracles. Many of our loyal supporters, of whom I was personally very fond, were simply aiming too high. Some had their sights fixed on jobs they were unsuited for. One of the most painful things I learned to do was bring the disappointing news.

Others came into conflict with their new bosses. Personality is more important in Washington than elsewhere. Few people hold political jobs because their expertise is indispensable. There were some who achieved that status: everyone thought Dave Stockman was the only one who could "crunch the numbers" on the budget, and Richard Perle was considered the nuclear arms guru, but for the most part people were replaceable. Without a bottom line to prove their effectiveness, political appointees rely upon the goodwill of their superiors to keep their jobs, and sometimes there were clashes.

One job aspirant, though, stands out in my memory above all the others. Nineteen-year-old Marc Holtzman, my pen pal from the 1970s who had gone on to play an active role in the 1980 campaign, came to see me. I thought I'd impress him by taking him to lunch in the Executive mess. I wanted to give him a thrill. I'll never know whether Marc was impressed. He had his mind on other things. After the salad had been served, Marc looked very earnest. "I'd appreciate your suggesting to President Reagan that I be appointed as Ambassador to New Zealand," he announced. I didn't laugh. Somehow I managed to say something about the government of New Zealand perhaps taking offense at being sent a teenaged envoy. Marc was ready with a reply. "But think of what it would do for Reagan's image with youth."

I couldn't resist sharing the story with the President. He had appreciated Marc's dedication during the campaign. "He could probably do it," he said, grinning.

Being involved in personnel naturally led into other areas as well. Because I was concerned that our longtime supporters not be forgotten, I started to meddle in the guest lists for White House functions. State dinners are a perfect opportunity to say thanks to supporters. It's a ceremonial occasion, so there's no danger that anyone will be deemed unqualified to attend (as can be the case with political jobs), and it gives the invitees an unforgettable feeling of importance which lasts beyond one evening.

State dinners were held every eight weeks or so. They coincided with visits from foreign heads of State.

The First Lady's staff included a social secretary, Mabel (Muffie) Brandon, who was in charge of helping to compile the invitation lists. Each dinner had a maximum of about a hundred guests. But of those, forty or so would be the traveling party of the visiting head of State. Of the remaining sixty slots, I hoped to see some of our longtime friends and associates on the list.

I cultivated a very nice working relationship with Muffie, who was sensitive to the fact that she needed input from Reaganites since she wasn't one herself.

Mrs. R also relied very heavily on Mike Deaver for advice on invitations. After I saw the first state dinner list, I was appalled that not a single one of our loyal supporters had been included. I went to Mike and Mrs. R to lobby. They agreed that in the future I'd be allowed to suggest four couples per dinner.

It was quite a victory. The first people I named were the Max Rabbs, the Fred Eckards, the Paul Robinsons, and the Dan Terras.

I was ill at ease when I was invited to my first state dinner. After all, I worked at the White House. I didn't really feel like a guest. As Byron and I approached the military officer who was announcing people, I whispered "staff" to him in a dismissing tone. "Mr. and Mrs. Staff," he sang out, to my eternal mortification.

After that I tried to keep a watchful eye on the lists of guests. There were endless lunches, receptions, and dinners at the White House. If we'd been trying hard, we could have invited all of the Reaganites twice over. It was the "beautiful people" who were awarded this honor again and again. I remembered only too well that it was not they who had gotten us there.

When the President took his first long weekend at Rancho Cielo in California, I was part of the entourage. I was excited at the prospect of my first ride on Air Force One. I don't know why there's so much mystique about the President's plane—perhaps because Lyndon Johnson took the oath of office on it in Dallas in 1963. New Air Force Ones have been built since then, of course, and I was just as curious as anyone to get a look at President Reagan's plane.

The party traveling with the President assembled on the South Lawn and waited for Marine One, the President's helicopter, to fly us to Andrews Air Force Base. The helicopter flight goes quickly, affording a terrific view of Washington along the way.

When we arrived at the plane I couldn't get over how stratified everything was. Commercial airliners have first class and coach, but on Air Force One the differentiation goes much further.

The first section of the 707 is a sort of sitting room for the President and First Lady. It's equipped with a private bathroom and twin beds. Frequently the President would change into sweatpants during the trip so as not to wrinkle his pants during the flight. Next there's a VIP section, usually the province of senior staff and Cabinet Secretaries. The middle of the aircraft is reserved for working staff. It contains a table on each side of the aircraft, a typewriter, and the all-important telephones. I have to laugh when I recall how all of us would stampede to those phones just for the pleasure of hearing the operator (also on board) say to the party on the ground, "This is Air Force One calling." The rear of the plane is fitted like an ordinary commercial airliner, except that the seats are larger and better spaced. Members of the press, invited guests, extra staff, and Secret Service agents take those seats.

Each seat on the plane is assigned. As you board, the stewards know exactly who you are and where you belong. On each seat a card with the presidential seal and your name is waiting. The physical layout of the aircraft almost invites competition for seating. Still, I couldn't believe when some of my old pals began to take these petty status questions dead seriously. Having sections assigned made sense for working efficiency. But I thought it got a little crazy when the pecking order was such that every seat was assigned even on Marine One, which seats only ten people and usually involves trips of only ten minutes. In the same breath let me say that once you've flown on Air Force One, you're spoiled for life. Travel becomes such a breeze when you travel with the President. I'd arrive at work, park at my usual place, hand my bag to an advance man, and then relax. No rushing—the plane takes off when the President boards. No traffic. No hassle. And even the food was good!

Once in Santa Barbara, we Californians had our first opportunity in a very long time for some much-needed rest and recreation.

———

The President was relaxing, and while all of us could be summoned at any moment, we still felt freer than we had in months. Santa Barbara is one of the most beautiful spots on earth. We went for walks along the beach and enjoyed the salty breeze. The surrounding hills inspired me to go for long hikes by myself, as I had done when I was living in California. One of those hikes took me to the perimeter of the Reagan ranch, and I had quite a time persuading the Secret Service I wasn't some sort of flake.

The press seemed to enjoy Santa Barbara as well, though they may have been bored just sitting in a beautiful spot with nothing to do. I often wondered how the women with children felt about being dragged across the country and separated from their families just on the chance that a story might break while the President was in California.

The rest did me good. By the time we returned to Washington, I was refreshed and ready to face once again my extremely long days. At 6:45 A.M. I would struggle out of bed, make my way to the shower like a blind person, and then throw on some clothes. I've never worn much makeup or done anything time-consuming with my hair, so I was out of the house quickly. My terribly elegant old blue Pinto would take me to the White House. I'd buy a cup of coffee and a doughnut at the mess, and then speed-read the newspapers before the 8 A.M. staff meeting.

Technically, only Assistants to the President (I was a Special Assistant) were supposed to attend the early meeting. But I got Mike Deaver's permission to be there. My punctiliousness about the rules was scarcely necessary. Each morning several lower-ranking people would show up and it would have been ridiculous to eject them on the spot. Occasionally, Jim Baker would send a memo around to the Assistants reminding them that the meeting was restricted to them and not members of their staffs, but the rules continued to be flouted.

The meeting was held in the Roosevelt Room, the lovely rose-colored meeting room across the hall from the Oval Office. It got its name from Theodore Roosevelt, who was President when the West Wing was built, and it still contains memorabilia from his time, including the Nobel Peace Prize he won for negotiating the peace between Russia and Japan in 1906. There is also a picture of Franklin Roosevelt hanging there, as well as the flags of the five armed services.

Since I was not an Assistant to the President, I never used to sit at the conference table but preferred to be less conspicuous on the sofa along the wall. The others would customarily take the same places morning after morning: Jim Baker at the head of the table, Elizabeth Dole, at the time the only woman Assistant to the President, in the middle.

Jim Baker presided. He began the meeting with a summary of the President's schedule, a look at the legislative agenda, questions for the heads of certain departments if they were involved in the day's activities (for example, a question to Elizabeth Dole if Public Liaison was bringing in a group of businessmen to support the President's budget), and a discussion of press coverage. Baker always tried to shape that evening's news lead in the morning meeting. He'd say, "Okay, what's our story today?" I'd tune in at 7 P.M., and sure enough, "our story" would usually be their story.

The morning staff meeting was usually the highlight of my day. The atmosphere was relaxed and informal. Though Jim Baker always got right down to business, he made it pleasant and smooth. Later, when I became an Assistant to the President myself, I used those morning meetings as a good place to buttonhole people. Ironically, it was there, with the senior White House officials, that I really got a sense of being close to the center of everything—not outside the Oval Office. I just didn't have enough meaningful work to do.

12

POLITICS IS NOT
A ROSE GARDEN

*I*T WAS WONDERFUL TO WORK FOR RONALD REAGAN, of course. I've always loved and admired him. But my duties had become so circumscribed that I was getting a little stir-crazy. Dave Fischer was now escorting people into and out of the Oval Office—apparently every President has a personal aide de camp—so I didn't even have the "meet and greet" duties to enliven my day. From nine in the morning, when the President would come in smiling, or seeing me on the telephone, joke that "all my women are always on the telephone," until five in the evening, when he would tap on my French doors and remind me not to stay too late, all I had to do was shuffle papers. I answered the telephone, sorted through the mail for things I knew from long experience would interest him, and ensured that the President's briefing papers were in the correct order.

My clout, such as it was, inhered in my decisions about which phone calls or letters to put through and which to screen out. Mrs. Reagan and Mike Deaver periodically challenged my judgment by decreeing that a particular person was a "nuisance" whose calls or letters should not come to President Reagan's attention. I was torn. On the one hand, I had no wish to offend Mrs. Reagan (which could lead to early retirement) or my friend Mike, but my primary responsibility and loyalty was to the President. I didn't want to see him blindsided. We came to a modus vivendi. When there was something I thought he should see but which was on the Deaver/Mrs. R Index, I'd hand it to him in the Oval Office. When he made a move to put it in the pile he would later retire with upstairs, I'd say, "No, no. That's only for reading here. I need it back." We'd exchange a look—I'm sure we understood each other.

His day was much busier than mine. Though the President was often criticized for being a nine-to-five worker, it wasn't true. He found the Oval Office a difficult place to do serious thinking. So he used it more for meetings and ceremonial occasions than for real work. Of course, there were the personal touches he added to the Oval Office. He had several plaques on the desk. Some he had brought from California and some were new. One, a gift from the staff, read: "The buckeroo stops here."

Each evening, President Reagan left with a great sheaf of papers under his arm, and would go through them in the study on the second floor of the residence, sometimes drafting memos and even letters to constituents on yellow legal pads.

Whenever he had time to spare, in cars, on airplane trips, or between meetings, the President would open his briefcase and dig in. He was also a tireless reader of newspapers and magazines. There were rumors that Jim Baker and company tried to keep *Human Events* from reaching the Oval Office. I don't know if that was true or whether Mrs. Reagan and Mike were really the responsible agents—but I do know that the President was forever circling and checking items he found in newspapers and magazines like *National Review* and *Human Events*. Only on Wednesday afternoons did the President give himself time off to go horseback riding. He would go to Camp David or Quantico. Often he asked Bill Clark or Mac Baldrige to come along.

It seemed that everyone had a claim on the President's time. I know getting him scheduled for their event was always the highest priority of the Assistants to the President. After meeting with the Big Three in the morning, President Reagan would spend about a half hour with Dick Allen for the national security briefing. After that the schedule was nonstop. It wasn't unusual for him to have five meetings or photo "ops" (opportunities) in the space of a single hour. I was always worried that he'd lose track of whom he was seeing when. But he rarely did. And if there was a momentary confusion, he always handled it with aplomb and humor. I recall that one day he had a list of calls to make offering jobs to people. He called one of his ambassadorial appointments twice. When the surprised man picked up the phone for his second talk with the President in one day, Ronald Reagan realized his mistake and quipped, "I just phoned to make sure you haven't changed your mind."

If I were asked to describe a typical day, I'd have to say it would begin with the meetings just mentioned and then proceed to a meeting with Cap Weinberger to discuss a new weapons system, a courtesy call with the Italian Ambassador, several lobbying phone calls to key House and Senate members, a "drop-by" to a meeting with supporters of tax reform in the Old Executive Office Building, and a Rose Garden ceremony to honor the Indianapolis 4-H Club.

There were strict rules for handshakes, drop-bys, and photo ops, but the greatest violator was President Reagan himself. He was always willing and eager to listen to people and would get angry if we tried to pry him away before he was ready, particularly with young people.

The White House had not changed Ronald Reagan at all. He was as humble and thoughtful as I had always known him. If a letter I had prepared for the President's signature didn't quite suit him, he would try to doctor it up by adding PS's. Only as a last resort would he return it to be redone.

President Reagan's luncheons were as spartan and disciplined as his lifestyle, consisting of soup and crackers with perhaps Jell-O for dessert. He might splurge with a hamburger once in a while but he never went beyond drinking water or iced tea during the day. A glass or two of wine was reserved for the evenings. He never had coffee or snacks between meals and he would exercise regularly at his private gym in the White House residence.

Ronald Reagan never had an unkind word to say about anyone. Unlike most of us, who will praise someone and then go on to list his faults, he stopped with the positives. If there were buts, he kept them to himself, just like other observations he may have made. He always seemed oblivious to any infighting in the White House or to existing tensions. In time I came to agree with Bill Clark, who had always maintained that Ronald Reagan knew much more than he led us to believe. He simply chose not to get involved. And while its wisdom escaped me at first, what was there to gain by injecting himself in staff disputes?

I don't think I've ever known anyone with such an even disposition. It was very hard not to feel good when he was around. His sense of humor could be impish, as when he buzzed me and announced, "I've just declared war." I correctly translated this as "Get me Cap Weinberger." Or he could be self-deprecating, as when he appeared one morning wearing a tie tack in the shape of a horse's rear end. "It's to remind me what not to become," he explained with a wink.

I loved our private conversations, though there was very little time for them once we reached the White House. But from time to time, between meetings or when he had an hour free, we'd get a chance to chat one on one. I recall in particular a conversation we once had about the all-volunteer army. He was for it. I was opposed. It was a good-natured dispute and I left that evening feeling really high about life.

He was informal and warm in manner but formal in his

way of dressing and behaving. He always wore a shirt and tie, which he never loosened, when he was alone. President Reagan never fit the picture of a back-room politician in a smoke-filled room. He was never one of the boys with his feet up on the desk.

Anyone who got access to him, licitly or otherwise, was bowled over by his kindness. One morning he came into the office with the cryptic request that we find a letter which had been sent to him by a William Bell Smith, a sailor. It seemed that at seven o'clock that morning a call from "Bill Smith" had been placed to the White House. In their only failing in all the years I knew them, the operators blew it. To assist the operators the Big Three and I compiled a list of the Reagans' extended family and friends and Administration officials who were to have direct access to the President's private quarters. Anyone not on that list would have to be cleared by one of us. They must have assumed that William French Smith, the Attorney General, was on the line. Anyway, they put Bill Smith through and in a couple of minutes he was telling the President of the United States how disappointed he was that he'd never gotten a response to his letter. Ronald Reagan didn't find it strange. His principal concern was that people weren't getting prompt replies (there's an entire staff to handle the huge volume of personal letters addressed to the President).

———

The great "Does he or doesn't he?" debate raged in Washington during the entire period of the Reagan presidency. His Irish genes had given him the gift of lush dark hair and rosy red cheeks into his seventies. I was absolutely, positively certain that he never dyed his hair and never used rouge. But boy, you just couldn't dissuade some members of the press. Back in California they had actually tried to salvage his clippings after haircuts and have them chemically analyzed. Envy leads people to do some pretty foolish things.

———

My direct contact with Mrs. Reagan was limited. That was how things had always been in California and I didn't think about it much. I wasn't pining to be her friend, but I was distressed by some of her priorities. Those state dinner guest lists were only one example.

She knew that we were trying to give priority in hiring first to longtime Reaganites, second to conservatives, and third to Republicans. Yet Nancy Reagan chose as social secretary Muffie Brandon, a Kennedy Democrat. On pure merit, Muffie was an excellent choice, and I actually grew to like her a lot. We became friends. But that wasn't the point. Here we were telling Cabinet Secretaries that they couldn't bring their personal secretaries with them to Washington unless they were Republicans, and the President's wife hires a Democrat for a prestigious White House job. I raised the issue with Mike, and he just shrugged his shoulders and replied, "There's only one person who can talk to her about that and it's not me."

At the time I was baffled. But now, in retrospect, I think I understand. The motivation was just what it had been during the campaign, when Mrs. R refused to allow me to go to her wealthy Eastern friends to ask for money. Then, like now, her foremost concern seemed acceptance in what she regarded as the elite Eastern Establishment. But now the President's political credibility was undercut!

But since I'm on the subject, I do want to give Nancy Reagan her due. She restored a sense of elegance to the White House at a time when the country seemed to want a return to standards. She was careful about details: taste-testing the food for White House dinners in advance, taking charge of redecorating the living quarters, and making sure everything was perfect for official functions.

Moreover, she displayed a resilience I wasn't sure she had. The first year in office was not a good one for Mrs. R. The assassination attempt frightened her badly. And the press clapped a Marie Antoinette image on her which she did little to counteract. But then, to everyone's surprise, she proved that she too could roll with the punches at the Gridiron Dinner in March 1982. The Gridiron is a Washington institution: a once-a-year, white-tie occasion where press and politicians go behind closed doors (no cameras or tape recorders allowed) and take silly, but usually good-natured shots at each other.

When Nancy Reagan emerged onstage wearing a crazy-quilt bag-lady-type outfit and sang "Second Hand Rose," she brought the house down—and brought an end to the Marie Antoinette image. From that moment on, the press was always willing to give her the benefit of the doubt. Her crusade against youthful drug abuse was taken seriously, and she heard no more criticism about her extravagant clothes.

For the first few months I tried to compensate for my nine-to-five dissatisfaction by going to as many parties as I could handle. In Washington, where jobs, not people, get invitations, I was near the top of everyone's list. If Byron couldn't be there because of his job in New Jersey, I would invite one of President Reagan's visiting supporters to be my escort. Just sorting through all of the invitations took time: dinner with the French Foreign Minister at the State Department, a reception at the Greek Embassy, a yacht cruise on the Potomac, a testimonial dinner for a prominent senator hosted by a well-connected lobbyist. They were lovely. Fine food and drink. Elegant surroundings. But the party circuit gets old quickly. I have just so much small talk in me. The parties seemed to fall into two categories: either there were the same old faces or I wouldn't know a soul. After the first dozen or so parties, I began to send regrets more and more often.

Soon I attended only those parties hosted by or for friends. One I will always remember fondly was hosted in my honor by Washington public affairs consultant and longtime Reagan supporter Roy Pfautch. He is an extremely inventive host and all his parties are terrific, but I thought he outdid himself on my party. Together with Joe Miller, my former boss at AMPAC, he designed a "coming out" party at the Folger Shakespeare Library for me. Instead of numbers, the tables were identified by Shakespeare's plays, and at each place setting there was a line from that play. I still remember mine. It was from *Henry VIII:* "Still in thy right hand carry gentle peace."

The standard Washington story is of someone who comes to power town with a new Administration, is feted, and dined, and flattered by lots of new "friends," and is later disappointed to find that the invitations dry up when the job is over.

For me it was different. In the first place, I wasn't really in a power job. It was prestigious mostly. And unlike others who went to Washington parties to "work the room," I was trying to fill a void. A void inside myself. But I wasn't successful.

My job continued to dispirit me. Though I was serving a man I loved and admired, his style of management wasn't conducive to keeping a personal secretary stimulated and involved. He was never the initiator. He never even asked me to get Mac Baldrige or Bill Casey on the phone just because he hadn't heard from them in a while. He would make decisions as they were presented to him.

I have to admit it takes a certain chutzpah to be unhappy in the face of such glamour. I was constantly being told that people would give their right arms to be in my position. But I also knew that however much my position was envied, it was not in fact enviable. I think anyone with ambition and experience would have felt stymied after a while.

In truth I was undergoing a terrible inner turmoil about my position. In one way, I wanted to relax, take it easy, and just enjoy the perks of office. Traveling with President Reagan was a treat I'd never again be able to enjoy. And part of me did enjoy having everyone cater to my needs and treat me with deference. But the other part of me desperately wanted to risk everything on a career change. I knew there were no guarantees that I'd be able to handle a more substantive job, and yet, at age forty, I wanted to try.

The battle raged inside me for months. I tried to hide my torn feelings at work, but there were many nights when I went home and cried. I'd look at my tear-stained face in the mirror and say to myself: "Look at you. You have one of the plum jobs in Washington and you're crying!" I saw the irony. What I couldn't see was an answer . . . yet.

By spring, only the tulips in the Rose Garden outside my office cheered me up. It was time to brainstorm with my advisers and friends.

I was in a perfect position to job-hunt. Jim Cavanaugh, who'd by now returned to the private sector as president of Smith Kline & French Laboratories, wasn't surprised to hear that I was considering leaving the White House. "You're ready to move on," he agreed. Jim's idea was that I should look for a position in the Commerce Department. Dan Terra was quick to offer me a job on his staff at the State Department office on the arts. And Peter McPherson, head of the Agency for International Development, thought he could find something for me there.

But my principal concern within the Administration was still personnel. Within the White House there are two personnel departments, which sometimes can confuse outsiders. The White House personnel office handled the insurance forms and payment for the people who worked within the White House complex—everyone from Assistants to the President to clerks. But the Office of Presidential Personnel was responsible for filling thousands of jobs in the entire Administration. Presidential Personnel searched for and made recommendations on Assistant Secretaries, FTC (Federal Trade Commission) board members, the UN delegation, in short every job which, by law, the President is empowered to fill.

That was where I wanted to be.

My anxious meditation about future career prospects were interrupted, however, when I suddenly found myself the center of a scandalette (that's my word for the press's habit of seizing upon one fact of a public figure's personal life, interpreting that fact in the most incriminating light possible, and splashing it on the front pages).

When Fred Fielding, the White House counsel, phoned, I knew what it must feel like to have a *60 Minutes* camera team show up at your doorstep. Fred said he'd gotten a call from the Scripps-Howard papers asking for information contained in my financial disclosure forms. By law, Fred was required to release the form and he had done so. His call was to give me a "heads up." Given that my net worth was about $30,000, I searched my memory for what could possibly look bad, and could think of only one thing.

I phoned Bob Tuttle (no relation to Holmes Tuttle), a friend and financial consultant, in California. "I'd like to talk to you about the low-income housing investment I made in Baltimore on your advice," I started.

"Sure," he replied. "What about?"

I told him about the press inquiry. "Don't worry," he said. "Everything is absolutely fine. Nothing to be embarrassed about." I breathed a sigh of relief. I figured he ought to know, since he managed it.

The next morning, when I got my customary doughnut and coffee at the mess and sat down at my desk to read the papers, I went pale. There I was, in black and white, referred to as a "slum landlord."

I was horrified. It's hard to describe the feeling of shame and violation you feel when the press says things about you which aren't true. I was no slum landlord. I had made a small investment in some housing in a neighborhood that I was given to understand was undergoing "gentrification." I was not the manager of the property—indeed, I'd never seen it. Most of the press hadn't either, but they burned up the phone lines to Baltimore seeking my "tenants." Naturally, when the people were informed that the owner of their houses was a Special Assistant to the President, they were happy to provide complaints about their homes.

The New York Times, The Washington Post, The Baltimore Sun, the wire services, even *The Today Show* carried the story.

I got the distinct feeling that the press was playing with me like a cat with a toy. They knew there was no real news in it, but it was fun for a few days. And I was pained by the reaction of my colleagues. Everyone in the West Wing seemed to find the slum-landlady image hilarious. I was teased for days. Drew Lewis phoned to ask if I had an apartment to rent. Lyn Nofziger, who owned houses on the very same street, offered to buy mine if the price was right. I didn't want to seem humorless, but I just couldn't join in the merriment. My friends, my associates, Byron's family, and millions of people who had never heard of me were going to read this and assume it was true. Like most people, I care what others think of me. You have to be pretty hardened to shrug it off.

At least it was over swiftly. The press had their scandalette to liven up a dull day and soon they were off on another chase.

Interestingly, the one person who seemed to understand how badly hurt I had been by the whole episode (besides Ronald Reagan, who was very sweet and soft-pedaled the story, knowing it wasn't very big) was a member of the press: Lem Tucker of CBS. He started to rib me about the episode at the radio and TV correspondents dinner later that month, but quickly noticed that I wasn't smiling. "You know," he explained, "I went up to Baltimore when that story broke and I looked at your so-called slum property. It wasn't bad at all. The tenants seemed reasonably happy. I decided it wasn't a story." The following day Lem sent half a dozen red roses. I gave the property away after that!

The requirement that all appointees above a certain rank reveal everything about their personal financial holdings is part of the post-Watergate morality. I don't object to the idea that possible conflicts of interest should be examined by an impartial observer—say a judge or a member of the Justice Department—but I do very much object to the fact that all of that information becomes part of the public domain, available to anyone who asks for it. My own small experience, as well as the far more serious suffering I saw inflicted on others (particularly Ray Donovan), convinces me that our current system is playing fast and loose with people's reputations. And I know, through my experience in personnel, that fear of press distortion does keep many highly qualified people from serving their government.

HOW THE GAME
IS REALLY PLAYED

*M*ARCH 30, 1981, DID NOT BEGIN LIKE OTHER
days. I suppose I must have set the alarm clock wrong, for it
awakened me at four o'clock. Once awake, I have difficulty
drifting back to sleep, so I arrived at work feeling sluggish. For
some reason the phones were ringing nonstop (it turned out
that the *National Journal,* a Washington insiders magazine, had
published all of our private phone numbers in that week's issue). At ten, the President met with 140 sub-Cabinet appointees. I sat in. When Ronald Reagan quoted Tom Paine's famous line: "We have it in our power to begin the world over
again," the faces in the room were shining. I was starting to
feel better too.

That afternoon, President Reagan was heading up to the
Hilton to address the Building Trades Council of the AFL-
CIO. As usual, he wanted some downtime beforehand to give
his speech a last-minute rereading. As he was leaving, I nod-

ded toward the speech and asked if it was okay. He gave me a thumbs-up sign and was off.

At two-thirty that afternoon, Dave Gergen burst into my office. His face was contorted and blotchy. "Cancel all appointments," he gasped, "there's been an assassination attempt." I froze. Cold fingers of terror constricted my throat. Only by sheer force of will was I able to get up from my chair and run after Gergen, who by this time had flown down the hall. "Is he hit?" I cried. "No," Gergen called back, "but a Secret Service agent and Jim Brady were."

Amid all the confusion the press office seemed to offer the best hope of solid information. Lots of others had already gathered there in front of the television monitors. The networks were running the film of the shooting. I saw the bodies moving in slow motion. I saw Jim Brady lying in a pool of blood, and my knees started to buckle. Somehow I made my way to the bathroom. I vomited until I thought my stomach would burst. The worst was yet to come.

In those first few chaotic hours, we were bombarded by information, some of it horribly wrong. I will never forget the agony of hearing Dan Rather announce (incorrectly, thank God) that Jim Brady was dead. By that time, Richard Allen, Al Haig, Don Regan, Cap Weinberger, Bill Casey, and I had gathered in the Situation Room. Dick Allen asked that we bow our heads in silent prayer. Half an hour later, we heard that Brady was alive after all.

The biggest shock, however, was that, contrary to first reports, the President had been shot. I am not a religious person, having rejected the doctrinal rigidity of the Catholic Church at a young age. But during the hours when Ronald Reagan was lying on the operating table, and for several days thereafter, I prayed like a nun. The nightmare seemed to go on and on. The President's lung had collapsed from the bullet wound and he was very weak. Jim Brady might never regain consciousness. The staff was confused over who was in charge. Everyone recalls that Al Haig went to the pressroom to announce that he was in charge. When we in the Situation Room saw him on the TV monitor, Weinberger looked taken aback. Many doubted that Haig was constitutionally correct (he wasn't). Moreover, his bravura performance was considered unnecessary with the Vice President about to return. I was so drained that my movements were like those of a sleepwalker. I just knew that I had to see Ronald Reagan for myself. I knew if I could look at him, after all the years I'd known him, through good times and bad, I'd know whether he was going to live or die.

The following morning, Mike Deaver saw to it that I got my wish. The hospital was crawling with security, and without prejudice to the Secret Service (which wasn't to blame and indeed probably saved Reagan's life), I must admit to having thought they were closing the barn door after the cow had run free. When I reached the President's room I felt a little wobbly. I wasn't quite prepared for how weak he looked. Though there was some color in his cheeks, his eyes were lacking their usual light. It was obviously too painful for him to speak. So I spoke. I chattered about this and that: gossip mostly. People tend to reach for mundane things in dire situations. It helps to restore a feeling of security where there is none. But when I got up to leave I was overcome. I bent over and kissed his hand.

After seeing the President I washed my face, took a deep breath, and headed down the hall to see Jim Brady. Sarah, his wife, was spending twenty-four hours a day by his side. No one said it, but everyone assumed Jim wouldn't make it. He looked very grave that second day. But as time went by he steadily improved. A couple of weeks later, I decided to see whether John Hinckley's bullet had truly destroyed the Jim Brady I'd been so fond of. I leaned over his bed and whispered, "Who's your favorite slum landlady?" He smiled and answered, "Helene von Damm." And I knew the old Jim, though he might never fully recover, had not been destroyed.

Even in the midst of all that tragedy, the usual White House turf warfare continued unabated. Dave Fischer took the opportunity of the President's injury to try to make himself important by announcing that he would be staying at the hospital night and day. Mike rolled his eyes at this but permitted Dave to play his self-appointed role; needless to say, he took himself very seriously. The first few times I tried to visit, Dave wouldn't let me in. He kept me in a "holding room" down the hall, and bustled about trying to look very busy. When I finally did see the President, I mentioned Dave's attempts to become the "keeper of the body." The President smiled. "Yeah," he said, "I think he'd brush my teeth for me if I'd let him."

Mrs. Reagan and Mike Deaver put out the word within days that the President was hale and hearty. The first couple posed for the famous red bathrobe photograph. But it was actually months before President Reagan was fit again. At first he came downstairs for an hour or two. Later he increased his working hours. Perhaps it was good for the country's morale to believe that the President was bouncing back and that continuity of leadership was not in doubt. But I was also concerned about his morale. A few days after the shooting, he suddenly took a turn for the worse, running a high fever and having difficulty keeping food down. Sick people need time to be sick. I hoped he wasn't being too pressured to act like a superman.

Vice President Bush behaved most admirably during this time. He kept a low profile, wouldn't think of taking RR's seat at Cabinet meetings, but maintained a reassuring presence nevertheless. Rumor had it that Mrs. Reagan and Mike Deaver insisted upon it. If true, they need not have worried. George Bush is too much of a gentleman to be reminded of how to behave at a time like that.

––––

In the weeks and months following the assassination attempt, the balance of power within the White House shifted. Prior to the shooting, Meese had been top dog. Baker was second. And Deaver wasn't significant enough to be considered a rival of either. While it was true that Baker had presided at the morning staff meetings, Meese was clearly in charge at Cabinet meetings, where Baker scarcely said a word.

The Sunday news programs always requested Meese as their guest, and he was even described as "President Meese" in a *Wall Street Journal* piece.

But the assassination attempt had allowed Mike Deaver to come into his own. The situation called for public relations skill, and Mike showed an abundance of it. He was suddenly handling the "spin" of stories about the President's health, about the running of the government during President Reagan's recuperation, and about future plans. The concept of a troika, the Big Three, was born at this time. Speculation has it that an interviewer for one of the newsweeklies asked Mike who was in charge during the President's illness. He said, "We three are in charge," and he wasn't exaggerating. He seemed to be everywhere at once, and always—sometimes as often as a dozen times a day—he was on the phone with Mrs. R. Their friendship became a crucial axis of power.

It was a personal turning point for Mike as well. He seemed to have made a decision to leave behind the loyalties of his California days. Though he had worked for Ed Meese for six years in California, he chose to align himself now with Jim Baker. And in so doing the stage was set for a lonely and difficult road for Ed Meese in the White House. As time proved, Mike Deaver also dealt a severe blow to the hopes of conservatives for the Reagan presidency.

During the first few months in Washington, Mike Deaver and I kept up our warm friendship, although our busy schedules seldom permitted us to get together informally and laugh, eat, and drink as we had done so comfortably in California. When Mike first began to rave about the glamorous and wealthy Washington establishment people he was meeting— including Katharine Graham, the liberal *Washington Post* publisher—I didn't think anything of it. After all, the truth was, I was also impressed. We were all impressed. Wealth and power are very alluring. But Mike seemed to be losing his head. He wanted to be part of that glittering world and spoke more and more often of ways to earn big money. I'm not sitting in judgment of Mike. I lost my equilibrium too, but later, and in different circumstances. I just feel sorry that Mike's personal ambitions torpedoed his friendship with the California group (he had began to drop his old friends) and affected the course of the Reagan presidency.

I think one of the reasons Mike was instantly mesmerized and drawn to Jim Baker (and away from his old colleague and former boss, Ed Meese) was that Baker represented everything he wanted to be. In fairness, I also think Mike genuinely liked and admired Baker and felt more comfortable with his pragmatic, can-do approach to Washington than with Meese's conservative dogma. In those morning meetings, Deaver would usually side with Baker on the grounds that public relations would be better served by Baker's recommendation. In private, their cooperation and like-mindedness was even more visible. Both were good strategists and neither was above using all the weapons available: the press, the bureaucracy, delay, and political favors. For a time Mike's star rose very high. His alliance with Baker and Mrs. Reagan made him a powerful man. And he imagined that he was becoming part of the "beautiful people" set. If there's a moral to be drawn from Mike's experience, perhaps it's to be found in what happened to him when he got into trouble. He had alienated all of his old friends. And there's little evidence that his new friends came through for him when he was in need—at least not in public.

Mike Deaver's strengths did not include management and organization. While he enjoyed making decisions, he tended to shoot from the hip. It matched his harried behavior. He was always in a hurry, on the run, on the phone, or late. If you had an appointment with Mike it meant at best a wait, if it was not canceled or postponed.

And his staff was the most complaining and warring in the White House. Interestingly enough, not against staffers of other departments, as was usually the case, but rather among themselves. They were always feuding and fighting over turf. (Mike often became terribly frustrated and disgusted when they tried to buttonhole him to settle their disputes more or less. But the staff never really pulled together; nor did Mike ever seem to have them under control.)

But I had to admire the niche he carved out for himself in the White House. For someone who knew and cared so little about substance, he wielded a huge amount of power. Almost all major decisions were made with Mike's participation. Among other duties, he and a select group from the White House would meet once a week to discuss themes President Reagan should be associated with. Also, Mrs. Reagan consulted him on anything and everything and together they'd spin ideas and scheme. Mike was at his best on his own—to orchestrate, to troubleshoot, and to run interference. No wonder Mrs. R found him to be an indispensable friend and accomplice in the White House. He had caught on to the ways of Washington quickly.

Ed Meese was exactly the opposite. He was anything but a schemer. Ed was a thoroughgoing policy person. He and Ronald Reagan thought exactly alike on nearly everything—to the point where they scarcely had to speak to one another in meetings because they could rely on body language. During Cabinet meetings, Ed was always busily scribbling on a yellow legal pad and only every now and then—just when the President was shooting him a glance—would Ed look up. Their eyes would meet and they'd seem to understand each other. Only at the end of the meeting would Ed speak. He'd sit back in his chair and summarize everything that had been said. He had become a great synthesizer. And as he spoke, Ronald Reagan would nod vigorously. It was a fascinating process to watch. I'd seen them do this for years, first in California and then in Washington.

Meese was a solid conservative and was willing to fight for principle. In fact, he was ready to fight for the entire Reagan agenda: civil rights, abolishing the Legal Services Corporation, or defending his deputy Brad Reynolds. In a city that values compromise, Ed's steadfastness earned him little praise except from a small band of conservative admirers. It's a pity that Ed Meese never had a Mike Deaver to look after his image, because the truth is that Ed was one of the most honest, dedicated, and unselfish aides in the Reagan Administration.

But the die was cast. Deaver and Baker discovered that together they could overcome Meese's intuitive understanding with President Reagan. From April 1981 onward, the pragmatist's influence slowly but steadily increased in the Reagan Administration.

———

In the spring of 1981, Byron and I were married. We had known for some time that we were going to do it, but one thing and another kept postponing our plans. Finally, Byron suggested that we just grab a marriage license and head for the courthouse in Hackensack, New Jersey. It was a fairy-tale story coming to what I hoped was going to be a "happily ever after." It didn't. But for that I blame only myself.

Immediately following the simple ceremony, we headed for Kennedy Airport to fly to Austria for our honeymoon. My good friends Lisl and Karl Böhm met us at the airport. This was the second entry into Vienna that they had helped smooth. They were very kind to me when I first came to Vienna as a vulnerable young girl, and we'd stayed in touch ever since. As Byron and I made our way to the gate we saw Karl holding a newspaper high in the air. It wasn't raining. I couldn't imagine what he was doing. In a minute I understood. It was a copy of the Vienna *Kurier.* Karl wanted us to see that our marriage had made the front page. I felt like royalty.

One of my priorities on the trip was to be with my mother as she marked her eightieth birthday. For so much of my life I had been hundreds or thousands of miles away from her. I loved her, but the truth was, I never really had known her very well. I knew only the mother a child sees, not the person an adult learns to distinguish.

My brother was living in West Germany and we had talked and written about our mother regularly. We were both upset that her living conditions were so poor. She still lived in my grandmother's apartment, without running water, central heating, or a bathroom. We were particularly concerned about her in winter because keeping warm required her to trudge downstairs two flights, gather wood and coal in a basket, and carry it upstairs to her flat.

This eightieth birthday was especially pleasing for us because Mother had finally agreed to let us move her into an old age home. The spot was lovely, in a little town on the Danube called Grein, complete with a picture postcard castle. More important, my mother now had hot and cold running water, central heating, and a bathroom for the first time in her life.

On a deeper level, though, my mother and I weren't connecting. She was proud of me, because everyone told her she had reason to be. But I wanted her to understand what I had accomplished. Unfortunately, the cultural divide was too vast. In a parent-child relationship, that hurts, even though I tried to tell myself I was being ridiculous. She was a simple person and she did the best she could. If she couldn't understand the world of America, much less Washington, D.C., how could I blame her?

The trip wasn't exactly nostalgic. I hadn't, after all, left Austria full of warm feelings for my native land, and yet I was seized by an urge to take Byron to Ulmerfeld, where I grew up. It was fascinating. I looked up some of the girls I had gone to grade school with—the ones who didn't seem to question their place in the world as I did—to see what had become of them. As I would have predicted, one had married the town florist, and another had married the hairdresser. They remembered that it was my birthday and rushed out for a cake to celebrate. As we ate and talked, I watched their faces. Were they happy? Did they feel cheated of life's riches? I don't think so. My life had certainly been far more eventful, but I couldn't have done it any differently. It was my nature. If I had been a more placid, satisfied person, like the women I was now eating and laughing with, I wouldn't have roamed.

After two lovely weeks, Byron and I returned to Washington. We joined the ranks of commuting couples. I spent Monday through Friday in Washington and traveled up to New Jersey on weekends to be with Byron. It wasn't a hardship, because by the time I got home most weeknights I was too tired to do anything except eat a quickly thawed frozen dinner and fall into bed. On weekends, when I was more relaxed, I had more time for my husband as well.

On my first day back in the office, my head was still reeling with Viennese waltzes, but that came to an abrupt end when the ever bumptious Dave Fischer presented his bill of particulars. Dave had filled in for me during my honeymoon and he now announced that in the future he wanted to see all confidential materials sent to the President. "Listen," I said. "I'm glad you enjoyed my job while I was gone. But I'm back, and if you think I'm going to turn over all of my responsibilities to you, you're crazy." He never said another word about it. But three days later he had the gall to show up in my office, just as breezy as could be, and ask to borrow our beach house for the weekend. I told him the truth; that Byron and I planned to be there every weekend we possibly could for the duration of the summer. But I was glad that the answer could so easily be no. Dave Fischer had a lot of nerve.

I returned to find that the President's National Security Adviser, Richard Allen, was having problems. Everyone seemed to be down on him. Key people in the Administration saw him as a poor manager and ineffective.

Moreover, Al Haig let it be known that he was bypassing the National Security Adviser on important matters. Even Bill Clark had clashed with Dick. His days seemed to be numbered.

Things simmered for a month or two after the Israeli bombing of Iraq. I was trying to spend a lot of time at the beach house, and invited Bill and Joan Clark and Mike Deaver for the weekend. Carolyn was away with the two children. The subject of Allen arose naturally. There was general agreement that he would have to go soon. I was vigilant about personnel matters, so I interjected, "But who would you get to replace Dick?" Mike glanced over at Bill Clark and asked, "How about it, Bill?"

"If that's what the President wants," Bill replied. I was relieved. If we had to lose a conservative like Dick Allen, at least Bill would be someone who shared Ronald Reagan's instincts and worldview.

On Monday morning, when I got to work, I found our weekend described in *Newsweek* as a strategy session to get rid of Allen. It was an obvious leak. But from whom? I had never intended the weekend to be any such thing. I wanted to rush into Dick's office and explain. But then I hesitated. What could I say? I hadn't had any thought of discussing him when I invited the Clarks and Deavers for the weekend. Nevertheless, the subject had been discussed. Would Dick believe that my intentions were completely unbiased toward him? It seemed doubtful. I stayed in my chair. My relationship with Dick Allen was never the same again.

———

In Sacramento and Los Angeles, I'd been a trusted staffer for Ronald Reagan, but I'd never been included in the social circles he traveled in. Not that I longed to be. But in Washington, as my "prestigious" job got me invitations to all the best social events, the California socialites began to notice me as well.

Our first Fourth of July in Washington was the best we ever had. Earle and Marion Jorgensen hosted a joint Fourth of July–Nancy Reagan birthday party at the Woodlawn Plantation on the Potomac. I was feeling festive in my red, white, and blue dress. The food was specially flown in from Chasen's restaurant in Los Angeles. We were all more relaxed than we'd been since before the assassination attempt. In fact, things got a bit silly. When Mrs. Reagan admired one of her friend's shoes, she slipped them off and insisted upon making them a birthday present to Nancy. Natalie Robinson spent the rest of the day barefooted. We had chartered buses to take us back to Washington for the fireworks in the evening but we got stuck in traffic. Bill Clark began to sing "Jimmy Crack Corn," and before long we were all singing and giggling like schoolchildren. When the sixty or so of us returned, we all went into the

White House. Some of our party went down to mingle with the White House staff who were celebrating on the South Lawn and others stayed upstairs. The fireworks were magnificent—and our view, from the second story of the White House, was surely the most perfect in Washington. All was right with the world that night.

With the coming of spring, the President's economic agenda was heading for a crucial vote in Congress. We wanted to cut taxes by 30 percent over three years and cut the budget to avoid huge deficits. Dave Stockman at OMB had been working sixteen-hour days attempting to iron out budget compromises with Congress, and in April we got our first victory, a win on the Economic Recovery Tax Act. Tip O'Neill was so bowled over that he elected to spend his vacation traveling in Australia and New Zealand rather than continue the struggle. "I know when to fight and when not to fight," he acknowledged. With his mail running five to one in favor of the President, O'Neill chose a wise course.

We lost some ground a few weeks later when Dick Schweiker, a born-again Reaganite ever since 1976 who was now heading the Department of Health and Human Services, unveiled a plan to cut Social Security benefits. There are many sacred cows in the domestic budget, but Social Security is so holy that grown congressmen bow down before it. We got clobbered by the Democrats (who later used it to some advantage as a campaign theme in 1982) and incurred the ire of House Republicans. Suddenly, our whole program of tax and budget cuts seemed a lot less secure.

By the time it emerged from committee on the Hill, the tax plan had been scaled back to 25 percent over three years— not bad for a town that usually splits the difference. Since Republicans controlled the Senate, everything rested upon one big vote in the House on August 4.

We geared up for it as if it were a military campaign. The President's daily schedule was two full pages long. Every spare moment was spent dialing congressmen. I thought the White

House operators' fingers were going to become frozen into the pattern of dialing 225, the first three numbers of most congressional offices. I kept track on our call sheets of who stood where on the tax and budget bills, and what particular concerns individual congressmen might have.

The President also made a speech to the nation, one of many in his first term which would strike fear into the hearts of opponents on the Hill. When Ronald Reagan went directly to the people, congressional offices were flooded with mail and phone calls.

When the big day finally arrived, everything seemed to be moving in slow motion. The morning dragged on forever. The President didn't just want to sit around and wait, so he spent the morning calling fence sitters. "I wonder if they're avoiding me," he sighed as I explained that several would have to call back. But call back they did. At around four the lines lit up. Everyone was with us. It was a snowball effect. Late in the day, the House voted, and we won by a vote of 282–95.

I needed a good back massage. But first there was champagne in the Oval Office and jubilation everywhere. We called everyone in the Administration who had played a key role in getting the bill passed to come on over and celebrate. Amid all the merriment, Tip O'Neill phoned the President. Democrat leaders Dan Rostenkowski, Tom Foley, and Jim Wright were also on the line.

"We're all sitting here stunned," said O'Neill.

"I'm a little stunned myself," the President replied, grinning.

After speaking to the Democratic leadership, President Reagan phoned the Republican leaders: Howard Baker, Bob Michel, and Jack Kemp. There was a huge smile on his face and you could almost see the smiles beaming at the other end of the phone lines.

Then, in a move which seemed surprising, the President summoned Elizabeth Dole. Her role in the effort hadn't been very crucial. As director of Public Liaison, she'd brought some groups into the White House to try to get their support, but that hardly seemed to merit what the President said when she walked in. "Now here's why we're all gathered here. Happy birthday Elizabeth." How like Ronald Reagan. At the moment of one of his great triumphs, he was willing to share the spotlight with someone else.

———

Before the buoyant mood of victory had worn off, I decided to seize my opportunity to ask President Reagan if I could transfer to the Office of Presidential Personnel. Pen James's deputy, John Herrington, was going to another post, so the opportunity was there.

I had been agonizing about this decision for so long. Would I be able to handle it? Did I dare to be the first secretary to the President of the United States to look for greener pastures? Would my friends and colleagues approve? In the past, all of my career moves had happened gradually. A boss would suggest that I move up. Or I'd take on the responsibilities of a job in addition to the one I held and get promoted through "sweat equity." But I'd never really set my sights on something which others might consider beyond my abilities. Now I was. The inner drive which had always propelled me forward was churning inside again. Byron was very supportive and that gave me strength, but ultimately it was my own yearning that finally pushed me into a decision.

I spoke to Mike about it first, and he suggested, wisely, that I have a replacement for myself lined up who would be acceptable to both of the Reagans before I spoke to the President. Knowing that Mrs. R would be unlikely to part with her own secretary, Elaine Crispen, I next thought of Kathy Osborne, who had been my understudy in California for a few years. I knew that both Reagans were very fond of her. With Mike's approval, I phoned Kathy at the boutique she owned in Sacramento.

"How would you like to be personal secretary to the President of the United States?" I asked.

Kathy was thunderstruck. For a minute I wasn't sure she

had heard me. But then she stammered, "Yes, yes, of course."
I told her to apply right away (a formality), and wished her
good luck.

When I finally went in to see President Reagan about it, I
got the feeling that Mike must have already spoken to him. He
didn't seem surprised when I took a deep breath and told him
how very much I loved working for him but I wanted the
challenge of taking over as Deputy Assistant to the President
for Presidential Personnel. The President had already given
the matter some thought.

"I've been noticing your restlessness and fully understand
your desire to test your wings. But is it really what you want?
What if you don't like it? I'd have a heck of a time getting you
this job back at some later date."

I told him I understood that and wouldn't expect any such
special treatment. "Besides," I said, "you don't really need me
here. I feel like a dilettante."

"What's wrong with being a dilettante?" President Reagan grinned. We both laughed. "And are you really sure," he
went on, "now that you've just married, that you want to work
eighteen-hour days again?"

I nodded. "I just think I could be making a much greater
contribution to your presidency."

"Well," he said, "you're wrong about my not needing
you. Just knowing you're out there is reassuring to me. But do
you really think it'll be that much more challenging in personnel now that most of the major posts are filled?"

I assured him I did. He had one more caveat. "Pen tells
me he'll be leaving in a year. But even if you serve the full
year as his deputy, I can't guarantee that I'll promote you to
the top post when the time comes."

"Of course I understand," I said. "But I'd like to do it, if
you want me to, of course." The President nodded and
pressed his lips together in the gesture familiar to millions, and
said, "Okay, eagle, try your wings."

As I look back, it's interesting that this was the one career
decision I had not consulted Bill Clark about. I suppose I was

so worried already about whether or not I'd be able to cut it in the new position that I was afraid to hear similar misgivings from Bill. Sure enough, when I told him of my decision, he volunteered the opinion that I was making a terrible mistake. I didn't ask why. I had passed a milestone—I no longer needed my friend's approval for every step I took.

———

The month between leaving the old job and starting the new was extremely busy. I was training Kathy Osborne (whose initials, everyone noticed jocularly, were KO) and straightening out my files—what to take along and what to leave behind.

The White House was all abuzz over the Professional Air Traffic Controllers' Organization (PATCO) fight. The President was determined, but sad to have to take such a firm stand against a union. His own experience as president of the Screen Actors Guild had left a lasting impression on him and I think at heart he was always a union man. The firing of all the PATCO employees caused some disruption in every flying person's life, mine included. I took to driving to New Jersey for the next few months since the wait at National Airport was just too unbearable.

I had pretty much wrapped things up by the time the President left for Santa Barbara on August 6. I had stopped traveling with the President, so I was not going to California on this trip. I was grateful for the time with Byron, but also, I must admit, slightly sheepish that I expressed no eagerness to head out to the dry, pleasant atmosphere of California. Washington's summers were so sticky that I couldn't wait to get to the Jersey shore each weekend.

———

But then, I did have something else up my sleeve for that summer as well. One of the new friends I had made in Washington was Phyllis Kaminsky, an exuberant woman very much involved in supporting the State of Israel. She invited me to be part of a trip to Israel sponsored by the Jerusalem Women's

Study Group, an organization which got started just after the Camp David peace accords.

I was ecstatic to be invited. My familiarity with an issue was usually acquired by listening to others, reading the papers, or glancing at memoranda when time allowed. But here was a chance to form impressions firsthand on an issue which had already confronted the Administration several times since we'd been in office.

I suspected that the press might try to impugn the propriety of the trip if they got wind of it before we left. And sure enough, two days before departure there were stories that this was some sort of secret White House mission to the Middle East because Ursula Meese, Carolyn Deaver, and I were going. Fred Fielding got that "I told you so" look on his face when the reports surfaced. He had been very jittery about the fact that the trip was all-expenses paid. He was so conscientious and protective of the President and the White House that he was deeply bothered when the press or any outsider merely questioned the propriety of something. Ursula, Carolyn, and I were part of a twenty-woman contingent. The others were all from the business and media worlds. I was determined never to repeat my sheepish response to the slum-landlady story. Sometimes, you've just got to square your shoulders and say, "Let the press say what they want, I'm going."

Israel was fantastic. When we first landed at Ben-Gurion Airport in Tel Aviv, I couldn't believe that this tiny airport was really the gateway to Israel. Because the country looms so large in world news, I had expected it to be larger in size somehow. And that was a perception that would remain with me for the entire trip. Understanding how small and vulnerable the country is geographically is the key to Israeli politics.

Phyllis had outdone herself in ensuring that we would see as much as possible in our short time there. In addition to the cities of Tel Aviv, Jerusalem, Caesarea, Eilat, and Haifa, we visited the Gaza Strip and the Golan Heights. The Golan Heights, for me, were an important symbol of Israel's predicament. From where I was standing, I could look down on miles upon miles of Israeli farms and villages. Prior to 1967, the Syrians had used the heights for their big guns and had terrorized the people below. I now understood why, when Israel was attacked in 1967, seizing the Golan had been a major objective. And I understood why they didn't want to return that region to Syrian hands.

Phyllis made sure we were given the opportunity to speak with both Arabs and Jews separately and together. The charismatic mayor of Jerusalem, Teddy Kollek, spent an afternoon with us. And we were able to meet Colonel Hadad, the Lebanese Catholic ally of Israel, who was equally interesting. Though Hadad was dressed in military fatigues and spoke with us while perched in his jeep, I got a very strong sense that he was more thoughtful than the average military man. His political sophistication was truly impressive.

Another wonderful aspect of the trip for me was the pure sensual enjoyment. The landscape was lovely, in a stark sort of way. I loved it because it bears a startling resemblance to southern California. There was time for hiking up Masada and swimming (in the Dead Sea!). And while I'm not a deeply spiritual person, there is something about being in the places where Christ lived and taught, particularly Jerusalem, which is very moving.

I returned feeling enriched in many ways. When I discussed my trip with the President, I was bursting with enthusiasm. "It's changed my perceptions of so many things," I explained. He understood. "Yes, my first trip to that part of the world had a similar impact on me. It's not something you'll soon forget." And he was right. I haven't.

GROWING WISE
TO THE WAYS
OF WASHINGTON

AT LAST, IN SEPTEMBER, I MOVED OVER TO PRESI-
dential Personnel. There's a huge, Victorian gray building
next to the White House which tourists often can't identify.
It's called the Old Executive Office Building, and to all those
who work within the gates of the compound, it's as much a
part of the White House as the white building next door. Well,
almost. The West Wing does house the very top handful of
Assistants to the President. But plenty of important people
have offices in the OEOB: Bill Casey, David Stockman, and
Lyn Nofziger had offices in the building, the Vice President
had his principal office there, and back in the 1970s President
Nixon used to work from a "hideaway" office in the OEOB,
preferring it to the formality of the Oval Office.

Still, it was a bit of a comedown for me. Instead of fresh
flowers on my desk and a view of the Rose Garden, I found
myself in a stuffy, overheated room with one grimy window. It
seemed to be miles to the ladies' room and the halls were so

alike in appearance that it was easy to lose your way in that building even after months of working there.

But aesthetics aside, my new home suited me. Any worries I had had about being able to handle the work vanished. There was an overabundance of work to do and I scarcely had time to reflect or worry.

Pen was a talented headhunter, and he spent most of his time seeking out the best people and running interference with Cabinet Secretaries. But he wasn't particularly interested in the mechanics of running the department, so he left the day-to-day management to his deputies. For a variety of reasons, there had already been three before me—I would be the fourth in nine months—and things needed to be tightened up.

I got a sense of just how loose the personnel department had become at our first staff meeting. The office employed fifty people, including support staff. There were six associate directors (the rank just below Special Assistant), each responsible for a cluster of related agencies and departments and each supervising a staff of their own. They were by and large competent, so I didn't have to make many changes. Among my able associate directors was even a familiar face: Maryann Urban, our teenybopper from the Sacramento days.

I called my first meeting for 9 A.M. Four associate directors simply didn't bother to show up. They gave no advance notice that they'd be unable to attend, nor did they think it necessary to explain their absence. This was going to stop.

I knew that in order to be taken seriously I would have to be somewhat tough in the beginning. I think women usually do in positions of authority. And in my case there was the added stigma of having been "just a secretary" to overcome. The following morning I announced that attendance at meetings was mandatory, and that failure to attend without prior written notice would not be viewed favorably. Meetings went fine after that.

Next I set about improving morale. The coin of the realm in the White House was perks, so I went to Jim Baker with a bill of particulars for the people under me. I wanted parking spaces, mess privileges, the works on an equal basis with the staff of Elizabeth Dole, which was comparable in size and setup. It took a lot of haggling and sheer persistence, but in time I got almost everything I asked for. The staff was very pleased.

I named three deputies under me: Becky Norton Dunlop to handle political clearance, Mike Farrell to supervise appointments to boards and commissions, and Lynn Wood (who had been in personnel since the transition) to handle administration. Lynn, bless her heart, also took care of our "must" placements. And she did so with aplomb.

Later I had a chance to appoint two new associate directors, both of whom turned out to be stars: Bonnie Newman, now president of the New England Industrial Council, and Dennis Patrick, who later became chairman of the Federal Communications Commission.

Because Pen was much like the President, I found myself in a position curiously analogous to Jim Baker's over in the West Wing. Pen approved all important decisions but gave me lots and lots of discretion. The Office of Presidential Personnel is key to the ideological tone of an Administration. We had the responsibility for seeing to it that the Reagan Revolution was being waged by true Reaganites. The federal government employs over a million people, not counting the military and the postal service. Most of them are nonpolitical, career employees who are protected by the Civil Service Act. A President gets to appoint only about two thousand people to full-time government jobs—political appointments. I was a great believer that those few jobs we were empowered to fill (compared with the overall size of the vast federal machinery) should not go to people who were indifferent to the President's political agenda. What else are political appointees for? I looked for qualified, competent, intelligent people who had been activists in the campaign or who shared our philosophy. In this, I was very grateful to Becky Norton Dunlop. Her political and ideological radar was dead accurate. She could spot a liberal at twenty paces. I relied on her judgment often and was never disappointed in her advice. I was also fortunate to have Ron Mann handle State—probably the most difficult department to make inroads into—and Dennis Patrick in charge of the second headache—Justice. Both were warriors as different in personality and style as could be, but effective. Where Ron was secretively operating behind the scenes, maneuvering through a network of Reaganites at State at all levels, Dennis was open, persistent, and persuasive and, if everything else failed, strident.

There was strong institutional pride among the lawyers at the Justice Department, and therefore strong resistance to political appointments. Dennis and I spent hours combing over names to suggest for Justice posts. It was important that they be top-quality people. But we were also looking for those who shared the President's political philosophy, and it never hurt if they had good political credentials as well, such as affiliation with the Republican Party or with conservative causes.

Dennis was also extremely adept at negotiating the tightrope one needed to walk when dealing with the Justice Department. He helped to fill dozens of top political positions there and still held on to the admiration and respect of the career Justice lawyers.

I asked Dennis to sit in for me at the weekly Thursday afternoon meetings which were held in the Roosevelt Room of the White House to pick nominees for judgeships. Those nominees were then submitted to the President for his approval.

The meetings were chaired by Fred Fielding, counsel to the President. The regulars were Ed Meese, Jim Baker, Mike Deaver, and representatives from the Justice Department. Since issues of criminal justice, civil rights, and judicial activism were so close to the President's heart, Ed Meese was able to dominate these meetings. Everyone knew that he very much spoke for the President on these issues.

The President, subject to approval by the Senate, has the power to appoint all federal judges, from the district court level to the Supreme Court of the United States. By custom, senators submit names to the Attorney General for the court vacancies which occur in their states. But for the first time, an Administration moved the decision-making process directly into the White House and away from the Justice Department. They would still try to accommodate the wishes of senators who were supporters of the President. But some were inevitably disappointed. It was important to President Reagan that the judicial selection group come up with names of young judges—he wanted his influence to be felt on the bench for years to come.

We also made an effort to find women judges, but that turned out to be difficult. Not that there weren't lots of qualified women jurists—there were. But it was awfully difficult to find qualified women jurists who were also conservative in outlook. I was so proud of Dennis for finding Pam Rymer, a Stanford, California, lawyer, when one of the federal district court slots in California opened up. He was responsible for making her Judge Rymer.

I think that when the accomplishments of the Reagan Administration are tallied by historians, the effect upon the judiciary will have to be counted among the greatest accomplishments. It will become the Reagan legacy.

———

The first high-level appointment I took on personally was the chairman of the National Endowment for the Humanities. I was a bit of a novice in the area, but soon came to understand that this had long been a sore point with conservatives. I mentioned the post to Becky Norton Dunlop over lunch one day and she launched into an impassioned denunciation of the liberal dominance of the agency. There were stories of the National Endowment giving money to Marxist and quasi-Marxist organizations, to counterculture-style entertainments, and to other recipients who were less than wholesome.

I believed that the post needed someone who could articulate conservative values without seeming to be a fuddy-duddy. William Bennett was in my eyes the ideal choice. A lawyer and educator, Bennett was then the director of the National Humanities Center in North Carolina. He was also a

My mother and father (Helene Pehamberger and Josef Winter) during their courtship.

My brother Pepi and I. I was furious, Mother remembers, for having to submit to being photographed. It shows!

My high school picture, taken in 1952. I'm the smiling fourteen-year-old in the front row, second from the right.

In 1963 my mother visited me in the United States for the first time. My friend Marvin Lowe and I took her sightseeing around Chicago.

Baker, Meese, and Deaver: the "Big Three" (and Dave Fischer) during their morning staff meeting with President Reagan. PHOTO CREDIT: THE WHITE HOUSE

The typical commotion and chaos of a photo opportunity in the Oval Office. PHOTO CREDIT: THE WHITE HOUSE

Saying good night in the early morning hours after a splendid evening in the White House. Occasion: Ronald Reagan's seventieth birthday celebration with friends on February 6, 1981. It was also my first black-tie dinner dance at the White House. PHOTO CREDIT:/THE WHITE HOUSE

Bill Clark loves to show off his cooking—be it at his ranch, in someone else's kitchen, or here, in formal Blair House (the government's guest house for foreign dignitaries). The occasion: a 1982 Christmas party hosted by the cook, William P. Clark, then National Security Adviser. PHOTO CREDIT: THE WHITE HOUSE

New Year's Day brunch at the Annenbergs'. Mrs. Reagan with her women friends (from right to left): Jean Smith, Carol Price, Lee Annenberg, unidentified, Nancy Reagan, Marion Jorgensen, Betty Wilson, and me.

My swearing-in ceremony as Ambassador to Austria, with President Ronald Reagan, Mrs. Selwa (Lucky) Roosevelt, me, Byron Leeds, and Bill Clark. PHOTO CREDIT: THE WHITE HOUSE

Dear Helene — There are no words. God Bless you & Keep you — "Sincerely" — Ronald Reagan

President Reagan congratulating me after my swearing-in as Ambassador to Austria. PHOTO CREDIT: THE WHITE HOUSE

Reviewing the Honor Guard on my way to the Imperial Palace to present my credentials to Austria's President.

The diplomatic scene is still a male bastion! Occasion: the celebration of the thirtieth anniversary of the signing of Austria's State Treaty in the Belvedere Palace, June 15, 1985.

Party at the U.S. Ambassador's residence in Vienna after the benefit concert with Frank Sinatra. Next to him are his wife, Barbara, me, the world-renowned race car driver Niki Lauda, and Byron Leeds.

Conquering the highest peak of the Rosengarten in the Dolomites, Italy, with Hannes Gasser, head of Tirol's famous mountain-climbing school Alpinschule Innsbruck, in summer 1987.

fan of rock music. Unlike some conservatives, he was comfortable in the twentieth century. On the other hand, his values—courage, self-sacrifice, hard work, honesty, eternal truths, democracy—were exactly what the chairman of NEH would need.

Some in my department favored another candidate, Robert B. Hollander, a professor of comparative literature at Princeton. He was very conservative, but then so was Bennett, so it wasn't really a dispute about ideology.

The first part of considering someone for an appointment is always long hours on the telephone. You call people who know him and like him. You call people who know him and maybe don't like him. You try to find some neutral scholars who will give an unbiased opinion. Everyone praised Bill Bennett. I was starting to like him myself, even before I had met the man.

I was still in my first week on the job, though, and the work had piled up so high that I didn't get a chance to call Bennett from the office. Byron and I were going to Newport for the weekend, and I knew I would have about forty-five minutes at the airport to make last-minute calls. I rushed out of the White House lugging an overstuffed briefcase and a small overnight bag on Friday evening. Once at the airport, I realized that while I had remembered to bring along Bennett's phone number, I didn't have his file with me. The airport noise was deafening. I slipped into a glass-enclosed phone booth (why are there so few left in public places?), kept one eye on the departing flights board, and dialed the White House operators. They put me through to Bennett. A male voice answered. "Is this Mr. Hollander?" I asked. As soon as the words were out of my mouth I wanted to die. Hollander was Bennett's principal rival for the job and Bennett surely knew that. He politely dismissed my apologies and insisted that it was a perfectly understandable mistake. I felt better and tried to patch things up by inviting him to lunch with me at the White House. He accepted. There seemed to be smiles on both ends of the telephone lines. Until I said, "I'm looking forward to meeting your wife." Ugh. Bennett was single at the time. Without his file in front of me I had gotten his personal statistics confused with Hollander's. This time Bennett sounded mighty wary. "Listen, Mrs. von Damm," he said, "are you sure you've got the right guy?" I was sure, but I don't think Bill was truly convinced for a long time thereafter.

On Monday morning, I discovered that I had problems beyond my own mistakes with this appointment. Senators Jesse Helms and John East, both of North Carolina, had their own candidate in mind, Professor M. E. Bradford of the University of Dallas. I spoke to the Congressional Liaison people and they were extremely dubious about Bradford's ability to win Senate confirmation. He had supported George Wallace for President in 1968—and while roughly 13 percent of the electorate had also, it probably wouldn't go down well in the U.S. Senate. There was also talk that he had written a book highly critical of Abraham Lincoln. But, as so often happens in politics, the question had to be suspended for a while. The Administration was trying to win passage of legislation which would allow us to send AWACS planes to Saudi Arabia. Helms's support was critical. Accordingly, we were told to lie low on the Bennett thing for a while. Two months later, after considerable lobbying (I even went to Capitol Hill to try to win over Senator East), and with the AWACS deal approved, Bennett was quietly confirmed. I'm not sure if Jesse Helms was promised something in return for agreeing to drop Bradford or if he just lost interest, but I was extremely pleased. I like to think of Bennett as another of my stars. In later years, I noted with amusement that Senator Helms always introduced Bill Bennett as "North Carolina's own."

For the first month or two, September and October of 1981, things went smoothly. The department got to know me and I them. After the initial lines of authority were clear, I felt more able to socialize with my colleagues. We often had lunch together, and many evenings were spent gossiping and laughing either at one another's homes or in restaurants. I kept a supply of peppermint schnapps in my desk for our late evening wind-downs. Everyone gossips about people, of course, but when personnel is also your business, you get in the habit of looking over your shoulder at all times. We began to develop a wonderful esprit de corps. I was especially happy to have Lynn Wood and Tad Tharp working with me again. We often felt as if we were holding up the banner of Reaganism against the onslaughts of the entrenched bureaucracy. And they always knew how to work the system to their advantage. We were learning on the job.

Nor was it only bureaucrats we tangled with. I got a strong taste of back-room politics, the hardball kind, during October. At the time, Charles Percy was the chairman of the Senate Foreign Relations Committee. His daughter, Sharon Percy Rockefeller (she was married to Jay Rockefeller, then Democratic Governor of and now Senator from West Virginia), was chairman of the board of the Corporation for Public Broadcasting. Though Percy was a Republican, he was at the liberal end of the spectrum. His daughter was a Democrat. And a liberal Democrat at that. But that didn't prevent Percy from phoning the President to say that he very much hoped and expected that his daughter would be renominated for another term at the CPB.

I was amazed. Didn't philosophical agreement count for anything? Sharon Rockefeller not only didn't support Ronald Reagan for President, she had actively worked against him. Besides, the board had fifteen members, who served not at the pleasure of the President but had staggered-term appointments. So far we had had the chance to appoint only seven new members. Thus, the board was still controlled by liberal Carter appointees. If we reappointed Sharon, she would represent the crucial swing vote, and we would have to wait for several years until the next vacancy would give us a chance for control of the board.

I went on the warpath. I called Jim Baker and asked if he, Deaver, and Meese would meet with me. He said "sure" with that relaxed southern style of his which almost makes you question what you were so exercised about. I presented my case to the three of them the next day. Meese was unequivocally against reappointing Sharon. Baker and Deaver scratched their chins. They suggested that I have lunch with her and try to get her to compromise.

Sometimes I think Washington believes that lunches solve all problems. Three-trillion-dollar deficit? Why don't the leaders of Congress and the President have lunch. Soviets have invaded another country? Why not have lunch with the ambassador.

Well, I invited Sharon to lunch and I put it to her straight. "We both know what's happening here. Can you promise me that if we reappoint you to the board you'll step down as chairman?" I saw her eyes start to narrow. I pressed on. "Or if not, that in the case of a tie you'll vote with us?"

She smiled. She was charming. But she didn't answer.

"Look," I said, "for us to use up one of our few political slots to reappoint you, you have to give *something* in return. I hope, for example, that you'd refrain from testifying against us on the Hill" (as she had in the past). I swallowed some water and looked at her. Her eyes said nothing. She thanked me for lunch and promised to consider what I'd said. After lunch I remember feeling somewhat sad that she was now out of a job. I had some more things to learn about how Washington works.

A couple of days later, a storm called Senator Chuck Percy blew into the White House. His secretary called saying he wanted to speak to me, Ed Meese, and the President—in that order. Ed and I met with him the following day. Percy was upset, though in too theatrical a way to be totally believable. He reminded us of how important the chairman of the Foreign Relations Committee was to the Administration. We nodded. He allowed as how it would be awful if he was forced *for any reason* to cancel his planned trip to Thailand, where he was to represent President Reagan at that country's bicentennial celebration. We agreed. He then gave us a long lecture to the effect that it would be illegal for us to attempt to influence the Corporation for Public Broadcasting. That was too much! I wanted to scream. In the first place, he was obviously strong-arming us. To then piously invoke the law where there was absolutely no question of illegality was too much to bear. The President can appoint whomever he likes. That's what the law says.

Percy then demanded to see the President. Ed Meese said some soothing things and the "lecture" was over. I went back to my office in the OEOB (we had used Ed's West Wing office for the meeting) with steam rising from my ears. Emotionally I was ready to continue to fight, but on the other hand I was glad I didn't have to make the decision. When the Big Three invited me to join their next meeting on the subject, the die had been cast. The decision was to fold. Sharon Percy Rockefeller continued to appear on the Hill and elsewhere as a vocal critic of Administration policies. But now questioners could begin with: "Mrs. Rockefeller, you were appointed by this President, were you not? Therefore your criticisms must take on added weight."

―――――

By my second month on the job, I had fallen in love with the personnel office. Everything we touched was controversial —and therefore never boring. Where I had felt understimulated sitting outside the Oval Office, I was overstimulated now. Work began at 7:30 A.M. most days and frequently continued until 7:30 in the evening and beyond. The phone was constantly ringing. I could never in a single day return every call I got. I interviewed candidates only after they had been recommended by my staff and had reached the "finalist" stage. There's nothing like being in a position to fill prestigious jobs to make you popular. My phone at home rang all the time, even on weekends. But Byron was wonderful and never complained about the infringement on our privacy.

After the Sharon Percy Rockefeller episode, I began to see that moderate and liberal Republicans were not going to be bashful about pushing for advantage within our conservative Administration. All I could do was try to hold the line and hope that I'd get support from above. It wasn't always forth-coming.

Before I had joined the personnel department, Jim Baker had managed to get one of his personal staffers, Frank Hodsoll, appointed as chairman of the National Endowment for the Arts. I was upset that this guy was given one of the plum jobs in the Administration, particularly after seeing his résumé. He had few if any qualifications for the post. Further, Hodsoll was a liberal Republican who had nothing but contempt for conservatives. When the two of us discussed names of possible candidates for his board, it was as if we were coming from different worlds. Everyone he recommended was from the liberal establishment. Everyone I recommended he would dismiss as an "embarrassment." We butted heads for weeks. Finally, Hodsoll got tired of fighting me and apparently decided to resolve things in the usual Washington way. He successfully solicited the help of Armand Deutsch, a longtime friend of the Reagans, and suggested that what was really needed (instead of me!) was a President's Advisory Commission on the Arts. Moreover, what was needed was Nancy Reagan to serve as honorary chairman. She was delighted to accept. I had been outmaneuvered. Hodsoll filled that commission with people who had no place in a Reagan Administration. Some were Democrats. Some were incompetent. But because Hodsoll had friends in high places, I could do absolutely nothing. It was infuriating. President Reagan gave clear signals that he wanted us to hire people who shared his philosophy. But at a personal level, he rarely had the heart to fight about it. It was left to us top assistants, as I saw it, to fight some of those battles for him.

My move to the personnel office was a good political education. When I had been the President's secretary, I had, of course, known that the conservatives were restive and uncomfortable about the way things were going, but I didn't really understand their position. But over in personnel I saw that the conservatives were not paranoid; they were indeed being out-maneuvered in important ways by the moderates.

My loyalty had always been first and foremost to Ronald Reagan personally. But that extended to his philosophy, which I shared. It troubled me, as it troubled other conservatives who didn't necessarily have a personal relationship with the President, that his ideas were being shunted aside.

WE'RE LOSING OUR GRIP

O N TUESDAY, NOVEMBER 10, 1981, I WAS WORKING late in the office as usual. The television in my office was on but I wasn't paying close attention to it. Suddenly, I sat up straight and stared at the screen. Leslie Stahl was saying something about David Stockman. I heard the name William Greider. And then the terms "embarrassing," "explosive," and "revealing," and my heart froze. The next issue of *The Atlantic Monthly* would contain an extensive interview with our brilliant young director of the Office of Management and Budget. The Administration, according to Stockman, had used "Reaganomics" as a Trojan horse to disguise plain old "trickle-down" economics—giving breaks to the rich in the hope that the benefits would eventually reach the poor.

Stockman. I had never really trusted that man. He had betrayed his old boss John Anderson—and now he had betrayed us. I felt as if someone had punched me in the stomach. I knew the press was going to go wild with the story. I was enraged at Stockman, but also, in truth, a little angry at the President too. I was working twelve- to-fifteen hour days trying to ensure that we hired people who were loyal to him. Couldn't he take some interest in who worked for him?

The following morning, after the usual eight o'clock staff meeting, Mike Deaver, Jim Baker, Ed Meese, and Lyn Nofziger met with the President in the Oval Office. I heard later from Lyn Nofziger what took place.

"What the hell happened?" asked the President. Baker looked drawn. He explained that, as far as he knew, Stockman had been meeting with Greider once a week at the Hay-Adams Hotel across Lafayette Park from the White House since the outset of the Administration. There were expletives around the room. Mike Deaver said, "He's outta here." All of the Californians agreed wholeheartedly.

But then Jim Baker began to speak in that deliberate, dispassionate, almost lulling way. He said Stockman felt truly awful about the way this was being played in the press (Ronald Reagan was always a softie for people who felt misrepresented), that he was really sort of a victim in all this, and that we needed him to pass our economic program through Congress. He then suggested (what else?) that the President have lunch with Stockman and talk things over. President Reagan agreed to the lunch but nothing more.

The meeting ended, but I saw Deaver and Baker walk out together and I sensed that it was not going to be hard to get Deaver to switch sides. I knew he had been overawed by Stockman's brilliance. Sure enough, Mike soon lobbied Mrs. Reagan to go easy on Stockman, and Dave kept his job. A few nights later, I had dinner with Bill Clark. "You know, Bill," I said, "there is truly no penalty for treachery in the Reagan White House." He nodded with great sadness.

A few short weeks later, Bill was the ironic beneficiary of similar treachery when he was appointed the head of the National Security Council. Mike Deaver, Al Haig, and others had been gunning for Richard Allen for months. Suddenly, a silly item about a couple of watches Dick had received as gifts while on a visit to Japan, then residing in his White House safe, made headlines. They weren't particularly valuable as watches go, but as news they were gold. I couldn't help but wonder who had tipped off the press. Naturally, there had to be a Justice Department investigation. Dick decided to take a leave of absence to defend himself, but he never returned. The "scandalette" was sufficient fodder for his enemies on the inside to oust him. I was happy for Bill Clark, but I certainly hated what had been done to Dick Allen. When, in due course, Dick was vindicated of all charges of wrongdoing, no one noticed. It ran on the back pages of the newspapers and wasn't mentioned on the evening news.

We all handled being under that kind of pressure in our individual ways. I tended to discount the possibility of anything like that happening to me because I wasn't important enough. In retrospect, I know I was plenty important, but it gave me some comfort at the time to think I was below the line of fire. Later, not even I could persuade myself that I was inconspicuous, and I did indeed get shot down.

———

President Reagan never really appreciated the importance of who worked for him. Partly, I suppose, this was the consequence of his own personal history as an actor, speaker, and then politician; in those roles he was always a free agent who didn't rely on an organization. It was also true that he really hated to impose on people, and if he got an inkling that someone wanted to move on, he would never stand in their way. And finally, I suppose there was a kind of splendid isolation about the man. He really didn't seem to need close friends. He was warm and friendly, yet still slightly aloof and autonomous. In his free time he was quite content to be alone with Nancy.

The President and Mrs. Reagan spent most weekends at Camp David. They usually took along a movie or two, and the President always brought a big briefcase of papers: briefing materials, speech drafts, and memos. He was never one to just sit around doing nothing.

The President's detachment from personnel matters was illustrated by Lyn Nofziger's fate. Lyn had been a longtime friend and ally to Ronald Reagan. His loyalty was without question. And yet, the meeting about the Stockman affair in the Oval Office had been unusual. Lyn had been invited. Usually, he was excluded. I had noticed Lyn's fading star back when I had been working as the President's secretary. But I was busy with other things, and hoped he would find his rightful place in the scheme of things. I also thought Baker appreciated him to some extent. Why else make him political director?

But now, in the fall of 1981, it was increasingly clear that Lyn was being isolated. I don't think it was always intentional. Baker, understandably, gravitated to his own people. Besides, Nofziger's office was in the Old Executive Office Building, not in the West Wing, which made him slightly less accessible. Mrs. Reagan snubbed him by failing to include his name on invitation lists, and allowed talk to simmer in the press that she disapproved of his rumpled appearance and bearing. Questioned about this by a reporter, Lyn remarked mordantly that he chose his clothing with an eye to making Ronald Reagan look good. I loved Lyn's sense of humor. He was such a casual person in such an intense world. His presence always gave the reassuring feeling that politics wasn't completely detached from the world of "real" people. Moreover, Lyn was a conservative, and I saw in his exclusion the same forces (Baker, Deaver, Mrs. R) who were slowly diminishing the influence of all of the conservatives in the Administration. Mike Deaver's book has since confirmed what was only a feeling on my part. He says point-blank that he (and Mrs. R as his ally) tried to rid the Administration of conservatives.

I thought about Lyn's predicament a good deal. When I tried to raise the subject with him, he said something about wanting to make more money. I phoned Paul Laxalt and asked his advice. We agreed that money probably had nothing to do with Lyn's dissatisfaction. His pride was hurt. And understandably so.

I decided to raise the issue with the President. I didn't make a habit of lobbying him about specific people. My influence was a precious resource and I didn't want to dilute it by using it too often. But Lyn was special and someone had to go to bat for him. The next time I saw President Reagan alone I put aside my files and looked him right in the eye. "Mr. President, I must bring this up. Lyn really feels cut out."

The President looked genuinely surprised. "Why would he feel cut out?" he asked.

I explained how Baker and Deaver never consulted him or included him in important meetings. And then I pressed further. "When was the last time you called him or asked him to come to a meeting?" He looked pensive. "I guess I don't remember. I'll make a note of this. We can't have Lyn unhappy."

I left his office feeling terrific. I had taken the bull by the horns and accomplished something. Or so I thought. As it turned out, my feelings of triumph were quite temporary. The President didn't follow through after our talk in November. In December 1981, Lyn resigned.

I now think Lyn's departure marked a turning point in the Reagan Administration. Lyn was more than a loyal conservative. He was someone who had known Ronald Reagan for years, understood his weaknesses as well as his strengths, and would speak plainly to him when necessary. Lyn knew when Ronald Reagan was allowing himself to be talked into something which went against his gut instincts. Lyn shared those instincts. He also knew how to protect his political base. But President Reagan never seemed to grasp what a void was created when Lyn left.

Just after Christmas, Roy Pfautch, a longtime good friend of Lyn's, who was, like all Reaganites, pained by his departure, threw a farewell party for him at the Sheraton Washington Hotel. The event was planned to be bright and cheery, the way Lyn would have wanted it. It had a carnival theme— "Life's a Circus When You Know Lyn Nofziger." There were clowns, and cotton candy, and even an elephant. But I found all the balloons and merrymaking even more depressing. David Stockman gets to keep his job even after publicly betraying his boss, and Lyn Nofziger gets eased out. I was angry and sad and I know other loyal Reaganites felt the same way. Perhaps the most ironic twist of the evening came when a reporter cornered Lyn and demanded to know how he could possibly be resigning. "Why are you jumping ship?" she asked. "Must be my rat heritage," replied Lyn with a sad smile. There were certainly rats in the Administration, but Lyn Nofziger wasn't one of them.

My position in personnel required me to collaborate with Nancy Reagan a good deal. This relationship had come to be called the "Mommy account" (so named because the President sometimes called Mrs. R "Mommy" with his kids). And it was natural that it fell to me because of my long relationship with the Reagans.

It worked out better than I had been expecting. Mrs. R had known me as a secretary for so many years that I was afraid she wouldn't take me seriously as a Deputy Assistant and later Assistant to the President. To my surprise, she was quite cooperative and nicer to me than she had ever been before. I was proud of the relationship I was able to maintain with her, though at the same time I must admit that I found her priorities puzzling.

Mrs. Reagan always said that she was interested in "people, not policy," but what was the distinction? People are policy. That's why personnel struggles became so fierce. It wasn't just an argument about patronage, it was a matter of which direction the Administration would move in.

At that point in the Administration (late 1981 and 1982), she was very interested in appointments that touched on the arts in any way. Perhaps this was the influence of her own acting background, or perhaps it reflected her eagerness to please her friends, who had similar interests. In any event, I was more than willing to consult with her about those appointments.

But she was puzzlingly inconsistent. She would appoint a Democrat to her own staff one day and on the next be on the phone to me urging that I fight for Reaganites. Yet if a battle ever became public—a Reaganite versus a moderate—she'd back away. I did my best to accommodate her but I was never sure what she'd say next. She changed her mind frequently, and just as quickly would change it back. I understood that people who worked for her had become accustomed to her unpredictability.

On the other hand, Nancy Reagan's influence at the start of the first term was not what it would later become. She, like everyone else, was learning how to use power. Besides, initially she was busy redecorating the White House and polishing her own image.

During my time in personnel, I know that there was never a case of an important appointment, such as an ambassadorship, going through simply because Mrs. R suggested someone. Her recommendations were subject to the same scrutiny as everyone else's. She never made a suggestion for a post which I found unconscionable. If she had, I would not have hesitated to go to Ed Meese or Bill Clark. The Californians, unlike many of President Reagan's later advisers, were not afraid of Nancy Reagan. They would counsel the President as they thought best—whatever her views might be.

Slowly, though, her presence was felt. Jim Baker and Mike Deaver shrewdly saw that she could be a formidable ally. They encouraged her to become involved by using her as a sounding board and asking for her advice and help. Soon, she was thriving on it. No matter how much she denied it, the role of "power behind the throne" suited her to perfection. She was a schemer married to someone who was unable to conceive of a Machiavellian thought.

During the second term, I think her influence grew even greater because there was an increasing vacuum of power at the White House. The President's advancing age and illnesses made cooperation with the First Lady more imperative. But the new staff, particularly Don Regan, went much further in bowing to her influence than Meese or Clark or, I believe, Baker would have done. I cannot imagine that any of those three would have blocked out the President's calendar in obedience to Mrs. R's astrologer. They would have gently but firmly told Mrs. Reagan that her wishes couldn't be accommodated. In other words, they would have just said NO! Besides, by then she had learned to use all of the weapons in her arsenal: social invitations, leaks to the press, and intramural scheming to work her will. She relied on her savvy Washington friends, such as Mary Jane Wick, Nancy Reynolds, and Maureen Reagan, to act as conduits for her views to the press. Though she always claimed that her sole motivation was making her husband look good, I was very distressed by the open fashion in which she attempted to manipulate him over Don Regan's dismissal. Far from making him look good, her practically open interference made him look pathetic and weak. Most of the press played along with her fiction of being uninvolved in substance because they didn't want to lose access to her. In 1987, when Bill Safire, almost alone among the Washington press corps, criticized her influence in print, I commended him on his courage. "It's not courage, Helene," he said, "I just genuinely prefer eating hamburgers at home."

Whenever I got involved in one of my knock-down-dragouts, I could go for help and support to a large number of friends within the Administration. Ed Harper at the Policy Development Office, Fred Fielding, Elizabeth Dole, Max Friedersdorf, Bill Clark, Ed Meese, and many, many more, including, of course, my boss, Pen James. When I needed support for a job candidate, to prove that they were worthy of the task, I would line up the others to add weight to my judgment.

Though Bill Clark had initially disapproved of my decision to take the personnel job, once I was there he was terrifically supportive. I knew I could call on him at any time. Washington didn't have any effect on Bill. He maintained his integrity and even his slightly eccentric ways of doing things. Bill also kept me on an even keel by making social occasions as easy and informal as they had been in our Sacramento days.

We didn't have nearly as much time to entertain now, but Byron and I hosted a brunch at our new Watergate apartment for Lionel Olmer, Under Secretary of Commerce for International Trade, and his wife, Judy, Donald and Ivana Trump (whom I'd met while raising money for the campaign), Bill and Joan Clark, and our friends Ida and Joe Gotthelf. It was one of the few occasions when we found time to entertain and it brought back pleasant memories of my California days.

Bill insisted upon serving up his California-style western omelette. I'd tasted his cooking many times before and was more than willing to let him have the run of my kitchen. He put together a concoction which must have included twenty ingredients—eggs were in there somewhere but you couldn't find them easily. It tasted great, and everyone, myself included, was applauding the chef when suddenly this horrible sound began to emanate from the kitchen. The sink was backed up and overflowing, spewing greasy slime all over the countertops and floor. There was no stopping it. Donald Trump had built kitchens all over the country, but doubting that he'd ever actually seen a drain up close before, I felt it pointless to ask for advice. So I decided to cope with the mess myself. Marc Brazil, a young staffer from my office who'd tended bar for us that evening, and I were flinging paper towels around the kitchen like life preservers. Bill looked as innocent as a baby. I was dubious. It would be just like a man who fancies himself a great chef because he does nicely with outdoor barbecues to pour hot grease down a drain. He drew himself up to his full height and accused me of sexism. Well, maybe. In the end, we had to call a plumber to fix the pipes and a cleaning lady to scrub the grease off the kitchen. It certainly was a change of pace from the embassy receptions we all attended so often.

But while Bill was his old self with us, he nevertheless handled each of his jobs within the Administration with skill and finesse. When he had been Deputy Secretary of State, his steady advice to Al Haig had been important to the smoothing out of relations between Haig and the White House. That wasn't easy. Haig was a high-strung person who threatened to resign with regularity. The first time he did so was after the President passed over him and appointed George Bush to head a newly organized crisis management team. Bill asked Al to hold off for twenty-four hours and then persuaded him to (of course) have lunch with Mike Deaver and see whether the whole thing couldn't be worked out. It wasn't. But Al didn't resign. It seems so funny from this distance. The much-vaunted crisis management team turned out to be a big zero. It was never convened, so far as I know. Bill was also a helpful influence at the State Department, which is dominated by those who take an accommodationist view toward the Soviet Union. Since Bill's views on the need to maintain vigilance were fixed, he well represented what the first-term Reagan Administration was all about in foreign policy.

Bill moved over to the National Security Adviser's job when I had been at personnel for about four months. Bill was busier in the new job, and I certainly was, so while our offices were now only a few hundred yards apart, we saw each other less.

After all of the hounding Bill had received when he was before the Senate for confirmation to the State Department position ("Does he know where Europe is?" ran one newspaper story at the time), I was proud of the way he handled the NSC. It's one of the toughest jobs in the Administration, with poorly delineated powers and the inevitability of being squeezed between the Secretary of Defense and the Secretary of State.

When Bill became National Security Adviser in January 1982, he improved the status and authority of the position. Dick Allen had accepted a basement office, one flight down from the Oval Office, and below where past National Security Advisers had had offices. Moreover, he had not reported to the President directly but instead had reported to him through Ed Meese. Bill kept the basement office but one of his first reforms was to insist upon a daily national security briefing for the President which only he and Ronald Reagan would attend.

He got the Troika to agree that he could brief the President on national security matters whenever he needed to—and he did frequently brief him more than once a day.

He also improved the morale of the NSC staff by giving respectful attention to their opinions ("Opinions are their work product," he used to say), and by ensuring that they got credit for their ideas. Bill always made sure to include at the top of a memo which reached the President's desk the name of the staffer who had done the main work. Bill had terrific people skills.

I think Bill was also an effective National Security Adviser because he reinforced Ronald Reagan's best instincts about the world. He was so rooted in his California origins that the blandishments of the career State Department bureaucracy didn't corrupt him. His worldview was based on a lifetime's experience of watching world events unfold, and he wasn't going to change fundamental views because someone at State who spoke Russian fluently tried to explain how truly moderate the Soviets were. In this, he and President Reagan were much alike. It's a pity that when Bill left, President Reagan heard less and less from people who shared his worldview and more and more from those who took a softer line.

Bill Clark also continued to serve as a buffer between Al Haig and the White House. Unlike the others in the West Wing, Clark fundamentally agreed with Haig's conservative views. For that reason, he was more willing to put up with Haig's theatrical tactics and extreme sensitivity to slights. Yet, after a few months in the NSC job, the relationship between Haig and Clark began to change subtly. Clark was now responsible for balancing the views of the Secretary of Defense, the Director of the CIA, and others, and I think eventually it was difficult for Haig to accept the fact that Clark was no longer his man.

For the first year of the Reagan Administration, foreign policy got short shrift. I knew that this was terribly frustrating for Al Haig. He, alone among the President's close advisers, had extensive foreign policy knowledge and experience. He knew that the Administration had a rare opportunity to make progress in foreign policy because part of President Reagan's mandate was to reverse the perceived weakness of the United States during the Carter Presidency. Ronald Reagan was eager to increase funding for the U.S. military, but when it came to policy initiatives, he was less focused than he would later become.

After Bill Clark became National Security Adviser, foreign policy did become a much larger part of the President's agenda. He and the President formulated policies on Central America, Africa, arms control, and the Strategic Defense Initiative. As Jim Baker, Mike Deaver, and Mrs. R saw what a large influence Clark was having, they began to feel threatened. They didn't approve of the conservative line the Administration was taking on foreign policy and so began to undercut Clark.

Haig had been undercut too, but for different reasons. I can remember sitting in on Cabinet meetings during the first eighteen months of the Reagan term, where I was sometimes a silent observer, and understanding how frustrated Haig must have felt. Sitting around that table, who besides himself knew much about foreign affairs? Bill Casey? He did a terrific job at the CIA, but in the beginning of the Administration he was a novice. Meese? No. Baker? No. Weinberger? No. So when he tried to urge that the Caribbean was going to be a thorn in our side unless we dealt directly with the problem of Castro's Cuba, he might as well have been talking to himself.

What a pity that more attention was not paid back in the Carter White House or right in the beginning of our Administration to the emerging problem of Nicaragua. By the time our Administration did focus on the problems of Central America, the Sandinistas had become well entrenched with the help of Soviet money and Cuban advisers.

But Haig's real problem was not so much that he had few allies at the top levels of the Administration who could understand the strategic wisdom of what he was saying, as it was his inability or unwillingness to appear to be a team player. President Reagan always prized that very much. Haig was more accustomed to giving orders, I suppose, than to persuading others to make common cause with him. Eventually, this stand-offish, imperial style of his cost him the job of Secretary of State. I was sorry to see him go. I thought some of his arrogance was understandable. He was an extremely talented person with a résumé as long as your arm. If he didn't think a bunch of novices should be able to overrule his policy prescriptions so easily, who could blame him? Also, I wonder what direction the Administration would have taken if Haig had been able to stay on. When he left, it was a victory for Baker, for Deaver, for Jeane Kirkpatrick (who had a much-publicized feud with him from her post at the UN, especially over the Falklands war), and even a little bit for Clark. But it was a loss for the country.

When Haig left, the President asked Bill Clark whom he would recommend as a successor. Bill didn't hesitate. "Cap," he said. But it was really only a gesture on Bill's part. He knew, as I did, that someone had long before poisoned the well with Reagan on the subject of Weinberger as Secretary of State. There seemed to be unanimity among the staff that George Shultz would be a good choice. It fell to Clark to phone Shultz in London and offer him the position. Shultz accepted on the spot.

TROUBLES AHEAD

*D*URING THIS PERIOD, WHEN I SERVED AS DEPUTY
Assistant to the President, my work life was like a constant
military campaign. I had comrades-in-arms—Tad Tharp, Becky
Norton Dunlop, Dennis Patrick, Ed Meese, Bill Clark, and
others—and we went into battle for the things we believed in.
It was exhilarating at times, but also had the potential to be
quite depressing. I could never get over the lengths some
were prepared to go to protect their government sinecures.
Members of Congress protected some of them; bureaucracies
defended most others.

And yet, we had a lot to be proud of too. With help from
others in the government, the personnel office during my tenure was able to achieve real victories in placing conservatives
in key posts. Despite the difficulty, we were able to get State to
agree to at least one political appointment in every bureau at
the deputy assistant secretary level. Actually, all deputy assistant secretary slots are political appointments. But the career-

ists had so successfully incorporated them into their realm that we were grateful to get even one back. The lesson is, you can make a difference if you bring persistence and determination to the job.

My personal life was a placid retreat. Byron was always interested in the war stories I came home with on weekends, and he would ask pertinent questions and frequently come up with good advice. He understood politics, but more important, he understood people: their little vanities, their hopes, their fears. I frequently took Byron's advice, especially when there was some sort of personality conflict within my own staff.

On a June morning in 1982, I came to work and was greeted by a slightly pale Tad Tharp. He told me Fred Furino had been shot and killed in Manhattan. "I'm sorry, Tad," I said, confused, "but did we know him?" Tad said no, but there was talk of some connection to Ray Donovan. Sure enough, the next issue of *Time* magazine reported that Furino, a thug thought to have been associated with the Mafia, had been grilled by Leon Silverman, the independent counsel who had been assigned to investigate Ray Donovan. According to the *Time* story, Furino had repeatedly flunked a lie detector test when asked if he had had any dealings with Ray.

The press speculation went wild. Was Ray associated with the Mafia? It was just unbelievable. I called Ray to offer whatever help I could. He was grateful, but rather in shock. I don't think any innocent person can withstand that kind of onslaught without losing a sense of equilibrium. One day you're a respected member of the Cabinet. The next day you're a suspected mobster. It's crazy.

The Democrats on Capitol Hill immediately weighed in with demands that Ray take a leave of absence until he was cleared of all suspicion. In the White House, opinions were, as usual, mixed. Ed Meese defended Donovan and bitterly resented the fact that mere accusations could force someone from office (there had been no facts adduced at all). Stu Spencer, the political consultant who had known Ronald Reagan since the California days, called to say that Ray had to go. Mike Deaver and Mrs. R were distraught by the bad press and argued for Ray's dismissal.

But the President has a stubborn streak in him. There are times when he will do what he believes to be right no matter how many people try to dissuade him. He said, "I'm standing by Ray Donovan." I was really proud of him. And many weeks later, the President's confidence was rewarded when the independent counsel, Leon Silverman, released a 708-page report which concluded that there was "insufficient credible evidence" to bring an indictment against Ray.

Later, the charges were revived. Leon Silverman cranked up his shop again, and this time he was able to get an indictment alleging that Ray had improperly profited from the Schiavone Construction Company, of which he had been a part owner. The legal nightmare dragged on for four years. Ray had to spend millions on attorneys' fees. He went to trial amid great fanfare. But when it was over, the jury found him innocent. I will never forget the press conference he held outside the courtroom after the verdict. His voice choked with emotion, he thanked the jury for their fine service. And then he recounted what a shambles had been made of his life. "What office do I go to in order to get my good name back?" he asked. He spoke for every public figure who has ever been falsely accused. I think there must be limits. This open season on people in government is cruel and unjust and keeps talented people from serving their country.

But in July, a far crueler tragedy hit Ed and Ursula Meese. Their nineteen-year-old-son, Scott, a wonderful young Princeton freshman, was killed when his car spun out of control on the George Washington Parkway in Virginia. Scott, a straight arrow like his father, had not been drinking or using drugs of any kind.

Ed was shattered. I've never had children of my own, but I imagine that losing a child is probably the worst thing a person can endure. It robs you not just of a loved person but also of your future. I phoned Ed at home to offer condolences and felt foolish for not being able to think of anything comforting to say. Since that time, I have lived through the death of my mother, and I now understand that there's nothing anyone can say that's particularly comforting. The comfort derives from the fact that they called at all.

We all attended the funeral at the end of the week. Ed and Ursula could not contain their grief. I had never been as close to them personally as I had to Bill and Joan Clark or Mike and Carolyn Deaver, but at that moment I was overcome with tenderness for them. Fate's bitter twists can touch anyone. High government officials are not exempt.

Ed was never quite the same after that. He quickly resumed his old pace of work, and made a show of being as high-spirited as ever. But the light was gone from his eyes. In the years that followed he continued to fight for the right—but perhaps not with the same hope that he'd be leaving the world a better place for his children.

———

In my shop, things really began to fizz when the new Secretary of State was announced. If there's one thing that Ron Mann and I wanted to accomplish, it was to get some right-thinking (by our lights) people into that department. We were not pleased with our accomplishments under the Haig tenure and wanted to do better with our second chance. We wanted people who basically shared the President's belief in peace through strength and who had a healthy skepticism about the Soviet Union. It was tough. The State Department is the most hidebound, stubborn, supercilious agency in Washington. Their people are very bright, and they know every bureaucratic trick in the book to get their way—whoever the President may be.

The new Secretary of State, who was appointed July 16, 1982, would naturally be given the discretion to choose his top assistants but it was my job to be sure that the assistant secretaries and deputy assistant secretaries would be vetted through our office. I sat down and wrote a private memo to the President about it.

> Dear Mr. President:
> The Department of State traditionally considers itself autonomous, aloof from other departments and agencies. The Secretaries of State usually reflect this attitude, particularly when it comes to staffing. This is why it is imperative that ground rules are established with the new Secretary early in order to avoid a repeat of past experiences with State.
> To ensure that we do not fall into the same trap, certain understandings and agreements must be reached before our new Secretary of State takes office.

I went on to list recommendations for the selection of qualified but philosophically conservative people for the department.

I knew it would be a battle royal. The career State Department "professionals," as they like to be called have convinced the Congress and relevant portions of the press that their expertise on foreign policy is such that to hire outsiders —businessmen, educators, politicians—to important posts is to place the foreign policy stance of the United States in severe jeopardy.

I regarded their claims to expertise skeptically. Sure, they knew the languages and histories of the countries we deal with every day, but when it comes to the actual making of policy— do we or do we not send AWACS to Saudi Arabia, do we or do we not try to send aid to the freedom fighters of Nicaragua— they are in no better position than anyone else to make decisions. Those political decisions are placed by the Constitution in the President's hands. And in order for him to make those decisions, he needs people in key posts who are his allies.

The President never formally responded to my memo, but he must have mentioned it to Shultz, because Shultz called me the following Monday to arrange an appointment at his office.

Our first meeting went well. Shultz was an old Washington hand. His people skills were pretty good, and he used some of them on me. He was extremely pleasant and affable and spoke of developing a nice working relationship. I found myself feeling very well disposed toward him. He went through the motions of cooperation with our office, but went his own way on staff decisions. He seemed to want no interference. In the back of my mind, even in the first flush of enthusiasm about someone new, I was suspicious. People I admired and respected who knew Shultz well did not believe that he held the same values as President Reagan. As it turned out, the conservatives were right about Shultz's ideology. But something else about him made me furious.

I have rarely been more disappointed at a member of the Administration than I was several years later when Shultz paraded himself at the Iran/Contra hearings on the Hill as the great hero of the affair. If he had been so opposed to the arms shipment, why didn't he resign when the matter first came up within the Administration? I know he threatened to resign if the highly gifted Jeane Kirkpatrick was appointed National Security Adviser (a move which I believe would have prevented the Iran/Contra affair). And to allow the Congress to praise his wisdom and foresight at the expense of his boss was more than I could believe. But I suppose, at that point, he felt he had become invulnerable.

With the ascendance of George Shultz the Administration began its slow slide toward détente. It wasn't just that Shultz was eager for better relations with the Soviets (though my conservative grapevine assured me that was true). There were others, specifically Mrs. R, Deaver, and Baker, who were similarly inclined. It didn't happen all at once, but slowly the tone of the Reagan White House shifted.

Later, I found out through friends what had happened behind the scenes to grease the skids for a superpower summit. The official stance of the Administration was that there would be no summit meeting between the leaders of the Soviet Union and our country until the Soviets took concrete steps on human rights and arms control. But behind the scenes, Mrs. R and George Shultz were plotting to bring one about. I can't say what their motivations were. But I believe that Shultz was after the acclaim of the press and possibly a Nobel Peace Prize, while Mrs. R was hoping that summitry would prove popular with the public for her husband. They must have talked about it together for months, because in the early or middle part of 1983 they arranged to smuggle the Soviet Ambassador into the White House to see the President without the knowledge of the National Security Adviser. Anatoly Dobrynin was whisked into the East Wing (where Mrs. Reagan's offices were) and from there taken to the residence for the secret meeting. The press never knew about it, and until it was over, neither did most of the senior staff. But it was a critical turning point—the time when the Reagan Administration began to move toward détente.

Bill Clark was livid when the President told him what had happened. But the wheels were set in motion. At that point Bill Clark realized that the combination of Deaver, Mrs. R, and Shultz was undercutting his effectiveness. The following November, President Reagan and the new Secretary General of the Soviet Union, Mikhail Gorbachev, met in Geneva for exactly the kind of nonspecific summit meeting that Clark (and previously the President) had always opposed. They didn't believe that a summit with no agenda was good for the United States. All it did was provide legitimacy to the Soviets.

In Latin America, an area of the world critical to the United States, Shultz paid only lip service to the Reaganite perspective. In practice, he hired, promoted, and took advice from careerists who were suspicious of if not hostile to the Reagan doctrine of aiding freedom fighters battling Communist regimes around the world.

An example was Shultz's announcement, early in his tenure at State, that the new Deputy Assistant Secretary for Inter-

American Affairs—the department within State which dealt with Latin America—would be Miles Frechette, a careerist foreign service officer who had been serving as head of the Cuban desk.

I was aghast. During the Carter Administration, Frechette had been a point man in the attempt to pursue a rapprochement with Castro's Cuba. All of my feedback was that he was reviled among Cuban-Americans, who were an extremely loyal and vocal constituency for Ronald Reagan. He had inflamed them as the State Department officer who took the lead in forcing the return of a Cuban stowaway who tried to gain asylum in the United States. Some in the Administration even considered him sympathetic to Castro.

While he was on the Cuban desk, there was little I could do about Frechette. As a career foreign service officer, he was protected and could not be fired for political reasons. But Shultz was now proposing to place Frechette in one of the few slots which were specifically reserved for presidential appointees. Since Shultz been on the job for only a short time at that point, I was reluctant to provoke conflict between us. But all of our other political appointees at State I talked to assured me that Frechette would send out all the wrong signals. I decided I had to act.

In the days that followed, I made an appointment to speak with the Big Three. I presented Frechette's history, the opposition of the other political appointees, and my own sense that perhaps Shultz was too new on the job to fully appreciate the seriousness of this step. Baker, Deaver, and Meese agreed that Frechette's appointment should be vetoed. Satisfied, but sorry to have to be the bearer of bad tidings, I phoned Shultz to explain the decision. To my dismay, he responded blandly that Frechette was already doing the job on a de facto basis—without clearance. I protested, and asked Shultz to move him to another position. But Shultz replied that he didn't think that would be appropriate. Frechette wound up doing the job of Deputy Assistant Secretary for Inter-American Affairs for another month, until he himself found something that suited him better.

Meanwhile, Frechette's boss, Thomas Enders, was little better. Enders was known as an Eastern Establishment liberal —not a McGovernite, but certainly not one of us—and yet he had been appointed Assistant Secretary for Inter-American affairs under Haig. In January 1983, Enders drafted a memo which suggested that the United States ought to pursue a two-track policy in Central America: holding the line with countries like El Salvador and Guatemala and also negotiating with the Sandinistas. Enders wanted to get a promise from the Sandinistas that they would cease trying to subvert their neighbors. In return, the United States would cut off aid to the Contras. Bill Clark, who saw the memo when it reached the White House, was appalled. The President's policy was to support the Contras until genuine democracy was brought to Nicaragua. Bill sent the memo on to the President as proof of Enders's unsuitability. Not long thereafter, the memo found its way into *The Washington Post.*

I knew then that while Enders deserved credit for being honest enough to put his views on paper, he was out of sync with the President's views and would have to go. Conservatives within the Administration banded together to put pressure on Shultz. Of course, people were never outright fired because they were too liberal for the Reagan Administration. That just wasn't done (though plenty of conservatives were forced out through a variety of means). We in personnel had to find him the government equivalent of a golden parachute: an ambassadorship. I put my staff to work looking for an available slot and within a few short months Tom Enders was Ambassador to Spain.

With the slot open, several heavy hitters within the Administration weighed in with recommendations for a replacement. Bill Casey and Jeane Kirkpatrick wanted a gifted scholar who had also worked in the CIA, Dr. Constantine Menges. But Shultz was adamantly opposed to Menges. He wanted a State Department man. Shultz prevailed. The post went to Anthony Motley, then serving as Ambassador to Brazil. Motley was an Alaskan oil developer and was considered a Reagan supporter. Strong Contra supporters quickly became disillusioned with Motley because he bought the State Department line. But then, he couldn't have gotten away with that without Shultz's approval.

That wasn't the end of Menges either. Bill Clark hired him in the White House as the senior National Security Council officer for Latin America, to make sellouts more difficult for the State Department. But when Menges brought to the President's attention State's attempt to end run his Central American policy after Clark had left, he was first "promoted" out of his post into another area and later informed by Admiral Poindexter that "his tour of duty" at the NSC was completed. It isn't hard to guess who put the pressure on.

———

The State Department continued to be my bête noire for the length of my stay in personnel. I suppose if there was one area where I would say I and the Reagan Administration failed, that was it. Despite all of our efforts the State bureaucracy—the Foreign Service Association—won many more battles than we did. The President had his foreign policy, and the State Department had theirs. Frequently, theirs prevailed. There were several reasons for this. In the first place, the State Department is very smart and infinitely patient. We, as political people, would be in office only four or a maximum of eight years. But they would go on and on. And they used delaying tactics to great advantage. Also, I think there was a reluctance to take them on directly. Haig saw the problem but didn't do much about it. In the first place, it takes too much energy. But more important, it would make mortal enemies of the whole career foreign service, who could make a Secretary of State's job impossible if they chose to. Shultz actively cooperated with the careerists. He probably thought he needed them because his area of expertise was finance, not foreign relations.

Ronald Reagan's management style contributed to the problem as well. He was a strong believer in delegation and was quite reluctant to tell a Secretary how to staff his own department. Still, we Reaganites kept trying with State. We felt that the President had a responsibility to the people who voted for him to appoint those who shared his philosophy to important policy-making posts. And I almost wore my heart out trying.

———

On the other hand, I don't wish to condemn careerists as individuals or across the board. They are, by and large, a very gifted group. I, for instance, had no problem with Larry Eagleburger. He was suspect among conservatives for his Kissinger connection as well as for his tolerance of liberals working for him. But I found him to be a vigorous anti-Communist, who was also a dynamo and a good administrator. Unlike others, Eagleburger did not hesitate to declare his Republican affiliations. That made it easier for him to get appointments in Republican Administrations and should serve as a lesson to other foreign service officers. I think others should declare themselves politically. It's more honest, and I think, in the final analysis, the allocation of plum jobs would even out among Democratic and Republican Administrations.

Allegations that all foreign service officers are wimps aren't true either. The first example which comes to mind is my secretary, Peggy Buckley, when I served as Ambassador to Austria. She was career foreign service, a spunky lady and very leery of political appointees—a sentiment she wore on her sleeve. In time we became a great team, but only after I had proven myself. Or take Mort Abramovitz. Some, rightly or wrongly, considered him a liberal, and for that reason he had difficulty getting a position befitting his seniority and expertise. But I remember how impressed I was when he asked to be relieved of his post as Ambassador to the Mutual and Balanced Force Reduction Talks in Vienna. I urged him to stay, reminding him that he might wind up walking the halls within the department. But Mort took a principled stand. He didn't want an easy, comfortable life if the price was going through a meaningless charade of a job. I was also impressed with Tom

Niles, Deputy Assistant Secretary for Europe, and later Ambassador to Canada. He was an articulate straight shooter. And my colleague Bill Luers served very effectively as Ambassador to Czechoslovakia while I was serving in Austria. In short, the philosophical consistency and/or the perception of it was important. Whether or not a particular person was, in his heart, a liberal didn't really matter if he was known as one. Either way, his appointment by a conservative Administration would raise questions with its loyal constituency.

———

Ambassadorial appointments were always hotly contested between State and the White House. There is an institutional hostility at State toward political ambassadors, and a corresponding distaste for careerists at the White House. This has always been true, in presidencies of both parties. Over the years, a rough equilibrium on numbers was reached. Seventy percent of ambassadors would be State Department careerists, and 30 percent would be political.

Pen James was smart. He knew what a hornet's nest the ambassador fights were and so he happily gave that account to me from the very start. Wendy Borcherdt had handled ambassadorial appointments before me and I was lucky to build upon her strong start.

I got a sense of how difficult the appointment of ambassadors was when we were attempting to fill the post of Ambassador to Belize, a small Latin American country. As with judgeships, senators had clout on ambassadorships. For the Belize post, there were two candidates, both Texans who came recommended by Senator John Tower, chairman of the Armed Services Committee. One of the candidates, William Perrin, seemed to be Tower's preference, though, because he made several follow-up calls on his behalf.

But we preferred Shirley Abbott (a man, despite the feminine name), an El Paso optometrist and faithful Reagan supporter (which is why I favored him). I got a shock when we sent Abbott's name up to the Hill.

Senator Tower called me and asked me to meet him in his office. "Your nomination isn't going anywhere," he said.

"But you wrote a letter supporting Abbott," I protested.

"Yes," said Tower, "but he's not my candidate."

I asked him why he had written a letter of endorsement if he was now unacceptable and Tower explained that that's what he'd do for a constituent. He added that he was backing Abbott for a different post.

I didn't understand how powerful Tower was. "I'm going ahead," I said.

Tower just smiled. "You haven't heard of senatorial courtesy, have you?"

I pushed ahead with the nomination, as the President had already phoned Abbott to offer him the job and we had agrément from Belize. Agrément is the diplomatic process of a foreign country accepting an ambassador.

Later, to my chagrin, I discovered that any senator can veto the appointment of a constituent to any post without giving a reason and without sitting on the confirming committee and the other senators will go along. It's called senatorial courtesy. They don't call the Senate a club for nothing.

———

I was proud of myself that after six months or so on the job, the percentage of political ambassadors reached its peak of about 38 percent. But my pride was soon replaced by something else. The Foreign Service Association knows more than one way to skin a cat.

In April 1982, I received word that Mac Mathias, then a powerful senator from Maryland and a key member of the Senate Foreign Relations Committee, was considering legislation which would limit noncareer ambassadors to 15 percent of the total. The bill never really went anywhere, but I was getting a strong message from the State Department.

They could shoot arrows at me, but so long as they didn't score a direct hit, I persisted in looking for conservatives as ambassadors. The next post which became available was a plum: Switzerland. Our first ambassador there had been the very bright, outspoken Reaganite Faith Ryan Whittlesey. But at my suggestion and urging, she had been called back to Washington to take over the Office of Public Liaison in the White House when Elizabeth Dole moved over to become Secretary of Transportation. I was behind John Lodge. He was a former Governor of Connecticut and had served as Ambassador to Argentina and Spain. Moreover, he was an early and staunch supporter of President Reagan. I knew there would be a fight.

Sure enough, State shot down Lodge for an ambassadorship on the grounds that at eighty he was too old to handle the responsibility. I knew John. He was old, yes, but people age at different rates mentally. John was still very sharp and he seemed to have more energy than men half his age. Though I too would have liked him to be ten years younger, I pushed hard for Lodge, and even enlisted the President's help. State at last decided that Switzerland wasn't worth fighting the President for, and John Lodge went to Bern.

It was a sweet victory. John was exactly the sort of political appointee I was so eager to see placed in important slots. He had wide foreign policy knowledge and experience, but he was also a conservative. Much later, when I reached Austria as ambassador, I heard that John Lodge had been axed and that Faith Whittlesey had been sent back to Bern.

It took months before I found out what actually happened. Faith Whittlesey had made a big splash as Director of Public Liaison in the White House. She was a warrior for Reagan's policies across the board and tried to use every ounce of her power (which wasn't that significant) to advance the Reagan agenda. She was particularly forthright on the subject of Nicaragua, and expanded the role of the Office of Public Liaison to include a weekly program, to which the press and public were invited, outlining the situation in Central America and presenting the Administration position. In the process, she alienated all of the pragmatists in the White House, who were less than enthusiastic about the President's steadfast insistence on supporting the Contras. Meese defended her vehemently, but Baker and Deaver were resolved to get rid of her. There were nasty leaks about her in the press and she became almost a Joan of Arc figure to the conservatives in town who were tired of seeing all the Reaganites drummed out of the Administration.

But Faith couldn't withstand forever the furor she'd created. She lasted in the job a little over two years, and then they told her, "Faith, pick a country." Seeing she had no alternative, Faith said she'd go back to her beloved Switzerland and finish out the Reagan years as ambassador. Poor John Lodge was pushed out the door to make way. He returned to Connecticut a bitter and dejected man.

Faith remained persona non grata with the White House staff. A year or so later, when the President and Gorbachev met in Geneva, Deaver made sure that Faith was practically invisible. The humiliations of public life can really sting. She was the U.S. Ambassador, but she was never invited to the meet-and-greet sessions, and she was placed in the last car of the motorcade, the one which also included lower-level staff. I hate to blame Mike for everything, but he was in charge, even if Mrs. R—who had long before joined Faith's detractors—desired such actions. That was the treatment accorded to someone whose only offense was fighting vigorously for one of President Reagan's initiatives.

THE CHALLENGE: TOUGH DAYS

*I*N AUGUST, I TOOK SOME TIME OFF. IT WAS MY FIRST vacation in a year and I wanted to do something completely noncerebral and nonpolitical. At one of the embassy parties I'd attended earlier in the year, the Peruvian Ambassador had really fired my imagination with stories of how romantic it was to go trekking in Peru. Byron couldn't come along at the time because he was tied up with work, so I put together a group of my women friends—Monica Clark (Bill Clark's daughter), Bonnie Newman, Heide Kingsbury (my friend from California), and the wife of a foreign service officer from Peru—and the five of us set off for Lima. It was quite an experience. Mostly I recall getting Montezuma's revenge and thinking I was going to die. But the Andes were beautiful and my mind was cleansed by the clear air.

I knew that when I returned I would be getting a promotion to the job of Assistant to the President for Presidential

Personnel. Assistant to the President is the highest rank White House staffers can rise to.

My boss, Pen James, had announced in the early spring of 1982 that he would definitely be leaving in the summer to return to private business. Though the President had cautioned me, back when I first told him I wanted to move to personnel, that he couldn't guarantee that I'd be promoted, there didn't seem to be any real question in anyone's mind that I would be the next head of the shop. I think I had been a success as deputy in large part because of my willingness to surround myself with people who were better than I. I suppose I never felt threatened because I was politically secure. Because of my relationship with the President, no one could touch me. The Big Three had no objections to my appointment, and the President was delighted to promote me.

I was excited, but with a slight feeling of anxiety in the pit of my stomach. I was still self-conscious about my lack of formal education. Even people three levels below me had college degrees. Many had doctorates or were lawyers. Though I felt that I deserved the promotion, that I had earned it by doing a good job as deputy, I still worried that someone would think I was unqualified. It's ironic, since I was now in charge of finding the best-qualified politically compatible people to work for the President, that I still worried about my own qualifications. Byron teased me for refusing to fill out the form sent by Who's Who in America. "Send it in," he urged. I resisted. I didn't want the humiliation of not being a college grad to be in black and white for all to see.

But no one in the press seemed to notice my new job. And my nightmare that someone would write a story about me going over my background did not materialize. After a few days, I moved into my new office on the second floor of the West Wing. The Oval Office, Baker, Deaver, and Meese were on the first floor, and Clark was in the basement. My new office was next to Ken Duberstein, who was now Congressional Liaison. Down the hall were Elizabeth Dole, Fred Fielding, and Ed Harper.

My daily routine didn't change very much from the time when I had served as deputy under Pen. I still woke at 6:40 A.M. and arrived at the office one hour later. I read the papers for twenty minutes and then went to the morning staff meeting chaired by Jim Baker. I had attended those meetings before, when I was the President's secretary, or sitting in for Pen. Now I was a full member of the senior White House staff. Even so, I still kept my seat off to the side of the room instead of taking my place at the big conference table. Old habits die hard. There were only two women holding the rank of Assistant to the President: myself and Elizabeth Dole.

After the 8 A.M. staff meeting, all of us would disperse and I would walk across West Executive Avenue to the OEOB, where I held morning meetings with my own staff. I'm sure all Assistants to the President did pretty much the same thing: summarizing what had transpired at senior staff and then moving to office business. I enjoyed my staff immensely. We understood each other so well that we could speak in a kind of shorthand. And the day usually began with lots of humor and teasing.

I kept the same organizational structure I had used while I was deputy. I was intent on remaining a hands-on manager. By then I knew I could rely totally on my professional staff and wanted them to report to me directly. And I always relied completely on my wonderful secretary, Lindy St. Cyr, who joined me back when I was President Reagan's secretary. She not only managed to keep on top of everything but was a step ahead of me at all times.

Every Wednesday at 4 P.M. I met with Baker, Meese, and Deaver. I'd discuss and clear with them all presidential appointments before presenting them to President Reagan. I brought with me to these meetings Tad Tharp, whose discretion and judgment I trusted completely. Tad took notes—that is, until one day Baker noticed him scribbling during a particularly heated exchange between himself and Ed Meese and demanded that no more notes be taken. We'd sit around the table in Baker's office with a list of the positions open and the qualifications of the top contenders. I'd prepare a rundown of all the ramifications: whether there was a congressman or senator pushing for a particular candidate, whether someone had poor political credentials, whether a department head was resisting a candidate, whether we'd get criticized in the press, etc. The Big Three usually approved of my suggestions without too much fuss. If there was disagreement, it was usually hammered out around the table and a compromise arrived at.

The atmosphere of these meetings was usually relaxed—that was the way both Ed Meese and Jim Baker conducted themselves. These meetings were the most concentrated exposure I had to the working habits of the Big Three. I found Jim Baker to be a low-key Chief of Staff. Perhaps out of awareness of his own outsider status he rarely opposed a Reaganite candidate. Only in cases where he believed Ed Meese or I was suggesting someone who would be an embarrassment to the Administration would he object.

Of course, in politics as in other areas of life, personnel always has the capacity to become personal. Naturally, each of the Big Three came to meetings with their own favorite people in mind. I never objected to this; it's human nature—I had my favorites too. I also observed that Jim Baker showed more political skills in handling personnel matters than did Ed Meese. For instance, Baker always requested in advance that I send him the agenda for the coming meetings so that he could be prepared—which, I suppose, included lining up Mike Deaver's support in areas of special interest. Ed Meese never asked. But I made sure that Ken Cribb, one of Meese's brightest deputies, got the same agenda that I sent to Baker. I wanted it to be a level playing field when ticklish political issues came up. Meese was vigilant about placing Reagan conservatives in certain posts like the Board of the Legal Services Corporation, which bore directly on the President's agenda.

Mike Deaver tended to side with Jim Baker on personnel matters, and when he didn't, Jim Baker's considerable persuasive talents could frequently be brought to bear, as was the case with Stockman.

I'd usually know in advance if a position was going to cause friction between Baker and Meese. Frequently, I'd speak to each of them privately first to avoid a confrontation in which neither would feel comfortable backing down. If there was a sensitive area, it was always about issues, not, as Deaver was convinced, about power. Meese stuck to conservative principles above all else and Baker didn't. It was that simple. Though usually, if tension filled the air, one of the three men would break it with a joke. I recall one episode when Baker sat back, smiled, and said, "Okay. I'll get rid of —— if you get rid of ——."

Only once do I recall a meeting becoming acrimonious. It was just before Ed Meese's son was killed. There was an endless drumbeat in the press about the supposed rivalry between Baker and Meese. In truth, I think there was more rivalry between their staffs than between the two men.

One exception to this rule was the working relationship between Dick Darman, who was Baker's deputy, and Craig Fuller, Cabinet Secretary who reported to Meese. It was amazing. These two men were the nuts and bolts of the Meese and Baker operations and the White House and worked in total harmony. They were probably too busy for anything else.

On this particular morning, the acrimony spilled out into the open. We were discussing the usual things, Reaganites versus pragmatists. But suddenly the tension between Meese and Baker became so palpable that Tad and I were extremely embarrassed. The meeting had to be adjourned early. But that was a rarity. Cooperation, however grudging, was far more common.

The Big Three seemed to work well initially. They met for breakfast at seven-thirty to talk over issues, and worked closely together. But in this unworkable system, frictions had to develop and periodically tempers would fray. Baker and Meese got into a shouting match one day over the annual United Way fund-raising drive and someone leaked the story to *The Washington Post*.

Deaver was the first one to stop coming to the breakfast

meetings. Before too long, rumors circulated that a shake-up was coming. Baker would go back to his law practice and would be replaced by Bill Clark. Deaver was setting up a consulting firm. One particularly complicated story had it that Weinberger was going to resign as Secretary of Defense and would be replaced by Texas senator John Tower and the Texas Republican Governor would name Baker to Tower's Senate seat.

That the Troika worked as well as it did was the result of a certain balance of power and competition. Ed Meese made sure the policies and issues reflected Ronald Reagan's philosophy. Mike Deaver protected the body and image. Jim Baker made sure the apparatus worked and moved. It's also a tribute to the three individuals involved. Somehow, they made it work. It cost all of them a great deal of energy, I am sure, but Ronald Reagan was pretty much the winner.

———

After I had received the approval of the Big Three and consulted with the Cabinet Secretary for the relevant department (Defense, Commerce, Agriculture, and so on), I would present our personnel recommendations to the President at a weekly meeting on Thursday afternoons.

At first, it was a little strange to enter the Oval Office as his formal adviser, and no longer as a secretary. My self-image had changed dramatically in the year since I had been outside the Oval Office. As I stopped to chat with Kathy Osborne, I felt so proud and happy that I'd had the courage to make the move. So often, the only obstacles to our own advancement are inside ourselves.

But at the time, I didn't dwell on the milestone I had passed. My way is just to forge ahead with the next project instead of sitting back and savoring where I've come from.

Besides, there was too much business to accomplish at these weekly meetings. I presented the President with a rundown of all the leading candidates for each position, a short explanation of the job's relevance (where required), and the reasons for our recommendations. In most cases, the President approved our choices. But not always. He sometimes over-ruled us if he had a personal relationship with someone who was a job applicant, or if he had spoken with someone from the outside (a member of the kitchen cabinet, or a friend) who recommended a particular candidate other than our choice.

I was able to use my time alone with the President for other things as well, as when I raised the matter of Lyn Nofziger. I also urged upon him the idea that he should make it a practice to address a gathering of the political appointees within the Administration—a kind of pep talk. He agreed and made it a regular event. I was also able to get permission from him to address the Cabinet on personnel matters, with him present. It was important to sensitize them to political realities and enlist their cooperation. But my paramount purpose was to prove—for all to see—that my efforts to put Reaganites, including women and minorities, in important jobs had the President's full backing. He readily agreed, suggesting that they ought to hear from Dick Wirthlin, his pollster, first. A few weeks later, on January 17, 1982, I found myself address-ing the full Cabinet in formal session:

> As those of you who have vacancies in your depart-ments will probably have noticed, we are no longer satisfied routinely to fill those openings with whatever candidates the traditional network pro-duces. To be sensitive to the political realities Dick Wirthlin just described to us does not interfere, nor is it inconsistent, with good government, as long as we don't sacrifice ability and philosophy.
>
> To varying degrees you have all been recep-tive to Presidential Personnel's suggestions and recommendations. But we must do more. Together we really need to take every single opportunity starting now to translate our political beliefs into appropriate action. The appointments process is a very crucial and visible building block toward end-ing whatever gender, minority, or ethnic bias still

exists. Those voting blocs or groups are waiting to be invited to participate in our Administration. They want to be shown that we care, that we don't take them for granted, and that we want their help. There are lots of Republican white males and that's fine. But we also want more Republicans of other stripes.

When I joined Presidential Personnel, I studied the appointments process during the last several Administrations and very quickly came to the conclusion that who gets appointed determines the stamp of a President. The process has ranged from a total heavy-handed approach by the White House to one of total abdication of responsibility.

In many of your departments, there are legislative, public affairs, and confidential positions open. For each of those, there are Reaganites or political activists who are always contacting my office looking for leads. As the positions still held by Carter holdovers become free, it would be easy to simply promote the deputy, or appoint a friend or acquaintance. Understandably it is easier for all of us to surround ourselves with people we know. But that does not help the President.

There is no such thing as a nonpolitical agency in Washington. We all share a responsibility to build the Republican Party, to be responsive to our people, to strategize as to where we want to be down the road. Right now, we have dozens of good Republicans who have worked the political trenches and would be delighted to join the Administration. It would help them and us. But much depends on you. If we don't seize control of the appointments process now, we will never get a tight grip on government.

The weeks flew past. Before I knew it we were facing midterm elections in 1982. The President campaigned actively for Republican candidates all across the country and there was eager speculation about how strong his influence would turn out to be with the voters. Presidents who come in strong in their own elections frequently lose seats in the Congress at midterm, but we were all hoping that we could avoid that fate.

A few days before the election, I began to get very nervous. I was concerned that our eight-vote majority in the Senate was in jeopardy, and I was worried about what would happen in the second two years of the Administration if we suffered a severe setback at the polls. The Democrats had made hay out of the Social Security issue, accusing the President of wanting to cut benefits to the elderly. The President denied that was his intention, but it wasn't clear how well his denial had been absorbed by the elderly voters.

Byron and I decided to watch the returns at home. We'd been to so many official functions at election time, we decided that this year it would be more fun to make some popcorn, sit in front of the television with a notepad, and cuddle up in our bathrobes. The first two hours or so were very dull. We heard mostly local returns. But then the big ones started coming in.

We did manage to hold on to our eight-vote majority in the Senate, which was key, but we had some scares also. Bob Michel, the House minority leader, almost lost his seat in a very close race. Margaret Heckler, an eight-term Republican from Massachusetts, was defeated by an ultraliberal. I was sorry to see that Millicent Fenwick, the congresswoman from New Jersey whom I had met during the campaign and who impressed me so much with her intelligence, grace, and good spirits, lost her bid for a Senate seat to a businessman named Frank Lautenberg. But we all got a huge lift from the fact that Pete Wilson narrowly defeated former Governor Jerry Brown for the Senate seat from California. Byron proposed a toast and we drank to the new senator from California.

We were disappointed, though, that Bill Clements, a

voluble supporter from Texas, lost the governorship to liberal Mark White. It was one of seven governorships we lost.

At around midnight, we switched off the TV and chatted for a while. We speculated as to whether this was a bad omen for the 1984 election but decided that it was much too soon to tell.

For the next several days, everyone in the White House was talking about the election returns. An important part of politics is taking care of the people who help you. There's nothing sinister about it. It's the nature of the business. Unlike the world of private enterprise, where you can reward people who help you with contracts or money, the usual way to repay a political debt is with a return favor or a job. Margaret Heckler, though a liberal Republican, had been very supportive of the White House during the first two years of the Administration, and the President wanted to show his gratitude.

After the President let it be known that he wanted to help out the victims of November 4, particularly Margaret Heckler, I huddled with Baker, Deaver, and Meese to come up with something. The Department of Health and Human Services seemed like a good choice because we wanted a woman in the Cabinet and because Heckler had the political skills to sell our policies to the public and on the Hill. At the same time, we weren't sure whether or not she had the administrative skills to handle such a large agency and thought it would make sense to appoint a good deputy as well who could help her with that.

Ed Meese and I met with Heckler several times and sold her on taking Jack Svahn (a Meese man) as her deputy. She barely knew him but agreed.

But it was an arranged marriage and it soon ran into difficulties. Jack apparently offended Heckler by presuming too much in terms of authority. People in the Secretary's office claimed that Jack was calling staff meetings without even informing Heckler, conveying the impression that he was really the one running the agency. I was in no position to make a judgment about who was right, but it was clear that the problem was serious. I tried various forms of intervention: new staff people at lower-level positions, talks between Heckler and Lyn Nofziger on strategy, and talks with Svahn. But Heckler's reputation as a poor administrator, unwilling to work with Svahn or the White House, stuck and began to damage her within the White House.

I felt badly for her. She had always been a staunch defender of President Reagan, especially on his record on women's issues, where he had too few articulate women supporters. While she was at HHS, she was also having serious personal problems—an ugly divorce which had leapt into the newspapers. She remained at her post after my departure for Austria, but I don't forget people who've been loyal to Ronald Reagan and I kept tabs on what happened to her.

In the second term, when Don Regan became Chief of Staff, the White House drumbeat to dump Heckler really stepped up. Feeling embattled, she asked for a private meeting with the President. This was granted, but it was given out to the press that the purpose of the meeting was that the President was calling her on the carpet. That's dirty pool. Finally, when the top White House aides, particularly Don Regan, had convinced the President that she had to be reassigned, she was called again to the Oval Office. She had no idea what the meeting was about. But the next thing she knew she was being hustled to the White House briefing room and her new appointment as Ambassador to Ireland was announced. She could barely choke back the tears in front of the assembled cameras and reporters. It was a humiliating moment and one of the low points of the Reagan Administration. Still, if living well is the best revenge, Margaret Heckler got it. The Irish were a bit wary of the new ambassador they knew had been "dumped" on them because she was no longer wanted in Washington. It's absurd to think they would be unaware of the circumstances of her appointment. And yet she moved to Ireland and became a great hit as ambassador. I think she even had some much-deserved fun.

Byron and I had purchased an eighteenth-century flag-stone farmhouse in New Jersey just around the time of the presidential election. Restoring it became my release from the pressures of Washington. It was a wonderful project for both of us. We spent many weekends searching around New Jersey for the right antiques to decorate with. We were proud of our achievement and enjoyed being around the "real" people who were our neighbors.

When I wasn't decorating and repairing the house with Byron, I found other outlets for my excess energy. When Bill Clark bragged that he had flown in an F-15 fighter aircraft, I just knew that I had to do it too. I spoke to people in the Pentagon and they were very cooperative (military officers always addressed me as "ma'am"). But I had to go through flight training first. The training involved being carried aloft in a huge compression chamber aboard an airplane to about 35,000 feet. I sailed through that part just fine. But when the time for my great flight in the F-15 came along, the whole thing was wasted. I buckled myself into the back seat, gave the thumbs-up to the young pilot, and promptly passed out when we reached three G's.

18

THE REWARD: UNITED STATES AMBASSADOR TO AUSTRIA

O F ALL THE REAGANITES I KNEW FROM THE CALI-
fornia days, the one I admired the most (with the exception of
Ronald Reagan) was Cap Weinberger. He is so bright, such a
gentlemen, so honest, and so patriotic. I could never understand why he got such bad press. I just loved him. But that is
not to say that we didn't have our little run-ins over personnel
matters. When it came to staff, I seemed to take everyone on at
one time or another. Bill Clark chided me for this. He said,
"Helene, Baker, Deaver, and Shultz give Cap a hard enough
time. You're his friend. Why don't you lay off?" Bill was referring to the fact that Cap was frequently embroiled in policy
arguments with the others. "Cap is my friend," I replied, "and
I am his. But we must each do our jobs as we think best and
this is an important aspect of mine."

In the spring of 1982, Cap and I disagreed about who
should be appointed to the very important job of Pentagon
comptroller. The comptroller supervises a staff of 3,700 audi-

tors, accountants, and other number crunchers. And in light of the fact that the Democratic Congress is more inclined to scrutinize the Pentagon's spending habits than, say, the Department of Health and Human Services, you need someone as comptroller who can testify effectively on the Hill.

Cap wanted Vincent Puritano, who was then serving as executive assistant to Cap's deputy, Frank Carlucci. I was dumbfounded. Puritano may have been a fine executive assistant, but I saw no evidence that he understood the requirements for the comptroller's job, and I told Cap that. He had never prepared a budget, and hadn't had experience in the fiscal realm. Cap replied in the mild, gentlemanly way he always used (I've never heard Cap Weinberger raise his voice) that he still favored Puritano, and was confident he could do the job.

I huddled with my staff. "Listen," I told them. "We've got to come up with some people who will be so outstanding that Cap will just have to see the light." Dick Kinser, our "professional" recruiter who came from the executive search business, quickly compiled a list of three names, all culled from private industry. He suggested Philip Cowen, the senior vice president for finance at Pneumo Corporation and a former vice president for finance at General Dynamics; Frank Alfieri, the executive vice president for finance at Clark Equipment Company and formerly of ITT; and Donald H. White, the senior vice president and chief accounting officer of Hughes Aerospace. I was delighted with Dick's work. As I was riding over to the Pentagon to meet again with Cap, I felt like a card player who is carrying a trump.

But Cap was unmoved by what I thought were simply overwhelmingly qualified candidates. He was sticking with Puritano. He knew the guy and I suppose Cap was relying on his own intuition. But I was really frustrated. And I told Cap so. He was firm. "Well," I said, after we'd argued about it for ten minutes or so, "I guess we'll both have to go see the President." He agreed.

When we got to the Oval Office several days later, I had

my arguments all prepared. "The Defense Department is under attack from all sides, Mr. President. Liberal senators are trying to cut the defense budget. The Soviets are looking for any sign of vulnerability. We need to have the very best team possible."

As Cap presented his counter arguments, I let my eyes wander around the office. I noticed that some of the family pictures on the credenza behind the President's desk had been rearranged. I wondered if that was on purpose or whether they had gotten out of order during one of the periodic security sweeps for bugs. I admired the bronze Remington figurines decorating the tables around the office. They were so American, so appropriate. Exactly what I would have expected to find in the office of the President of the United States back when I was a young Austrian girl watching John Wayne movies in Vienna. I was called back to the present by the President's voice.

He sided with Cap. Puritano got the job. I pretty much knew that that's what would happen. The President always sided with Cabinet officials on personnel matters. I suppose he figured it was preferable to have me a little upset than to have them a lot upset—as they would be if I was successful in pushing on them a candidate they didn't want. But I had to occasionally force a confrontation in the Oval Office because it gave me clout in later encounters. Even though the President almost always took their side, Cabinet officers didn't like being dragged before the boss that way and would work harder the next time to avoid it.

The next time with Cap came more quickly than I expected. In the middle of the Puritano fight, Frank Carlucci announced that he was leaving to join a private firm. It was as if the bell had been rung in a boxing match and Cap and I resumed our places in the ring (though it was a good-natured fight). Cap wanted to replace Frank with William Howard Taft III. But I urged him to consider Paul Thayer, chairman of and CEO of LTV Corporation, a large aerospace contractor. For a change, I wasn't backing Thayer because he was a Reaganite.

In fact, he hadn't been very politically active. But everyone I spoke to insisted upon his sterling credentials and I became convinced that we couldn't do without him. Cap resisted.

Back we went to the Oval Office. But this time, before the President could support his Cabinet officer, Cap backed down and agreed to hire Thayer.

I wish I'd lost that one. Two years later Thayer was indicted for insider trading before he joined the Administration and went to jail. How could it happen? He had passed a complete security investigation and the FBI had given him a clean bill of health. This is an illustration that the FBI doesn't always uncover everything which would make a candidate unsuitable for public office. I don't blame the FBI for slipping up once in a while among the thousands of investigations they perform every year, but I found it unfair that the media blamed the Reagan White House. Cap was kind enough never to raise the subject with me, though he certainly would have been entitled to a few good I-told-you-so's. Maybe he could resist because his old trusted aide Taft got the job after all.

Our disagreements over personnel never affected our warm feelings for each other. I would do anything (except agree to a bad job applicant) for Cap and he for me. And that is true down to this very day.

Whenever I give lectures about my experiences in government, someone in the audience always asks me about whether I encountered sexism. The answer doesn't come easily.

I think my immigrant status affected my sensitivity to things like sexism. I was just so grateful to be in the United States that I wasn't inclined to find fault with the way things were. I also didn't expect anything at all. I never had a sense that I was entitled to anything. More the opposite. I felt that everything I got was the result of good fortune. I was grateful and just not in the habit of asking myself questions like "Is he treating me with respect or just as a secretary?"

When we were all in California, I used to like it when Bill

Clark, Ed Meese, and Lyn Nofziger teased me about my accent, my misuse of idioms, or my flighty female habits. They teased one another about equivalent things and it was always out in the open, never behind one another's backs. It made me feel like one of the gang.

In Washington things were different. Perhaps it was just that I had changed, grown up, come into my own. I'm not sure. But I did begin to notice and resent some of the sexist attitudes of my colleagues. It was one thing for my friends to tease me. But I was shocked when I heard "the boys" (as the male aides in the West Wing were frequently called) making light of Elizabeth Dole. Elizabeth was a Cabinet Secretary, a former commissioner of the Federal Trade Commission, and a graduate of Harvard Law School. Yet they could get downright patronizing, deriding her organized and detailed presentations at Cabinet meetings as "schoolmarmish."

They were even more brutal about Jeane Kirkpatrick behind her back. I remember how shocked I was, after Jeane had taken a particularly tough stand at a meeting, to hear the boys wondering if "it was the wrong time of the month."

If there was one thing I learned while I served in the White House, it is that women are definitely not more petty than men. I had heard about the pettiness of women for so long and so often that it didn't occur to me to challenge it, but no more. I have witnessed too many male fights for perks and turf. The staff level had nothing to do with it. I will never forget the scramble and panic when Baker and Deaver, who were not part of the Cabinet, asked for chairs around the table rather than along the wall where all the nonmembers sat. "What's all the fuss about?" I remember asking John Rogers, the White House administrator, who had been summoned. "If you are short two chairs take them from my office." He shook his head. "You don't understand," he replied as he rushed out the door, "I need two of the same kind as the chairs around the table." And sure enough, he found them—in a warehouse. They arrived in time for the meeting by special truck and a crisis of possibly major proportions was circumvented, or at least those involved felt so.

The President was not a sexist. Neither was he particularly a feminist. His attitude was always that he'd be happy with whoever could do the job. It was his idea to hire Jeane Kirkpatrick after he read an article of hers in *Commentary* magazine. And he certainly welcomed the opportunity to appoint the first woman to the Supreme Court. But as in other areas, he was somewhat laissez-faire about women's status within his Administration.

But there were quite a few women in the Reagan Administration who did make a special effort to recruit women. I know that Faith Whittlesey was always on the lookout for qualified women candidates (she also had a soft spot for women lawyers since she was one herself), as was Elizabeth Dole, who picked as a protégée the very young but very gifted presidential speechwriter Mari Maseng. I too tried to pull my oar.

With the President's vigorous approval, I set up a task force to seek out qualified women as soon as I joined the personnel office. There were obstacles. One of the biggest was that women who are politically active and interested tend to be disproportionately on the left end of the spectrum. Even within the Republican Party, most of the women were moderates or liberals. That left us with a very constricted pool from which to recruit. Senator Nancy Kassebaum, Republican from Kansas, refused to see our point about this. She told *The Washington Post,* "I really get very tired of hearing, as I did one day from a Cabinet Secretary, that we just haven't had any names sent over to us. I resent it when I hear there aren't women with the qualifications."

Well, if you include philosophy as one the qualifications, as I always did, then it was hard to find names. All the same, in the first two years of the Reagan Administration, more women were appointed to top policy-making posts than in any previous presidency. There were 96 women in top-echelon jobs and a total of more than 700 in other important positions.

Try as I might, I was never able to persuade women's

groups that we had done a good job on this count. I think they must have been blind, or simply so hostile to Ronald Reagan's other policies that they wouldn't admit that his Administration had done well for women. Still, I was gratified to note that when it was rumored that I would be leaving my post at personnel, *Newsweek* published an item in their "Periscope" section saying that I would be missed by conservatives who viewed me as an important ally and by women who viewed me "as their consistent advocate."

Back in 1980, just after our victory, Holmes Tuttle took me aside. He was a member of the kitchen cabinet and someone I had always been very close to. "The President ought to appoint you Ambassador to Austria," he said. I laughed. We were all feeling giddy and I was sure Holmes's idea was more champagne than substance. Later, in solitude, I let my fantasies play with the idea a bit. What a fairy-tale story it would be. Poor girl leaves Austria at eighteen and returns as Ambassador to Austria! But then another voice said, "Sober up. You can't become an ambassador just because you've been a finance director for the campaign. Besides, you've got to be wealthy." And then I remembered how stratified Austrian society is. They'd never accept someone as ambassador who had so little formal education and who came from such a humble family, I thought. The fantasy came to an abrupt end.

The President appointed Ted Cummings, a member of the kitchen cabinet, who had also been born in Austria, as ambassador. I thought Ted was a wonderful choice. He was elegant, thoughtful, well-off, and about the President's age. He was quickly accepted in Austria.

Sadly, while in Vienna, Ted discovered that the cancer he had been living with for years had become active again. He suddenly began to deteriorate. I saw him at the Annenbergs' New Year's party in January 1982 and was shocked at how frail he looked. A short time later, he died.

The following spring, while traveling with the President in Santa Barbara, I had lunch with Holmes Tuttle. We were seated in his magnificent garden terrace which looked out over the Pacific. We chatted about politics for a while and then Holmes raised the issue of Austria again. "You may not believe me, Helene," he said, "but Ted Cummings wanted you to be his successor in case anything happened." "He said that?" I asked. "Absolutely," Holmes assured me. My heart began to race, but I reminded myself of all the obstacles, and tried to banish the thrilling prospect from my imagination.

I told Holmes how flattered I was but explained why I thought it would be impossible. "Nonsense," he replied, dismissing my concerns with a wave of his hand. "I'll talk to the President."

And he must have. Because when we got back from the trip to California, the President buzzed me on the intercom and asked me to come into the office and shut the door. I was still Pen's deputy in those days.

"Lots of people think you'd make a good choice for Ambassador to Austria and I've got to admit, I'm one of them," he said. I was embarrassed. When you think you're unworthy of something, it's hard to believe that others might really take you seriously. So I changed the subject, or made a joke. Anyway, I didn't really answer.

But a couple of weeks later, the President raised the issue again. This time, having had time to absorb the fact that he might really be serious, I said, "Mr. President, I've grown up with you without any ulterior motives and I'm not going to start now. But if you offer me this job one more time, don't count on me to turn it down."

After we talked, I filled out the paperwork required for someone being considered for an ambassadorial post and sent it over to the National Security Council. Since I perceived a possible conflict of interest, I wanted someone else to handle the final recommendation. For some reason nothing was done about it. The matter languished after that at the bottom of everyone's files and the United States went without an Ambassador to Austria for an entire year. The Austrians, I wasn't surprised to find out later, were wondering what they had done to offend us.

Months passed. While the NSC dragged its feet, I rethought the whole idea. By then I understood that you don't have to be wealthy to be an ambassador. But I was worried about other things. My memories of my homeland weren't exactly warm. They were memories of hardship, poverty, pain, and loneliness. Nor did I necessarily believe that my old countrymen would welcome me with open arms. Unlike Americans, Austrians have no special regard for people who are self-made. Birth counts for a lot more. Or so I remembered from my girlhood.

Besides, I was very happy in my job at personnel. I had, in the meantime, risen to become one of the highest ranking women in the Reagan Administration. I was proud of that and also of the work I'd done. I worried that if I left the personnel office to take a glamorous position like ambassador, I might be sacrificing real influence for the trappings of influence.

Yet while I was indulging these doubts, in early 1983, almost a year after the President spoke to me about the ambassadorship, he called me once again and offered me the job. Julius Caesar only refused the crown three times. Who was I to go for four? Rumors were rampant that I had already been appointed and I began to get some personal pressure. My mother heard about it in Austria and phoned me, sounding more excited than I'd ever heard her in my life. I thought about my mother's loneliness. She was eighty-two. She had lived alone for twenty-five years without a word of complaint. Neither my brother nor I had blessed her with grandchildren. Though I kept in touch through the telephone and letters, I didn't really know how she spent her days. This would be an opportunity for me to spend some time with the woman who had given me life, who had cared for me and loved me until I was eighteen, and whom I scarcely knew. She needed me now, and I wanted to be there.

Life sometimes works out so conveniently. Just as I was mulling over the idea of moving to Austria with Byron, he received a dynamite offer from someone to buy out his company. He had always wanted to retire early and now he would be able to put his feet up at fifty—except he'd be putting them up on a Viennese cushion.

The response to my news in the personnel department was exactly what I had hoped for. Everyone had mixed feelings. They were happy for me, but sad to be losing me. The phone was ringing constantly with good wishes from friends, acquaintances, and colleagues, since the news had already leaked to the press. My spirits were soaring. That is, until I received a call from Mrs. Reagan. She asked me to come and see her in the residence for a "private talk." This was one of the few times Mrs. Reagan had asked me to come up to the residence. She saved these personal meetings for things she considered extremely important. Everything else was handled over the telephone.

I walked through the West Wing, past all the photographs of the Reagans at ceremonial occasions and relaxing at the ranch, past the press office with its banks of television monitors, through the Rose Garden, and into the ground floor of the residence. A tiny, wood-paneled elevator, installed for Franklin Roosevelt and only large enough to fit three people comfortably, took me up to the Reagans' private quarters. Mrs. Reagan was waiting for me. She asked me to sit down and came right to the point.

"I've heard that you've been offered the job of Ambassador to Austria." I nodded. Apparently her husband hadn't told her that I had already accepted, because her next words were: "I expect that you'll turn down the President."

I was taken aback. I was so surprised that I didn't have the presence of mind to say that it was too late. I stammered, "Well, why?"

"You know the President," she continued. "He never thinks of himself. He needs you. You can't go. At least not now. Perhaps in the future there will be another appointment."

I couldn't understand why she was saying this to me. It

made no sense. During my tenure at personnel, we had been getting along so well. But I never got the impression that she considered me indispensable. She didn't consider anyone indispensable. Far from it.

I could only conclude that for some reason this posting was something she simply did not want me to have. Apparently, in her eyes, my career had progressed far enough. I felt as if someone had slapped me across the face. I had been so jubilant for the past several days, accepting everyone's congratulations, and chatting eagerly to my mother on the overseas telephone. Now the wife of the President of the United States was telling me not to go.

I left the residence trembling with anger and anxiety. I ducked into the first ladies' room I could find and stared into the mirror. I looked pale but not as shaken as I was feeling. I decided it was safe to head back to my office, that no one would stop me and ask if I was sick. Naturally, the first thing I did was phone Bill Clark.

He was like a tonic. First of all, I could tell from the sound of his voice that he was angry, which gave me courage. Second, he gave me the feeling that everyone was on my side except the First Lady. "Everything has already been prepared," he told me. "We've done all the groundwork. We've filled out all the forms. We've gotten everyone's approval from the NSC to State—and dammit, there's no reason in the world that you shouldn't go. The President wants you to go. He loves a fairy tale ending as much as anyone."

I thanked Bill and told him I didn't know what I'd do without him. And then, for some reason I can't fathom at this remove, I phoned Mike Deaver to tell him what had happened (as if he didn't already know!). I explained to Mike that I had accepted the position and wasn't going to change my mind. He just said, "Um-hmm," and we hung up. I then tried to reach Mrs. Reagan. But Mike must have used his special line to reach her (he could call her private line by pressing just one number on his phone) as soon as we had rung off. I tried several times that afternoon to get through to her. But Nancy Reagan never took another one of my calls.

The only person I confided in other than Mike Deaver who knew Mrs. Reagan was my old friend Mary Jane Wick. She was sympathetic, but urged me to see things from Mrs. Reagan's perspective. "She's always concerned about her husband. Try to be a little patient. Time heals all wounds." I hoped she was right, but in any case, I was going.

I knew there would be opposition from some members of the Department of State, since we had tangled so often on the subject of personnel appointments. In fact, the Foreign Service Association, the union for foreign service officers, had threatened to oppose me when the Senate held confirmation hearings in April 1983. I was a little worried about that since the Foreign Service Association has very close ties to some members of the Senate Foreign Relations Committee.

I decided to meet with the executive secretary of the FSA. I wasn't sure what I would say to him. I certainly couldn't deny that I had been trying to stymie the State Department bureaucracy at every turn. But I was lucky. When I arrived, he was very polite and promised me that they would not testify against me. I think I owe that bit of luck to the fact that in 1983 President Reagan was at the height of his power. Few people in Washington wanted to offend him gratuitously. It was known that he and I had a strong relationship spanning many years and that he would not take kindly to attacks on me.

Still, I was concerned about the confirmation hearings. I recalled all too vividly the way liberal senators had set out to embarrass Bill Clark at his confirmation hearings and succeeded. I couldn't become a foreign policy expert overnight, but I could certainly cram. Friends and colleagues helped me to think of potentially embarrassing questions. I carried stacks of books home with me each night: the history of Austria, American diplomacy, Austria-American relations, and even international law. For weeks I was like a first-year law student, buried in books and emerging only to go to work, to eat, and to sleep. The old fear of being labeled as unqualified haunted me.

When I felt ready, I asked Larry Eagleburger if he would hold a mock hearing for me. Larry had been in the foreign service for years. There were no tricks of the trade he didn't know, and besides, he was extremely bright. He was also happy to oblige. Larry and several colleagues set up a long table complete with water pitchers and ashtrays and sat me at the head of it. And then for several hours they threw question after question at me. "What was the nature of the negotiations on Austria's neutrality following the Second World War?" "Who were the last five Ambassadors to Austria?" "What was the cause of the demise of the Austro-Hungarian Empire?" They also seized the opportunity to play with me a bit over my role in Presidential Personnel. Since I was now going to be working with the foreign service on a daily basis, I was questioned closely on my record of increasing the number of political ambassadors.

I knew all the right answers and then some. They gave me high marks. The time had come for courtesy calls on members of the committee.

The courtesy call is really an antiquated tradition. It dates from the pre-mass media days when the President would submit the name of a candidate for ambassador or Supreme Court justice, or whatever, and the senators who would be examining the nominee in committee hearings wouldn't know anything about the person—not even what he looked like. The courtesy call was thus a chance for the senators to give the nominee an informal once-over before the actual grilling in public. Of course, in our era, the senators always know at least a little about the nominee from television and the print press. But the tradition endures. And sometimes it can be a useful opportunity for the nominee to make a good impression. I visited with my senators from New Jersey, Bill Bradley and Frank Lautenberg, and also with Senators Kassebaum, Percy, Pell, Mathias, Lugar, among others. Neither Kassebaum, with whom I'd had a public disagreement over the question of recruiting women into the Administration, nor Percy, who was chairman of the Foreign Relations Committee and with whom I'd tussled about the reappointment of his daughter to the Corporation for Public Broadcasting, gave me any trouble at all.

The hearings themselves turned out to be a breeze. I woke up quite early, picked out a tailored two-piece knit suit, and silently quizzed myself with note cards over breakfast. Byron and I then drove to the Capitol. We had trouble at first finding the correct hearing room; the Capitol is so vast it's easy to get lost. But with the help of the endlessly courteous Capitol police, we finally found the way. There were no senators present when we arrived—we were a bit early—just staffers roaming about and some press, both American and Austrian. When the senators did arrive, it was all extremely cordial. We all shook hands and exchanged pleasantries before I was formally sworn in. It was over before I knew it. The questions were incredibly easy, or maybe it just seemed that way because I was so well prepared. I was confirmed without a dissenting vote.

Byron took me out for a special celebration dinner the night of my confirmation. We ate lobsters and drank white wine at the Palm restaurant. But that was just the beginning of the celebrations. I was given an embarrassing number of farewell parties. It got to the point where I was afraid of running into people who'd already been to one (or two or three!) of these parties for fear that they'd say, "Haven't you left yet?"

I was extremely touched by the outpouring of warmth and affection. It was now clearer than it had ever been before that I had really made a mark during my two years in Washington. My colleagues were paying me tribute not just because I was fun to be around, or because I was one of the gang, but because I had made a difference in the Administration. I had accomplished a great deal and I was proud of it.

I had fabulous parties given for me by John Shad and Roy Cohn in New York; by Ambassadors Alejandro Orfila of the Organization of American States and Thomas Klestil of Austria and my special friend Roy Pfautch. One of the most exquisite was one hosted by Dan Terra in the elegant State Department dining room. The crème de la crème of the Administration was there: the Clarks, the Meeses, the Nofzigers, the Eagleburgers, the Jameses, the Fieldings, and many, many more of my friends. During the final toast, Dan unveiled the going-away present, which was the combined gift of my friends. It was a magnificent painting by Leon Gaspard, one of my favorite artists, and inscribed on the back was: "Für Helene von Damm. Wir mussen dich an Österreich zurückgeben. Lass unseren herzlichsten Dank dich begleiten. Viel Glück!" (For Helene von Damm. We must give you back to Austria. Let our heartfelt thanks accompany you. Good luck!)

———

Ambassadors are normally sworn in at the State Department, but Bill Clark and the President wanted mine to be special and arranged to have it held in the Rose Garden, a rare privilege. Mike Deaver, knowing Mrs. R's opposition to my appointment, scurried around trying to block the Rose Garden ceremony. It was humiliating. Mike, who had been one of my closest friends from the California crowd, had now sunk to this level of pettiness. And for what? Because I had the audacity to accept a position the President had offered me? Or was he under pressure from the First Lady?

Mike was unsuccessful in persuading the President to hold the ceremony elsewhere, but weather intervened. It poured on the appointed day and so it was moved into the graceful and glittering State Dining Room. The President gave a beautiful speech about me, and I gave a short one in return. Then, as Byron held the Bible for me, the oath was administered by Bill Clark. "I, Helene von Damm, do solemnly swear that I will faithfully execute the office of Ambassador to Austria: that I will to the best of my ability preserve, protect, and defend the Constitution of the United States of America, against all enemies, foreign and domestic, so help me God." Everyone was there, with two notable exceptions: Mrs. Reagan and Mike Deaver.

After that there were seemingly endless details to work out. We needed special diplomatic passports. We had to be sure that we packed the important things to travel by air, and the less important things to travel by boat. Both of our income taxes had to be paid before we left the country, and there were endless briefings for me to attend at the State Department. But finally we were ready. Larry Eagleburger gave me a great parting gift, in the form of a quote to the press: "Helene doesn't have power, she is power!" When I called to thank him for the dizzying buildup, he laughed and said "Never mind, just concentrate on enjoying your time in Vienna. You'll never have another experience like it."

ARRIVING IN VIENNA: THE FAIRY TALE

*T*HE PLANE RIDE OVER TO AUSTRIA WAS UNLIKE ANY I had ever flown before. While I had traveled in great style on Air Force One, this was, in a certain way, better. All of the special attention was for my sake. We flew first-class and the stewards knew that I was the new ambassador. We were greeted by the captain, who came back to chat with us in midflight. Once on the ground, we were met at the foot of the stairs by the top embassy staff and a storm of reporters and cameramen. The staff took care of everything. They handled our luggage, our passports, our transportation to the city, everything. My friends Karl and Lisl Böhm were at the airport and they had brought my mother along with them.

It was an incredibly emotional experience to return to Vienna. As I gazed out the window of my official bulletproof sedan with flags flying on the hood at the elegant boulevards with their ivory buildings and elaborate gratings, I struggled to remember how it felt to be an eighteen-year-old girl from

Ulmerfeld coming to this city to make her way in life and walking the same streets through which I was now chauffeured in such comfort. Though I can't say that my life flashed before my eyes, I can say that I felt a sense of completeness I had never known before. It was hard to hold back the tears.

The Austrian press obviously saw it just as dramatically. They portrayed my story as the homecoming of the poor girl who had made good. It was the biggest news in Austria. Polls showed that 85 percent of Austrians recognized my name. The newspapers, magazines, and television were filled with stories about me. I was an instant celebrity. Austrian politicians and other public figures were clamoring to have their pictures taken with me.

It was exhilarating yet also frightening. I had not always had pleasant experiences with our press back at home. Though the coverage I was now getting was more than positive—it was glowing—I knew that it also established high expectations of me. Any mistake was bound to be magnified. For the first time, I was at center stage.

It was like floating on top of the world. I was successful and celebrated. I had the support of a devoted and secure husband, and I felt as if I were embarking on a fairy tale. I kept thinking of Larry Eagleburger's send-off: "Concentrate on enjoying your time in Vienna. You'll never have another experience like it."

There was much to enjoy. But it was also somewhat overwhelming at first. I was prepared for the substance of the job, but the pomp and ceremony almost took my breath away.

One of the first official acts of a new ambassador is to present his or her credentials to the head of government of the host country. Austria has a particularly beautiful ceremony.

We arrived in the morning at the Imperial Palace. Stationed outside was a smartly dressed honor guard. With the Austrian chief of protocol I was supposed to walk slowly past them, rather like an inspection of the troops, and in the middle somewhere, stop, turn to the honor guard, and bow my head slightly. But I wasn't able to keep my mind on the exact formalities. There were cheering crowds on either side of me and I was terribly tempted to wave at them (who doesn't love being onstage?). Byron was in the crowd snapping pictures. Spouses are not invited to official presentation of credentials. I forgot about stopping and acknowledging the honor guard until I was at the end of the line.

The actual presentation of credentials took place inside the palace and looked like something right out of Hollywood. A red carpet stretched through a series of five ornate rooms, with doors opening onto the next room. All the way at the end, the President of Austria, Dr. Rudolf Kirchschläger, stood very erect in a morning coat, awaiting me. It was a momentous moment. I walked down the length of rooms and we exchanged greetings.

Kirchschläger was a kindly, gracious man. After the formalities were accomplished, we sat down with the Foreign Minister and a few top aides for some small talk. Now I was really at a loss. It suddenly dawned on me that I'd never really learned the art of small talk. My life had always been nose-to-the-grindstone. Small talk was for people who didn't have work to do, I thought. But now, small talk was part of the job. I knew I'd have to learn to do it well.

———

All my life I've taken a ribbing for my strong German accent. It's ironic, then, that my first serious problem in Austria was my German. Now the accent was flawless. But the vocabulary was so thin as to be embarrassing. I could carry on a very rudimentary conversation about ordinary things. But as soon as the conversation moved into abstractions like political ideas I was at a loss. In all of the frantic preparations for my departure, I just hadn't thought that language lessons would be necessary.

So I improvised. People said they never noticed that my German was weak. I'm glad. But that was no accident. I tried to use the words I did remember as well as I could. But whenever possible, I would write out my speeches, toasts, and even informal talks beforehand with the help of my devoted Austrian press secretary, Karen Czerny, or my able public devoted officer, Walter Kohl, who spoke fluent German. Then I would try to memorize it in the bathtub or under the hair dryer.

My first crisis, though only a small one, came a few months into my term. The Austrian Defense Minister requested an urgent meeting. He asked me to be seated and without saying a word handed me a letter with my signature which said that the United States considered Austria to be a de facto member of NATO and would come to her defense if she were attacked.

I was dumbfounded. I didn't remember writing any such thing. How could I? I knew that Austria valued her neutrality more than almost anything. Yet I hesitated in answering him. The letter certainly seemed to be on American Embassy stationery. There were so many possible screw-ups which could have caused this that I didn't want to just stand up and indignantly label the paper a forgery. My mind raced. Had I signed this along with many other "routine" papers that morning without reading it? Not likely. I read everything I signed. Was it possible that someone had actually forged this or slipped it into a batch of form letters and was trying to set me up?

The Defense Minister waited. "I have no immediate explanation for this," I said at last. I was mortified. I sensed that a career ambassador would have known better how to handle the situation.

News of what had happened leaked to the Austrian press. They could easily have raked me over the coals, but thankfully they were restrained. Soon thereafter, Washington confirmed that the paper was indeed a forgery, possibly Soviet disinformation. I was filled with revulsion. What President Reagan had said about the Soviets after he was elected was indeed true. They would lie, cheat, or do anything to pursue their interests. It was a sobering experience and it brought home to me the stakes of the game I was now playing.

———

I threw myself into my work. Not all ambassadors are aggressive about their duties. Some are content to clink glasses at official functions and let it go at that. But I had worked hard my entire life and I certainly wasn't going to just shut it off now. Just as when I was personnel director I believed that the purpose of political appointees was to promote the President's policies, I was equally adamant that ambassadors had a duty to promote the President's foreign policy.

Besides, my official duties were not that overwhelming. I had to meet and keep in touch with top Austrian government officials, the press, and other diplomats from around the world on a regular basis. But I'd become inured to the glamour of all that when I was in Washington. Only one ceremonial handshake stands out in my memory: the one with the Pope.

John Paul II had visited Austria on a trip which also included Poland and Germany. The entire diplomatic corps of Vienna assembled to meet him. As he made his way down the line shaking hands (and usually managing to address the diplomat in his native language), he looked right past me and reached out to the second row where spouses were assembled and shook Byron's hand, saying, "Hello, Mr. Ambassador." I wasn't angry or upset. Ronald Reagan might have done the same thing. It wasn't sexism, just the understandable assumption of a man of his generation. Maybe he thought Byron was being gallant by allowing me to stand in the first row.

As far as the office work of ambassador goes, a large part consists of reporting back to the State Department on a continuing basis about what's going on in the host country. This includes everything from summaries of the daily newspapers to longer political analyses. I was content to allow the career people in my embassy to handle the more routine reporting. But when it came to political analysis, I kept a very watchful eye on what went on.

Being an ambassador confirmed all of my preconceived ideas about the importance of political appointees. There was no question that the career people were qualified and "professional." That wasn't the issue. Everyone has political prejudices and they creep into every report and every summary that gets sent home. For example, if a country is undergoing a "leftist" insurgency, a political liberal would be inclined to report back to Washington that the movement was broad-based, indigenous, and democratic. A conservative would be more likely to look for Soviet or other Eastern bloc involvement and would be less likely to give the insurgents the benefit of the doubt on their democratic philosophy. Those differences in basic outlook can be critical—as they were in Nicaragua and El Salvador, to name just two recent examples. I wanted to be sure that if prejudices were going to affect our reports, they'd at least be *our* prejudices.

We didn't, thank God, have those kinds of problems in Austria. Because Austria is neutral, the main sources of friction between our two countries were commercial. I was able to help negotiate a favorable specialty steel quota for Austria. In return, we got an agreement from the Austrian government to pass legislation which would crack down on the illegal transfer of Western technology to the East. I was terribly proud of that. It had been a long-standing goal of American foreign policy.

I was less successful when the Austrians were shopping around for a new jet fighter. The Defense Minister told me that whoever submitted the most attractive bid would receive the order. I naturally lobbied for the American F-16. Only after the contract had been let to Sweden did I understand why I'd failed. Austria, being a neutral country, could not compromise that neutrality by buying arms from either the United States or the U.S.S.R. In choosing the Swedes, who are also neutral, they took the safest course.

But I was steamed about it. In the first place, I had been led to believe that the bidding was going to be completely open and that the best plane would win. In the end, for political reasons, we weren't even considered. Now I suppose I can understand that the Austrians don't want to seem to be taking sides between the United States and the U.S.S.R. I certainly think that by now they should have the independence to buy things from whomever they choose without worrying about what anyone will think. I was also angry at myself for being so naïve. But after that I was never innocent about the political content of economic decisions.

When we lost out, I was not shy about expressing my dismay and disappointment. Because I was so vocal about America's interests, Austria's Communist Party newspaper, *Volkstimme,* editorialized that "in a banana republic with some self-esteem an ambassador like her would be packed in a crate and sent back to Washington with thanks."

I clipped the article and sent it to the editor with a handwritten note attached: "Alive, I hope."

Volkstimme sent me a Christmas card that year. And when I resigned my office in June 1985, *Volkstimme* ran a charming cartoon showing three men trying to kill themselves, with the caption: "When Helene von Damm goes, I don't want to live anymore." Something tells me the editor isn't quite a dyed-in-the-wool Communist.

Ambassadors do only half a job if they focus exclusively on government-to-government relations and neglect business. I made it my priority to promote trade between the United States and Austria. I was always on the lookout for ways to help American business get a foot in the door. I helped put together an exhibition of American computers and persuaded the clothing designer Geoffrey Beene to bring his collection to Vienna, the first American designer to do so. The response to both was ecstatic.

But by far the most important work I could perform in neutral Austria was what we call "public diplomacy" and others call making your case. The idea was really born with Charlie Wick and the Reagan Administration. Ambassadors were urged to use their posts to explain American foreign policy directly to the people of the host country and not just to ministers of government and top opinion makers. After all, in democracies the people ultimately control the government.

In no case was public diplomacy more crucial in recent years than in the struggle to emplace Pershing missiles on European soil. Anti-U.S. demonstrations swept European capitals, and while neutral, Vienna was not exempt. That there were no demonstrations against the Soviets when they had several years earlier installed SS-20s capable of reaching Europe makes one wonder. And another irony was that the governments of Europe had asked the United States for these missiles to counterbalance the Soviets. Yet it was portrayed by the leftists as the United States forcing these Pershings down Europe's throat.

I wasn't about to allow the disinformation and misinformation to go unanswered. In the midst of the controversy, a youthful group of anti-Pershing demonstrators announced that they were going to form a human chain between the Soviet Embassy and ours. My aides urged me to get out of town. That would have been the classic, safe, careerist approach to a problem of this kind. But I overruled them. I wanted to use the opportunity to make America's case. I instructed my staff that I would indeed be in my office at the time of the demonstration and asked them to invite a delegation of the protesters in to meet with me. I also told them to make sure the press and TV were there. When the marchers arrived, I was sitting in my office. The staff person in charge came up to inform me of their arrival. "Is TV here?" I asked routinely. He said no, he hadn't been able to find them. I fixed him with a Nancy Reagan glare and said, "You'd better find them." He stammered, "But what do I do with the people downstairs?" I said that was his problem. He vanished, pale and nervous, but soon did manage to return with the TV people.

It worked just as I had hoped it would. That evening, Austrian television portrayed the United States as sympathetic to the concerns of young people. The Soviets were so upset that they complained about biased reporting. It was a delicious victory.

As for the staffer I had been so hard on, I congratulated him later for bouncing back. I was a tough boss and I knew it. But I had been a staff person for most of my life and I knew the difference between good and bad staff work. And I tried always to be fair.

The Pershing protest coup whetted my appetite to get out into the country more and talk to people informally. I found that there was widespread misunderstanding, even among opinion leaders, of the differences between our constitutional system and their parliamentary system. Many couldn't understand why the President had to go around talking about our need to build up our defenses. Why didn't he just do it? I explained about Congress and the role of public opinion in the United States. They were always eager listeners. However much the United States gets criticized in other parts of the world, there is nonetheless a ceaseless curiosity about America. Before long, I was spending more time on the road than in the office. I met student groups, businessmen, church groups, and local government officials. I tried never to pass up an opportunity to make America's case.

I also introduced some good old fashioned American traditions to embassy life. On the Fourth of July, I invited five hundred Austrians to join us for square dancing, country music, hot dogs, hamburgers, and baked beans. Tony Faillace, a special events genius came over bearing generous donations from Burger King and Coca-Cola, and acted as emcee. Joey Adams (he and Cindy were our guests at the time) delighted the crowd with an impromptu soft-shoe number and Byron brought the house down when, late in the evening, he appeared dressed up as Uncle Sam. We capped the evening with a fabulous fireworks display ending with the words "Happy Birthday America" glittering in Vienna's night sky.

I knew that there were other Americans who might be able to explain and defend our policies in particular areas better than I could. So I made a special effort to promote exchanges of officials—the biggest program in Austrian-American relations. During my two and a half years as ambassador, I brought most of the members of the Cabinet to Austria to meet their counterparts, and also lured Bill Buckley, Jeane Kirkpatrick, and Henry Kissinger to come and speak. This is not to denigrate my own influence. I was widely known in Austria and had no difficulty getting articles published, comments reported, or press conferences attended. I was even able to see an article justifying the rescue of Grenada in a Socialist Party newspaper.

I wanted Austria to know that we cared about her problems as well and weren't just there as Ronald Reagan's public relations firm. Drawing upon my own fund-raising experiences during the campaign, I was able to get ever generous Frank Sinatra to give a benefit concert that raised $300,000 for the poor children of Austria. I also hosted a garden concert at the residence to raise money for the Freud Museum with internationally renowned Lorin Maazel playing the violin and Rudolf Buchbinder playing the piano.

The concert was such a success that I sponsored another, this time with Leonard Bernstein conducting the Vienna Philharmonic. It was a breathtaking concert and it raised quite a bit for the museum.

As busy as I was, I also managed to squeeze in time for appreciating the sheer physical beauty of Austria, something I had never recognized while I was growing up. I went mountain climbing on Austria's highest mountain and got stuck in a freak July snowstorm. I also went trekking through the countryside with Prince and Princess of Liechtenstein. And then there was the steady stream of friends from home who came for visits. In addition to many of my former peers and staffers, Carolyn Deaver (despite the souring of my relationship with Mike), Janice and George Abbott, Evie and Seymour Holtzman (Marc's parents, who had also been active in the campaign), Mrs. Charles Price II (wife of our new ambassador in Great Britain), Fred and Helen Gottfurcht (Fred was my indefatiguable chairman of the private embassy fund), Tom Bolan, fashion designer Leamond Dean, and many, many others.

I was at my peak. Word got back to me that my name had come up at one of President Reagan's press conferences. The President was being asked about some confusion in the embassies in Central America. He replied that sometimes slip-ups occurred and an ambassador doesn't get informed of something important. "As a matter of fact," he added, "I received a cable from my most recent appointee, the Ambassador to Austria. And Helene von Damm let me know that something had taken place, and she hadn't been told about it in advance. And when Helene speaks, I listen." I was thrilled.

To complete my sense of accomplishment, the University of New Hampshire invited me to deliver the commencement address in the spring of 1984, bestowing upon me an honorary doctorate of law degree. Having been bothered for years by my lack of academic credentials, I was as thrilled as if I were informed I was the sole heir of a rich uncle.

The only clouds on the horizon were stories I was hearing about Mrs. R. According to my sources, her position was hardening toward me: more and more with each new success I achieved.

DISAPPOINTMENTS
EVERYWHERE

*B*ACK IN WASHINGTON, THINGS WEREN'T GOING
nearly so well. I kept in touch with my close friends and former associates and tried to keep tabs on internal White House
gossip. That's how I found out about Bill Clark.

I was meeting with a delegation of young Austrian musi-
cians in October 1983 when I received an overseas call from
an extremely distressed Tad Tharp. Tad, like me, took personnel changes extremely seriously.

"Bill Clark is leaving the NSC," he said. "This will be a
disaster for the President's foreign policy. Do something
about it!"

What could I do from six thousand miles away? For the
first time since I'd arrived in Austria, I felt frustrated to be so
far away. And, I must admit, I was a little hurt that Bill hadn't
called to give me the news himself. Still, my personal feelings
had to take second place. I agreed with Tad that Bill's departure would present an insurmountable loss to the conserva-

tives. There was still Cap at Defense, thank God. But I figured the constant infighting and intrigues were behind Clark's departure and now Shultz would probably have a large say in who his replacement would be. I told Tad I'd try.

I put in a call to Bill, but strangely his secretary asked me to hold on and then told me he was out. I tried not to take it personally. Bill isn't the kind of person who'd want to talk if he was feeling down. But his unwillingness to talk confirmed my worst suspicions about the circumstances surrounding his departure. So I dialed the President next.

He was out of town.

People kept calling me from the United States for the rest of the day to tell me what had happened. I was at least able to get the "official story," which was that Bill was moving over to become Secretary of the Interior at the President's request. Of course, I knew that wasn't true. What could have happened?

I thought back to the early days of the Administration. I recalled how enthusiastic Mike Deaver, Jim Baker, and Ed Meese had been about Bill's appointment to the NSC. There was lots of hopeful talk about the "judicial" approach he'd bring to the job. But by "judicial" they must have meant impartial. And that Bill could not be. Nor should he. Part of his job was to serve as a clearinghouse for the views of the State Department, the intelligence community, and the Department of Defense. But an equally important role was to give the President his own best advice.

As far as I could piece it together later, Bill got worn down as the conservative who stood in the way of the pragmatists. Just when I was trying to win over the demonstrators who formed a human chain at our embassy, the unfavorable press the United States was getting all over Europe was causing turmoil in the White House. The feedback I received—backed up by press reports and media speculation—was that Mrs. R decided that her husband's tough stand against Communism, the tyranny which had destroyed more lives than any other in our century, was simply costing too much politically. And it didn't remain a secret that she thought Clark was "abrasive" on the Soviet issue and began to push the "peace President" idea. Bill was adamantly anti-Communist. He hated the idea which was now starting to be circulated that President Reagan and Soviet leader Andropov should meet at an unconditional and unstructured summit. What Clark objected to was the sym bolism of the thing. They were talking of a summit for the mere sake of a meeting—something the President had always said he was against. Bill urged that if the President met with the leader of the Soviet Union, it should be only after an agenda had been carefully worked out and agreed upon beforehand. Otherwise, we'd be granting legitimacy to the Soviets and getting nothing in return. But Baker, Deaver, and especially Shultz loved the idea.

From the negative comments Mrs. Reagan freely made to friends and others in the administration about Bill Clark, it can be concluded that she was poisoning the water with the President as well. I can't imagine that she would have tried to impugn his character—the relationship between President Reagan and Clark was too solid for that. But I'm sure she told him that he wasn't getting along with the Baker/Deaver wing of the staff (Ronald Reagan always wanted team players). It was a plausible complaint, since Bill did have a tendency to be a bit of a lone ranger. He never really teamed up with anyone else on the staff. And he usually kept silent in general staff meetings (except when he was with the President), in part to keep the lid on leaks. At any rate, Bill began to feel the effects. He could still see the President alone whenever he desired, but Ronald Reagan seemed less and less inclined to take his advice on Soviet issues. Clark decided that it would be in the best interests of the country to step aside.

Meanwhile, Deaver had arranged for Shultz to meet alone with the President for two hours each week to the exclusion of Clark, the NSC, and the Department of Defense. Thread by thread, the ties that bound Clark to Ronald Reagan were being severed.

When Clark discovered that, without NSC coordination, the Soviet Ambassador, Anatoly Dobrynin, had been sneaked into the White House to meet with the President, he was fit to be tied.

But the straw which broke the camel's back was not a liberal versus conservative dispute. It concerned our policy toward Lebanon. Along with Cap Weinberger, Bill had been opposed to stationing U.S. Marines in an essentially undefended position at the Beirut airport. He and Cap argued that the Marines should be moved offshore to ships. Shultz was opposed, believing that this would be a sign of weakness. The President sided with Shultz. Two weeks later, a suicide terrorist drove a truck filled with explosives directly into the Marine barracks and killed 243 of our men.

Bill was ready to return to his ranch. However, Jim Watt, the controversial Secretary of the Interior, who had a tendency to put his foot in his mouth, had gotten himself into trouble with some imprudent remarks and had to resign and when the President asked Bill to replace Watt, he agreed.

But that was not the end of the drama. Baker and Deaver had cooked up a little scheme for the post-Clark White House. They wanted Baker to become National Security Adviser in Clark's place and Mike Deaver to become Chief of Staff in Baker's place. Everything was all arranged. All of the players were in their places. But the curtain never went up. It was Clark who got to rewrite the ending.

The setting was the final National Security Council meeting at which Clark would have presided as adviser. Everyone was assembled in the Situation Room in the basement of the White House. (NSC meetings were always held there, both by tradition and because the room is secure.) Bill kept looking at his watch. The President was late and that was unusual. Bill wasn't the type to send a staffer to find out what the delay was all about; he got up and went to see for himself.

Clark found the President still in his office, looking pensive. He saw Bill come in and said, "Oh, I'm still going over in my mind how I'm going to make the announcement."

"What announcement, Mr. President?" said Clark. President Reagan seemed surprised that Clark didn't know.

"I'm going to announce to the press that I've decided to make Jim Baker National Security Adviser and Mike Deaver Chief of Staff."

Bill nearly fell over.

"Mr. President," he said simply, "I urge you in the name of fairness to hold off. You can't make appointments at that level without consulting your other advisers who are affected by this move. You must speak to Casey, Weinberger, and Meese. I'm sure none of them knows that you have this in mind."

The President objected that if he delayed the announcement it would leak out and force his hand that way. Bill argued that it was worth the risk. The President finally relented. He attended the NSC meeting but said there'd be a delay in the announcement of a replacement for Bill Clark.

After the NSC meeting was adjourned, Mike Deaver went directly upstairs to the pressroom to await the President's arrival. But the President went into a smaller room and huddled with Bill Casey, Bill Clark, Ed Meese, and Cap Weinberger. It was a tense, white-knuckled meeting. No one sat. For a full hour, the four men told the President that the "incompatibility" problem would be so great that it simply would not work. They didn't directly threaten the President that they'd resign unless he took their advice, but it was hinted that they'd find it impossible to work with Deaver as Chief of Staff and Baker as National Security Adviser.

While they talked, Deaver was pacing up and down the hall next to the pressroom and demanding to know why the President was late for the press conference. Several times, he called down to the Situation Room to find out what was keeping him (no doubt suspecting exactly what was happening—his plan was being foiled!).

The President decided not to make the appointments and called Baker and Deaver into the Oval Office to explain his decision. Someone who witnessed the encounter among the three men told me that Baker took it like a gentleman. But Deaver lashed out. "You are weak," he said in an emotion-laden angry voice to the President. "I'll never trust you again." On that, he turned on his heel and slammed the Oval Office door behind him. Deaver behaved more casually with the President than many others because of their long familiarity. But his outburst that day was unusual even for him. I don't think he ever recovered from the blow he received in being fired from the campaign during the Sears episode. That long-simmering resentment must have flared anew when he lost the chance to be Chief of Staff.

Everyone's first choice for Bill's successor, Ronald Reagan included, was Jeane Kirkpatrick. Everyone except one. Shultz. I don't know how he talked the President out of appointing her, but he finally settled on a compromise candidate, Robert C. McFarlane, who had been Clark's deputy. As for Baker and Deaver, they would stay exactly where they were.

———

While Bill Clark and Mike Deaver, once close friends and colleagues, were coming almost to blows in Washington, I too was feeling the effects of politics in my personal life. In one area, I lost a friend. In another, I lost my husband.

The friend was Mary Jane Wick. We had been so close in the California days. I had dined at their home countless times and shared confidences of the most personal nature. I liked both Wicks very much, but of the two, I was much closer to Mary Jane. During the first two years in Washington, we had maintained that intimacy, speaking at least once or twice a week. But since my arrival in Vienna, though we'd started out calling and writing, her responses became colder and fewer.

In February 1984 I traveled with the President of Austria on a ceremonial visit to Washington. On the plane coming over I decided that I was going to find out what was wrong with Mary Jane no matter how many times I had to call.

But first there were official engagements to attend. One was a reception for the President and First Lady of Austria, hosted by the Reagans at the White House. I had hoped that Mrs. R would have forgiven me by now for defying her wishes. But she is not a forgiving woman. The only person I have ever seen her forgive was Stu Spencer. (He was persona non grata after he joined the Ford campaign in 1976 until he was perceived as needed again by us at a later stage.) Her snubs were so public—she would look right past me even when shaking hands. But I reminded myself that the Austrians seemed to like me very much and that the President said he was pleased with the job I was doing. Her ire was the price I was paying for all of the other wonderful things.

As soon as I was able, I got in touch with Mary Jane. I figured there was no easy way to broach the subject, so I just asked her bluntly why she wasn't acting like a friend. She was huffy. "Do you think I can forget what you did to Charlie?" I was heartsick. What had she been thinking?

"What did I do?" I asked, stunned.

"You know very well you got Gil Robinson a job," she snapped.

This was bizarre. She was referring to a minor episode two years earlier in which Gil Robinson, once Charlie Wick's deputy at USIA, had gotten into a dust-up with Charlie. Shultz, Clark, and I all agreed that Robinson deserved another post, at least for the time being. It was no big deal. Mary Jane and I had been friends at the time, and long afterward. But her tone now was so cold I started to doubt my own memory. Just to be sure, I checked through some old correspondence and found that yes, indeed, Mary Jane Wick had written me a beautiful and warm letter of congratulations when I was named ambassador, and this was after the Gil Robinson episode. Memories of her goodbye hugs and kisses were still warming my heart.

There was only one conclusion. Mary Jane felt she had to take sides as between Mrs. Reagan and me. She chose Mrs. Reagan. I suppose I can understand her solidarity with Mrs. Reagan. But I can't forgive her the cruelty with which she did it.

I couldn't help but contrast Mary Jane's handling of the situation with the way the Annenbergs handled it. Byron and I had been on their much-coveted New Year's Eve invitation list for several years. First and foremost, this was because of my relationship with the President. But I also think that over time a genuine friendship had developed between us. Before I left for Austria, Walter Annenberg told me he was looking forward to seeing us at New Year's again.

As the time drew closer, though, I got a call from Walter while I was in Austria. He was warm, as always, but it was clear there was something he had to say and he wasn't comfortable about it. He seemed to ease into the topic by saying, "Helene, you know how fond we are of you."

"Yes," I replied eagerly. "And you know I'm crazy about you and Lee."

"Well," he said slowly, "this makes it harder to say what I'm going to say, but could you and Byron come and visit us sometime other than New Year's?"

He didn't have to say another word. I knew it was Mrs. R. He was so clearly embarrassed and the conversation was obviously painful for him that I cut right in and said, "Walter, before you go on, we could not get away from Austria anyway at this time. It's been on my mind for weeks now to call you, so it's all for the best."

I admired the way Walter handled an impossible situation. He was straightforward, yet he never betrayed his friendship with Mrs. Reagan. And he was loyal to me too by considering my feelings and doing what he had to do in the least painful fashion. He's a gentleman.

It was gratifying to me to be able to visit my mother every week. She lived about two hours from Vienna. Aside from the trip she made on the day of my arrival, she was too frail to move very much, so I went to her faithfully. It became an interesting echo of my life in Washington, where I had worked in the White House from Monday through Friday and then escaped to New Jersey on weekends. Now I was the ambassador during the week, chauffeured about in an armored car. But on weekends, when I visited her, I drove myself. In Grein, at the old-age home, I was just another daughter visiting her mother: taking her for walks or to a coffee shop for lunch or a treat.

———

My ambassadorial duties were keeping me constantly on the run. But I did find time to spruce up the residence a bit. The setting was very lovely: five acres of property, a tennis court, and grounds beautifully tended by our gardener, Herr Schmidl, who nurtured each flower. The house itself was not in the grand eighteenth-century style. It was of the twentieth-century Bauhaus school of architecture. But it had become somewhat run-down and worn. The previous ambassador had started to do repairs but much remained unfinished. We put on a fresh coat of paint, replaced the carpets, and bought new garden furniture.

Money is scarce at the State Department, so we raised funds for the redecorating of the embassy residence privately. Unfortunately, the State Department has now disallowed such private funds and I think I know why. The careerists resented the ability of the political ambassadors to raise money through connections. But they were cutting off their nose to spite their face by opposing the practice. If a career person followed me as ambassador to Austria, he or she would be able to enjoy the improvements I was able to make. But more important than that, the improvements made the embassy more effective. The old piano in the residence was in such terrible condition that none of the pianists I invited to the house would play on it. Thanks to Fred Gottfurcht and his committee, I was able to purchase a Steinway.

Byron was a big help with the improvements, but unfortunately Byron was bored. He was a vigorous, healthy man of fifty who had just achieved his dream: to retire early. And while he had become co-chairman of Republicans Abroad, I'm afraid it just wasn't enough for him.

He tried to keep busy—by helping me with my work and by trying to learn German—but he felt like a fish out of water. It was the first time in his long, very successful career as a businessman that he didn't really have anything to run. Moreover, the strangeness of a new country was hard on him. In the United States, every stranger is made to feel at home. But Austria and most other countries make a stranger feel like a stranger.

It was tough on both of us. I was rediscovering my roots and being celebrated and feted while he was doing his best to be a good sport. We wound up suffering our own private turmoils without really going through the experience together. Still, I am sure we would have made it if another person hadn't come along—but that's water over the dam, because another person did come between us.

I knew it was a strain for Byron and I did everything I could to make time for him and to make him feel that I didn't take him for granted. But he started to find reasons to make trips back to the United States. At first he would go for a week. Later it became several weeks.

Byron, being Byron, never complained. For years he had always been my emotional anchor when I needed him. Now he needed me but wouldn't say so. He was the most unselfish person I've ever known. He kept silent about his own unhappiness because he didn't want to put a damper on my enjoyment. He felt that I deserved all of the attention, respect, and admiration I was now receiving. He was proud of me and happy for me. And yet . . .

As I look back now, I don't know how I could have been so insensitive. It wasn't just that I was too busy and didn't care to notice. The title of ambassador hadn't changed my whole personality. I think I was reluctant to probe into the relationship with my husband because I was afraid of what I'd find. I was afraid that if I reached out to him, I'd feel how strained our marriage had become. The truth was that, while I still loved Byron, I was feeling emotionally lonely in the relationship at the time. And there was no one I could confide in. My close friends were all back in the States. In Austria, only my assistant, Dorothy Tyson, Charles Tyson's stepmother, could be called a personal friend. But even though we were very close and I trusted her completely, I didn't want to discuss this with her because she was practically living in the official residence with us and it would have been too uncomfortable for her and for us. So Byron kept silent about his unhappiness for the sake of my happiness, and I kept silent about my unhappiness for the sake of the marriage. It was a recipe for disaster.

———

I met Peter Gürtler during my first week in Vienna. Owner of the legendary Sacher Hotel, Peter was the sort of man who fills the daydreams of schoolgirls. Handsome, sophisticated, charming, and wealthy, he was the most eligible bachelor in Vienna. But his charms eluded me during that first meeting. He appeared to me to be a superficial playboy and I had far weightier matters on my mind. Besides, my marriage seemed to be very healthy.

But in the weeks and months which followed, I kept running into Peter everywhere I went. He always sought me out at receptions, parties, and other public events. And he seemed to get my name placed on lots of private dinner lists as well. He was flirtatious, but that made little impression. As a woman ambassador I was getting more male attention than I'd ever gotten in my life. With all due modesty, I must say he was only one of many men who flirted with me.

Strangely enough, Bill Clark had a role in propelling this harmless flirtation into something more.

Bill had been after me for ages to learn how to ride a horse properly. In Austria, I finally had the time to do so and also a reason. During the visit of Austrian President Kirchschläger to the United States (the same visit on which I was snubbed by Mrs. Reagan), I would be required to accompany him to the Hearst ranch in California, where he was to go for a ride. Bill Clark phoned me and asked if I was planning to ride along. I knew he was teasing me. "At least learn how to get on and off a horse properly," he pleaded, "for the honor of the United States of America."

We both laughed. The last time I had been riding was at the Clark ranch on a Sunday afternoon years before. With Bill's help, I had gotten onto the horse's back by sitting on a fence and having Bill bring the horse up alongside. But as for getting off—well, I'd seen the horse heading straight for a fence and threw myself off. I hit my head on a rock and had to be rushed to a local hospital.

I decided to humor Bill and take lessons. But where? It turned out that my official driver was a horse enthusiast. He recommended the St. Hubertus Riding School on the outskirts of Vienna. I signed up.

It just so happened that Peter Gürtler, who was a champion dressage rider, kept his horse at the very same place. We exchanged pleasantries on my first day of lessons. He glanced over at my awkward first attempts at getting into the saddle with just a hint of amusement—but not mockery. Soon he was giving me pointers. When I had reached a level of proficiency where I could control the animal, he suggested that I accompany him and some friends riding in the Vienna woods.

It was glorious. We set out early in the day and enjoyed the silence and the beauty of nature. At first these outings were in groups of four and five. But after a while it seemed innocent enough to go out riding with Peter alone. It didn't even occur to me that I was doing something questionable. As a professional woman, I had many male friends and was as comfortable around them as I was with women friends. I didn't think of myself as someone who had to consider the appearance of impropriety.

In time, it was more than appearance.

On some rides, we would take rest stops at little villages and cozy country inns Peter knew about. We'd share a glass of wine or a meal. He was so entertaining. He seemed to have endless stories about people in Europe and the United States. As a hotel owner, there was no one he didn't know. His manners were always impeccable. I felt so pampered when I was with him. And I found that the time seemed to fly past.

When winter came, we gave up riding and took to the ski slopes. Just as with riding, Peter was the expert and he proved an excellent teacher again as well. Byron was by this time spending lots of time in the United States, and I found myself spending more and more time with Peter. The innocence was gone and I was in love.

My situation was impossible. I knew that. I desperately needed someone to confide in. Someone who could help me get my feet back on the ground and make some sensible decisions. But I couldn't discuss this over the international phone lines. The closest friend, the person who knew me better than anyone, was Byron. Tragically, in my blindness I turned to him.

When he got back from America I told him everything about my relationship with Peter. Naturally, he was crushed. What else did I expect? He wasn't going to be able to give me advice when I had just stabbed him in the heart. It was awful of me. I was being totally selfish.

Byron reacted as would any man who was still very much in love and felt betrayed. He was devastated and asked for a divorce. And I stood by and let it happen, paralyzed despite the fact that we'd spent ten great years together. I loved, admired, and respected Byron more than anyone else in the world, even then.

Peter, at the same time, was putting on a full-court press to win the lady ambassador. I had lost my grip. I began to drift and just allowed Peter to make decisions for me. He wanted us to be married.

Even now, I'm not sure why I lost my bearings as I did. I had worked so hard to get where I was. I enjoyed the job as ambassador and for the first time in my life I didn't feel insecure about my abilities. I was doing a great job and I knew it. There was nothing more that I felt I had to prove to myself or to the world. Perhaps that's why I let my self-control slip a bit. Maybe a handsome, dashing European was my reward to myself for having achieved as much as I had?

Or perhaps there was a deeper reason. Despite the incredible gains of the women's movement over the last several years, I think many of us are still in conflict about what our proper roles ought to be. Perhaps part of me felt that I really did need a dominant male in my life to be complete as a woman. Perhaps, despite all of my career accomplishments, there was still a wish to be swept away by romance?

I'm not sure, but the sheer emotion between Peter and me was like a powerful drug. I can try to psychoanalyze myself in hindsight but at the time I was awash in feeling. I would decide one morning that I was definitely going to end the relationship with Peter, and then I'd see him and my resolution would melt like butter. I decided that if he wanted me to be his wife and settle in Austria permanently, I would do it.

The first person I told of my decision (other than Byron, of course), as soon as I had an opportunity to come to the United States, was Bill Clark. I'd never seen him look so disappointed in me.

"You are not serious," he sighed.

I nodded with tears in my eyes.

"Then you're out of your mind," he said. "Can't you for once in your life just have an affair if you must? Or do you want to throw away thirty years of hard work?"

I argued that he was wrong. I told him I could weather the storm because my popularity was so high in Austria.

He shook his head. "That's irrelevant. With this move you'll destroy all of that respect. People will think you're just acting like a stupid woman instead of a professional. It will appear that, just as in the stereotypes, you're allowing your heart to rule you instead of your head. And by the way, I think you are." And he wasn't finished.

"You're also playing into the hands of your enemies. In case you've forgotten, you have some tough ones."

I'm not sure whether that was a reference to Mrs. Reagan or not, but if so, it was certainly prescient.

At the time, however, I convinced myself that Bill was wrong. Hadn't he discouraged me from moving over to the personnel department? And hadn't that turned out to be the best career move I ever made? He was wrong this time too.

I could have told the President about my decision but I didn't. I'm his Ambassador to Austria, I told myself. He needs to know anything which bears on that role. But this is my personal life. I won't bore him with it.

Actually, I think I just didn't want to hear another person I loved and trusted tell me the truth: that I was making a terrible mistake.

———

I returned to Austria and put the wheels in motion. It was agreed that Byron would file for divorce in New Jersey. Peter and I would be married as soon as the papers came through. The three of us agreed to keep the whole thing a secret. I was terrified that if the matter leaked before I was ready, it would cause a scandal. It didn't leak. But once the divorce was final, the press did serve up the story with relish.

My divorce from Byron came through in the middle of January 1985. Three days later, one of the Austrian papers carried a short item saying that I was getting a divorce in order to marry an Austrian. I waited like a trapped animal for the deluge of calls. It didn't happen immediately. There was certainly a great deal of whispering in diplomatic circles, but nothing that really made national news. Washington was caught up in Inaugural fever, among other things.

Until the wedding. We were married in the first week of February in a civil ceremony in Kitzbühel, a fashionable ski resort in Tirol. Sixty reporters crowded outside town hall. We were asked to reenact the ring exchange for the cameras.

But it wasn't a happy wedding day for me. My mind was full of Byron and how hurt he must be. So every smile hurt. I was also thinking about my position. It was my responsibility to present the United States in the best possible light and I was worried about what effect the publicity would have.

I also had a bit of a heavy heart toward Peter, because I wasn't enjoying our wedding day as I should have. He was relishing the whole experience, including the press attention, very much (maybe too much).

To my great surprise and delight, the press reports were not negative in the least. It wasn't, after all, as if I were carrying on a long affair while also serving as ambassador. I was properly divorced and properly remarried. After the initial shock wore off, Vienna warmed to the idea. The Austrian press seemed to think this marriage was the perfect fairy-tale ending to my poor-girl-makes-good story. It became the wedding of the year. In their eyes I had married an Austrian national symbol: the Sacher Hotel. When we returned to Vienna, Peter and I were the guests of then Finance Minister, and now Chancellor, Franz Vranitzky and his wife at the annual Opera Ball. And we were treated like Prince Charles and Princess Diana.

THE FALL FROM GRACE

*T*HINGS BACK IN WASHINGTON WERE SO EVENTFUL
that I hoped my personal life would escape notice. Jim Baker
and Don Regan had exchanged jobs. Mike Deaver had finally
left the White House staff to open his own public relations
firm. And the President's upcoming trip to the Bitburg cemetery was causing a furor.

Though I was caught up in the whirlwind of my personal
life, I was still interested in what was going on back home. The
Administration and all its players were still part of me. So I was
intrigued to hear that Jim Baker had finally succeeded in winning his prize: a seat at the Cabinet table. Only later did I
discover that my old friend Drew Lewis was blindsided in the
process.

Apparently, toward the end of the first term, Baker was
tired of the punishing hours and headaches of being Chief of
Staff and let it be known that he'd be moving on. The consensus candidate to replace him was Drew Lewis, who had served

as President Reagan's first Secretary of Transportation and was then in private industry. Lewis traveled to Washington and met with Baker, Meese, Deaver, and Mrs. R. It was understood among all of them that he would be offered the job by the President.

But all of this took place before Baker had talked to Regan and cooked up their little switcheroo. No sooner had they come to their arrangement than they quickly presented it to the President, who gave his approval. I heard later that Baker confided to friends, "This coup is too good to be true." (A footnote: Two years later, when Don Regan was doing such a poor job advising the President on the Iran/Contra affair, Drew was again offered the Chief of Staff job. He turned it down. He had to. He wanted to help the President, but back in 1984 he had given notice to his company, Union Pacific, and then retracted it. They demanded, and got, a commitment from him that he wouldn't consider another Washington job again in the Reagan Administration.

———

Peter moved into the residence with me and I settled back remarkably quickly into the normal pace of my activities. I had too many diplomatic responsibilities to make time for a honeymoon in February, so we postponed it until Easter, when we had a glorious time trekking through the Himalayas.

But upon our return to Vienna, I could tell by the looks on the faces of my staff that things were beginning to simmer back in Washington. They were starting to notice me. I never got the sense that what I had done was regarded as a scandal, but I knew it was being discussed—which was only natural. Oddly enough, I received fine support from the State Department. George Shultz very kindly sent a gift, and the department sent me a cable praising my work as ambassador. I had previously sought and received assurance from the European Bureau of the State Department that marrying a foreign national was no cause for resignation. The Austrian desk in Washington relayed word that in their opinion, U.S.-Austrian relations had never been better.

Articles in *The Washington Post* and *The New York Times* were not really negative. The problem became the gossip in Washington. It took on a life of its own. As I look back, I see that much of it was my fault. I hadn't confided in any of my friends, so they were in no position to come to my aid.

Soon my most loyal friends Lynn Wood and Phyllis Kaminsky were phoning every few days to express their growing concern. While it was still mostly party chatter, the gossip took on alarming proportions. It was whispered around town that Nancy Reagan had let it be known that I wasn't going to be around much longer. It was alleged in *The Washingtonian* that Nancy Reagan was "none too happy" with me, and that my four marriages were considered "unseemly."

That stung. I had never made a critical remark about Nancy Reagan to the press. We may have had our difficult moments, and I had many, many opportunities to criticize her anonymously, but I never did. My loyalty to Ronald Reagan extended to her and I would have thought that her loyalty to her husband would also extend to those who served him well.

But once word got around that Mrs. Reagan was after my head, the mood in Washington shifted from gossipy interest in my divorce and marriage to something else. All of the people I had alienated as Assistant to the President for Presidential Personnel, and all of the people who had been denied jobs because of me, could now feel freer to come out of the woodwork. Before Mrs. Reagan was known to oppose me, I was protected by my twenty-year relationship with the President. It had provided some insulation from the attacks of my detractors. But now that armor had a large chink in it.

I steeled myself. I'd seen people withstand the lynch mobs in Washington before, notably Ed Meese. I decided I'd hold on for six months and see whether things would cool off.

They didn't. And again, it was thanks largely to Mrs. R. She was reported in the press as having long objected to my fondness for low-cut dresses. Good Lord. She was making me sound like Mata Hari. If it hadn't hurt so much it might have made me laugh. I am one of the least glamorous dressers I know, a fact which was ratified when an Austrian fashion magazine named me to its list of worst-dressed women in the country, citing my frumpy clothes. I wore my one and only low-cut gown to the Vienna Opera Ball the previous February—only because décolletage is an old tradition at the Opera Ball. Anything less would have seemed underdressed.

But was I overreacting? What, after all, are a few catty remarks in the press? I hadn't worked hard for thirty years to be reduced to tears over an evening gown. I tried to focus on my work as ambassador.

I knew that the President was going to Germany on the trip which included the controversial stop at the Bitburg cemetery, so I contacted the State Department to see if a stopover in Austria might be added to his schedule.

"Forget it" was the response I received. I was stunned. The fellow at the other end of the line was a fourth-level State Department bureaucrat. It was unheard of to speak to an ambassador so rudely. And yet it was also highly instructive. If he felt he could speak to me that way, I must have fallen very far very fast in the State Department's regard. Soon the *Washingtonian* magazine carried an item saying that the President had canceled a trip to Austria because of me.

The effect of my fall from grace in Washington could be felt in Vienna as well. Austrian officials and press began to be skeptical about what I told them and began to double-check with their ambassador and the Austrian desk at the State Department. And even my staff in the embassy seemed less cooperative and respectful than they had been. Or did I imagine it?

I'd been in politics long enough to know that perception was just as important as reality, if not more so. Though I was sure that I was not in Ronald Reagan's bad graces, that was the perception. I began to accept the fact that I was beaten. It would be just a matter of time before the resignation.

———

In the midst of my gloom (I still loved being ambassador and hated the idea of giving it up) I was suddenly cheered up. On May 15, 1985, Austria was celebrating the thirtieth anniversary of the State Treaty. Each of the four allies who had occupied Austria after the war—Britain, France, the Soviet Union, and the United States—sent a delegation to the festivities. The American delegation included George Shultz, Bud McFarlane, and Richard Burt, Assistant Secretary of State for European Affairs.

I was as nervous as a cat before their arrival. I prepared every activity down to the minute for the length of their stay. I didn't want any awkward long silences. But to my great relief, they were extremely encouraging. Each one reassured me that I had his confidence and that there was no reason to think of resignation. Shultz simply cautioned me to be especially careful about the appearance of conflict of interest. They repeated their high marks for the job I was doing. Even Richard Burt, whom I had opposed as Assistant Secretary because I was unsure about his commitment to the President's ideas at the time, made a point of repeating in private that I had his full confidence.

It was like a cooling rain after a heat wave. I felt so refreshed. Later, I found out the reason for all this goodwill. Bud McFarlane told me that before they had left Washington, the President had announced that as of 1985 he wanted political ambassadors to stick to the same two-and-a-half-year rule of service that career ambassadors abided by. But, he added, there would be certain exceptions: Max Rabb in Italy, Charlie Price in England, Helene von Damm.

No wonder they were so kind to me. In the political world, there's usually only one reason for people's goodwill: power. Ronald Reagan had symbolically laid his protective hand on the top of my head, and now all of his lieutenants were bowing politely.

Unfortunately, the king's blessing didn't prove to have a very long shelf life.

Two weeks later, I returned to Washington for my annual State Department review. I was feeling so buoyant after the Shultz-McFarlane-Burt trip that I felt bold enough to request a private meeting with the President for Peter and me. I knew that was pressing my luck with Mrs. R—there's no way such an engagement would escape her attention—but I really wanted the President to meet my husband. I wanted to show them off to each other.

Nothing went right. It was almost as if Mrs. Reagan's influence reached even the airlines. Our trip over to the States was marred when the airline lost our baggage (it took two days to recover it). We were forced to attend a reception at the Bushes' in honor of Bob Hope that evening in the same clothes we had worn on the plane. At least no one could accuse me of looking too glamorous.

The following evening, Dan Terra hosted a wonderful black-tie dinner in my honor at the Jefferson Hotel on Sixteenth Street, just a few blocks from the White House. But there were conspicuous absences. Mike Deaver wasn't there. But that didn't really surprise me. I was hurt, however, that Bill Bennett, whom I had fought to place at the head of the National Endowment for the Humanities and who was now Secretary of Education, also stayed away without sending regrets. People said he had gotten close to Mrs. R in the last couple of years. He'll go far, I remember thinking ruefully. But I was bitter at the time. Much later, I talked to him about how hurt I had been and realized that I had overreacted. He had been so busy that he hadn't even known I was in trouble. His absence didn't mean he was disloyal.

Elaine Crispen and Kathy Osborne, both friends from my California days, were absent. So were other White House secretaries whom I had asked to be invited. I found an anonymous note in our hotel room later that night on White House stationery. It said simply, "Sorry, we were told to be busy tonight." Well, at least someone had had the urge to apologize. Still, most of my good friends did show up: the Hodels, Olmers, Nofzigers, Meeses, Tuttles (Bob Tuttle, Holmes Tuttle's son, had meanwhile taken over the top personnel job), Feulners, Whiteheads, and Roy Pfautch.

I felt certain that the meeting with the President, scheduled for the following day, would be canceled at any moment, because friends in the White House tipped me off that Mrs. Reagan was livid and that my sheer presence in Washington dominated her every minute. Had I not been so scared, angry, and hurt, I could have felt flattered by all the attention she gave me. But no call from the White House came that night. And no call came the following morning. It was a nice day, so Peter and I decided to walk to the White House. We entered at the gate on Pennsylvania Avenue. The guards remembered me and greeted me warmly. There are some people in Washington who don't calibrate their kindness according to who is up and who is down.

Once inside, however, I could feel a definite chill in the air. While we waited in the reception area (for a good twenty minutes), I called Kathy Osborne. She was nervous. I told her I'd like a photographer to record our visit. She seemed uncomfortable and stammered something about not being able to find one.

This was preposterous. There are several full-time photographers on the White House staff and one is always on duty to cover events in the Oval Office. It was all part of the icy treatment someone had decided I was to receive. It wasn't the end of the world. I had anticipated something like this. Stashed in my purse was a small 35 mm camera with a flash.

"I can't imagine what's keeping Don Regan," said Kathy, eager to change the subject from cameras and photographers.

"Why Don Regan?" I asked. She explained that he would be part of the meeting. More humiliation. I had always been able to meet with the President in private in the past. Now I was to be chaperoned. Besides, if anyone accompanied us it should have been Bud McFarlane, who arranged the meeting. Strange indeed.

Finally, Regan arrived and we all filed into the Oval Office. I introduced Peter to the President. He was all smiles and warmth as usual. I was certain that the poor treatment I was getting on this trip was completely unknown to him. Peter and I presented him with the Hungarian bridle we had brought as a gift. Before long we were having a lively conversation about horses and riding tricks. There was no mention of the rumors circulating that I might resign. Reagan was very much his old self. I couldn't sense any change in his feelings toward me. In fact, he looked somewhat disappointed when Don Regan made a conspicuous gesture of looking at his watch and announced that it was time to go.

"Oh, could we just take some pictures?" I asked. "Sorry," Regan replied. "There just isn't enough time." Having anticipated this, I responded by pulling my camera out of my purse. Regan looked dumbfounded. Was I actually asking the Chief of Staff of the White House, the man who had his own Secret Service detail, the man who liked to be called the "prime minister," to take pictures? Before he could say anything the President had jumped up and said, "Oh yes," and put his arms around Peter and me. Regan had no choice. He snapped pictures for us in several poses.

Peter could not believe how Byzantine the White House was. His experience in business had always been as the owner —the one others kowtowed to. He'd never before seen what it meant to be a staffer. And as a European, he was shocked at the kind of power apparently wielded by the First Lady. I shrugged. I was still feeling terrific because the President's fondness for me was undiminished and, I told myself, that's all that matters.

I was wrong again.

Still, the trip was not a complete disappointment. Nancy Reynolds, notwithstanding her close relationship with the First Lady, threw a wonderful party for me. It was Nancy at her best: a dinner on the terrace of her log cabin house in a woodsy suburb of Washington. Senator Pete Wilson (the one I'd had a crush on years earlier) was there with his new wife, as were Senator Hatfield and his wife, Antoinette, Craig Fuller and his wife, Karen, Dick and Gahl Burt, Bob Gray, Dennis Patrick, and many, many others.

———

On the way back to Austria, we stopped in London for a meeting of all the U.S. European ambassadors. At the end of the first day of the conference, I received word that George Shultz wanted to see me alone. He was staying with Charlie Price, our ambassador to Great Britain, and so I hailed a cab to Regents Park.

Shultz was affable as ever. We had tea. "How long do you plan to continue?" he asked after a decent interval of small talk. "The President thinks it might be a good idea if you started thinking of coming home."

I narrowed my eyes. "Did the President tell you that?"

"Not directly," replied Shultz. "Through Don Regan." I reflected ruefully on Don Regan's participation in my ouster. I had been instrumental in bringing him into the Administration in 1980. It must be true that no good deed goes unpunished! I could see the whole scenario before me. Mrs. R insisting that my time had come and leaning on Don Reagan to do something about it until he did. Why else would he bother with me? Anyone with the least bit of insight into White House operations knows that a Chief of Staff is much too busy to concern himself with an obscure ambassador. Out loud I protested that I had just seen the President a few days before. Nothing had been said about coming home. In fact, the President seemed as happy as ever with the job I was doing.

"Is that right," said Shultz mechanically. Obviously nothing I said was going to change anything. Nor was I required to respond now to his implied threat. We shook hands and I left feeling utterly defeated.

I pushed myself through the remainder of the conference like a robot. I didn't want the other ambassadors to know what had happened, though I was probably naïve to think they didn't already know. I was also considering my options. I felt sure President Reagan did not know what was being done in his name. If my resignation reached his desk, he'd have no reason in the world to assume it wasn't totally voluntary on my part. I thought of my options. I could do as Dan Terra did when he was once nudged to resign by Shultz. He simply told Shultz that Ronald Reagan appointed him and he would serve until the President told him otherwise. That was the end of that. Or I could contact Ed Meese or Holmes Tuttle, people who could see the President in private, away from the ever-present Don Regan. I knew he'd be shocked when he discovered what had been done behind his back.

Or was it really behind his back? I was suddenly beset by doubts. In the same way that the President might have reacted to a similar situation—I decided I didn't want to know.

On the plane ride over, I closed my eyes and began to think deeply. I always do my best thinking on airplanes. Something about being 35,000 feet over the earth and all its troubles helps to put things in perspective. I thought back on the many times during my tenure at personnel that I had told others in the Administration that bad press does matter, that their personal lives did matter, and that it was their responsibility to put the cause ahead of their own ambition. I thought about the fact that, to survive in my job, I'd have to lean on friends like Meese and Tuttle to intervene with the President and I really wasn't sure I wanted to impose on them. And if I succeeded in hanging on by my fingernails, what then? Would I still enjoy my job or would it have gone sour? In order to be effective, I had to be enthusiastic about my job. And finally, I wondered whether I wanted President Reagan to once again place his protective hand over me. If I asked for that, it was possible that the Helene von Damm issue would become a bone of contention between the President and his wife. Hadn't he already done enough for me?

By the time we reached the embassy residence, I knew what I had to do. Peter was sleepy after the trip, so I urged him to go up without me. I went into my study and got out a large yellow legal pad and began to compose my letter of resignation. I stayed up all night trying to find the right words. Finally I settled on these:

Dear Mr. President,
    You will recall that when I wrote you about my decision to marry Peter, I told you I was well aware of the potential consequences. For my own

part, I have always been cognizant of the priority
my official duties deserved.

Being at all times aware that public perceptions are as important as reality in the world in
which we live and work, however, I must recognize that there are voices that continue to assert a
conflict of interest between my professional responsibilities and my own personal situation. These
circumstances have led me to the conclusion that
the interests of our country and your own are best
served by your appointment of a new Ambassador
to Austria.

I noted in the postscript that I would always be Reagan's goodwill ambassador, and sent the letter off to be typed. I then
dragged myself upstairs, fell into bed, and cried.

The President accepted my resignation. It was over.
Though I've been to Washington several times since then, I've
never tried to see him and I've never called. Where would I
begin?

EPILOGUE

*T*HE COVERAGE MY RESIGNATION RECEIVED MADE ME livid. Newsweek ran a story titled "Playgirl Bows Out." The story said in part, "Always one to flout convention, von Damm stood out among the otherwise colorless White House staff. She favored striking, often low-cut dresses that were frowned upon by a First Lady who prefers women to be more demure."

I couldn't believe my eyes! Playgirl? I, who had worked since I was sixteen years old? Low-cut dresses? How ridiculous. I had never, ever worn a low-cut dress to work in the White House. The story was accompanied by a picture of Peter and me at the Opera Ball in Vienna—the one and only time I've appeared in public in a low-cut gown.

I had never been a crusading feminist, but I did wonder if a man would have gotten similar treatment. No, that's not true. I didn't wonder. I knew from my experience in government and as an ambassador that a man would not have been treated as I was. As Georgie Ann Geyer summed up in an article about me, "Perhaps we are witnessing a new stage, women can 'make it' but watch out! It's okay for men's lives to change and develop—and their home lives either change with them or become forsaken and irrelevant—but not for women's. It's not okay to do the frank things." The double standard is alive and well.

My biggest consolation was the Austrian press. There wasn't a paper which didn't editorialize about the great job I had done and express astonishment that my accomplishments didn't weigh heavier than any embarrassment the Administration may have felt about my new marriage.

After my resignation, I was hit by the shattering realization that my life for the past twenty years had revolved around Ronald Reagan. Suddenly, my life had lost its center.

Peter was a great socialite, so I was not at a loss for things to fill my time. There were dinner parties, concerts, plays, hunts, sports, hikes, and books. I enjoyed all of that. But my heart was still with Ronald Reagan and his Administration.

I still scoured the newspapers for stories about the boss and how things were going at home. I got several American newspapers and magazines delivered as well. I couldn't seem to cut the ties—less so with each unfolding drama.

Mike Deaver had finally gotten his wish at the start of the second term and had opened his own public relations firm. He quickly acquired prestige clients like TWA and the government of Canada. But Mike's ego got the better of him. He "went Hollywood," as we used to say. For someone who was such a great p.r. man for Ronald Reagan, he showed abominable judgment in allowing himself to appear on the cover of *Time* magazine, in a limousine, telephone to his ear, with the caption "Who's this man calling?" Nancy Reagan apparently told him after she saw the cover, "You're going to wish you hadn't done this." And boy, did he ever. Within a few months, Mike was under investigation by a special prosecutor for violating the Ethics in Government Act. The charge was that he had lobbied his former office—i.e., the White House—within one year of leaving office. In the end, they couldn't get enough evidence for an indictment on that charge, but they did get him for perjury.

I had mixed feelings about Mike. When he was really in trouble I was inclined to forgive and forget all of the insults and hurts we Californians had felt at his hands and his betrayal of the Reagan agenda. I felt sorry for him because there was no one there to lick his wounds.

In contrast, everyone's heart went out to Lyn Nofziger. Lyn was indicted by a special prosecutor for violations of the Ethics in Government Act. But unlike Mike, who was brought down by his own arrogance, I really believe that Lyn slipped up on some of the technicalities of the law because he was being Lyn—informal, unflappable, giving little attention to details.

And, of course, poor Ed Meese, the good government man who had become the bête noire of the liberals for reasons that I believe were mostly political (though there is no denying that his methods were sloppy and his judgment poor in allowing himself repeatedly to be used by others for their own gain). He was always the staunch conservative standard-bearer in the Administration, and so he was dogged every step of the way for almost his entire tenure in Washington. He was probably the most scrutinized and investigated senior official in any recent Administration who has been cleared of any offense.

And then, of course, the first Californian, Ronald Reagan, didn't do so well in his second term either. I was grieved to see how badly served he was by those around him: first on Bitburg (which I feel was the result of Mike's having one foot out the door already and not paying close enough attention), and then on the Iran/Contra affair.

I think his second term, though by no means a failure, took a course which was a real disappointment to true Reaganites. Despite a landslide reelection mandate, there wasn't a single major domestic initiative other than tax reform. In fact, as I look back at the entire Administration, I'd have to say that where Ronald Reagan erred was in failing to appreciate what the people around him did. If he had stuck with the original band of Californians—Meese, Clark, Nofziger, Deaver (who might not have sold out if Baker hadn't been made Chief of Staff), and Cap Weinberger—I think he and the goals of the Reagan Revolution would have been protected. For, unlike many others who joined the Reagan team later, they did not have their own agenda. It is ironic—but perhaps it was predictable—that Ronald Reagan's political and governmental career should end surrounded largely by advisers who in all probability had spent their earlier years laughing at him. This is not to say that an infusion of new blood and talent wasn't necessary, but that could have been accomplished without forsaking the others. But by the time he was hit with the most damaging crisis of his presidency, the Iran/Contra affair, only Meese and Weinberger were still on the team and their voices were drowned out by others who didn't know President Reagan as well.

I'm not saying that these advisers didn't want to serve him well. I'm just saying that they lacked time and memory with him. They didn't know his strengths and weaknesses. (Though this didn't show up as much during Baker's tenure since he had some of the Californians with him in the White House.) They didn't feel comfortable with his political instincts, and were always trying to move him to positions *they* thought would be more politically acceptable.

Just how little they understood him was revealed in the books Regan, Stockman, and Speakes wrote. They all felt unappreciated by Ronald Reagan. Regan noted bitterly that he received an impersonal form letter as his thank-you for his service.

No question, President Reagan could have saved himself a lot of trouble if he had learned to pat people on the back. He did it when we nudged him, but it was not natural for him to express gratitude or admiration for a job well done. We Californians knew this, but more important, we also knew that this didn't mean he was unappreciative or took us for granted.

I just know that the Iran/Contra affair would never have

happened if Bill Clark had remained at NSC. Bill was so careful. Under his leadership only the most carefully thought out options would have been presented to the President. Bill would also have been a cautionary voice where George Shultz was concerned. He would have reminded President Reagan constantly of first principles. Nor would he allow the President's attention to drift. Those who knew him for over twenty years knew all of his little habits. It got so we could feel when he was getting bored or distracted, and we'd find a way to bring his attention back to the subject at hand. Bill Clark and Ed Meese both cultivated very direct styles of speaking. No circumlocution. They got straight to the point, and they'd maintain eye contact with him as they spoke. As soon as his eyes wandered, they'd try another approach.

I felt sorry for Bud McFarlane when he lamented that he was never able to get through to President Reagan, to connect. But I think he badly misjudged the reasons. He thought it had something to do with the fact that he was a career military officer and not a self-made millionaire like Casey or Weinberger. But that had nothing to do with it. Ronald Reagan doesn't decide who to listen to on the basis of their bankbook. It was probably Bud's unfortunately dull style of speaking. He had lots to say, and he was articulate, but his delivery just didn't suit the President. It wasn't Bud's fault.

The Californians could also tell Ronald Reagan the truth without fearing that they were jeopardizing their jobs in the process, or that they were showing insufficient respect for the office. It's kind of interesting that the only aide who used to call Ronald Reagan by his first name was one of the first to be eased out: Lyn Nofziger.

It's ironic that until the Iran/Contra affair, President Reagan was constantly praised for his management style. He had innumerable strengths, but that wasn't one of them. In fact, never in his whole life did he understand how to manage a staff or appreciate the importance of staff work.

In his first career as a sportscaster he worked pretty much alone. The same was true of his acting days. When he was president of the Screen Actors Guild, he had a tiny staff of a typist or two, but that's all. As a writer and lecturer, he was again a lone wolf. Only when he was elected Governor of California, in late middle age, did he have the responsibility of choosing and managing a team.

But he didn't learn from the California experience. The kitchen cabinet more or less took over the personnel arrangements for him. They recommended a wonderful team which served him well for years. But President Reagan never understood how well.

Mrs. Reagan didn't understand either, and as her influence grew, the Administration came to lean more and more on traditional, mainstream Washington fixtures instead of on movement conservatives. She thought she was doing her best to make her husband popular, but without people around him with an institutional memory, she was actually robbing him of his best protection.

But in the last analysis, his shortcomings now being well known to the American people, Ronald Reagan will be remembered as one of the great Presidents of our century. By sheer force of personality, he lifted the spirits of an entire nation which had been languishing in a period of self-doubt following Vietnam, Watergate, and the Carter years. He rebuilt American prestige around the globe and he restored our economy and defenses. By rebuilding America's strength, he forced the Soviets to the conference table and a more cooperative attitude. President Reagan called into question the assumption that more government is always the answer to every problem. And he restored to their proper places of respect traditional Judeo-Christian values. It was a tall order, but he was a giant.

As for me, my Cinderella story did not conclude with the heroine living happily ever after with her handsome prince. When the cold light of dawn illuminated my new life as Mrs. Peter Gürtler, the romance was soon replaced by a nightmare.

I should have heeded my first impression of Peter. He

appeared to be a man not interested in a partnership or settling down. He was interested in wooing the Madam Ambassador—the most talked about woman in Austria—and wanted to conquer her, whatever the price. Peter apparently had never bargained for simply a wife because he quickly lost interest in Mrs. Gürtler. Already, six months after relinquishing my diplomatic post, he declared the marriage over. It was without warning, emotion, or a trace of guilt. I was totally shattered by it and feeling utterly helpless, for nothing I did or said made any difference. One might be tempted to analyze the deeper psychological reasons for such incomprehensible and brutal behavior, but in the end, all that matters is reality—and it was grim.

Perhaps I should have seen it coming. If that seems obvious, I can only say that it's hard to understand how people can be swept away by temptation until you are actually tempted yourself.

It was soon apparent that I had taken one risk too many—this time with too much to lose. I alone was paying the price for what had begun as a joint venture. I had given up my independence for the handsome prince, and now that I no longer had him, what did I have? I felt as if I'd fallen into an abyss. The fall was so deep and so hard that for the first time in my life I felt caught in the grip of despair.

At the age of forty-eight I suddenly found myself with no career, no income, no goals, and no country. It was deeply frightening—and it was ironic that I was feeling this fear in the same city where I had felt it thirty years earlier. But back then I had been full of restless energy. Now I was tired.

It took about a year for me to pull myself together and think about the future. And then something interesting happened. My outlook on my situation flipped 180 degrees. Instead of seeing myself as having thrown away everything I had built up over thirty years, I suddenly saw myself as free in a completely new way.

For the first time, I didn't need a job, a man, or a movement to make me feel worthy. In the past I had always pushed and pushed for the next accomplishment, the higher peak. I never rested on my laurels—in fact, I never rested. I was always trying to prove myself. But now, I knew that everything which had made my previous success possible was inside me, and I didn't have to prove anything anymore. Peace began to descend on my soul.

I don't say that my way is best. I have always been a risk taker and I've had my share of suffering as a result. But I do think I had incredible good fortune as well: the chance to know and serve President Reagan, the development of really deep and sustaining friendships, the chance to spend the last years of my mother's life with her in Austria, and the chance to participate in the government of the United States.

I have lived a full life. Now I'm not scaling any new mountains. For the time being, I'd like to slow down and reflect for a time. But I don't guarantee how long that will last. We are what we are.

I hope my California friends too are readjusting well to normal life, away from cameras and press calls. We fought hard. We did a lot of good. We made some mistakes. It was all worth it.

I truly believe President and Mrs. Reagan know it.

Index

Abbott, George and Janice, 111, 287
Abbott, Shirley, 246–47
Abernethy, Ann Elizabeth, 131
Abramovitz, Mort, 245
Adams, Joey, 286
Advance work in politics, 88–89
Agee, William, 94
Air Force One, 177–78
Alfieri, Frank, 263
Allen, Richard, 149
    assassination attempt on Reagan, reaction to, 193
    National Security Adviser, 183, 201–2, 223–24, 231
    presidential campaign of 1980, 117
Ambassadorial appointments, 246–49
American Medical Political Action Committee (AMPAC), 33–35, 38
Anderson, John, 122, 222
Anderson, Marty, 118
Annenberg, Lenore, 113, 175
Annenberg, Walter, 113, 295–96

Armstrong, Anne, 128, 129–30, 135, 136–37
Arnold, Capt., 19
Atlantic Monthly magazine, 222
Austria
    Anschluss, 1–2
    Soviet occupation, 6–9
    Von Damm's ambassadorial activities, 278–87
    World War II, 2–5
    See also Vienna

Baier, Kittie, 86
Baker, Howard, 130, 204
Baker, James A., III, 156, 182, 211, 213, 217–18, 220, 234
    Cabinet selections for Reagan Administration, 135
    Chief of Staff, selection as, 143–44
    Commerce Secretary, considered for, 128
    conservatives, actions against, 225, 233, 234, 240, 249

Deaver, relations with, 168–69, 196–97
Frechette appointment, 242
National Security Adviser, wish to be, 292–94
political appointments, involvement in, 252–55
as political moderate, 166
presidential campaign of 1980, 117, 122
press, relations with, 168
Stockman's interview, 223
tax hike of 1982, 167
Treasury Secretary, 61, 305–6
U.S.–Soviet relations, attitude toward, 291
Von Damm's assessment of, 165–68
White House barbershop dispute, 163
White House staff meetings, 179, 180, 252
Baldrige, Malcolm, 139–40, 144–45, 183
Baldrige, "Tish," 141
Battaglia, Phil, 45, 56
Beene, Geoffrey, 284
Belize, U.S. Ambassador to, 246–47
Bendix Corporation, 94
Bennet, Bill, 76
Bennett, William, 214–16, 310
Bernstein, Leonard, 287
Bird, Rose, 79
Black, Charlie, 111
Bloomingdale, Al, 62, 130, 138
Böhm, Karl and Lisl, 16, 199, 278
Bolan, Tom, 103, 111, 287
Borcherdt, Wendy, 147, 246
Boyette, Roger, 58
Bradford, M. E., 216
Bradley, Bill, 274
Brady, Jim, 193, 194

Brady, Sarah, 194
Brandon, Mabel (Muffie), 176, 186
Brazil, Marc, 121, 230
Brown, Jerry, 79, 258
Brown, "Pat," 66
Bryan, Jane, 62
Buchbinder, Rudolf, 287
Buckley, Peggy, 245
Buckley, William F., 286
Bulen, Keith, 115
Burt, Richard, 309, 312
Bush, George, 90, 159, 231
    assassination attempt on Reagan, reaction to, 195
    presidential campaign of 1980, 101, 117
    Von Damm's assessment of, 165

Cabinet selections for Reagan Administration
    Cabinet officers, 120–21, 126–40, 169–70
    substaffing, 144–45, 146–48, 150–51
Campbell, Glenn, 133
Campbell, Rita, 130
Capital punishment, Reagan's attitude toward, 66
Carlucci, Frank, 129, 130, 133, 144, 148, 263, 264
Carmen, Jerry, 115
Carson, Johnny, 154
Carter, Jimmy, 101, 116, 122, 123
Casey, William, ix, 128, 132, 170, 233
    assassination attempt on Reagan, reaction to, 193
    Cabinet selections for Reagan Administration, 134
    CIA directorship, 127–28, 137, 139

Clark's replacement at NSC,
  selection of, 293
Menges, support for, 243, 244
presidential campaign of 1980,
  101–2, 107, 117, 118–19
Cavanaugh, James, 145, 146, 189
Chancellor, John, 82
Chisholm, Shirley, 149–50
Christopher, George, 44, 55
Citizens for the Republic
  (Reagan's political action
  committee), 83
Clark, Joan, 49
Clark, Monica, 250
Clark, William P., 55, 68, 165,
  183, 184, 201, 202, 234,
  235, 262, 265–66, 299
  Attorney General, considered
    for, 136, 139
  Cabinet Secretary in California,
    46–47, 49–50, 52–53
  cars, interest in, 51 52
  Deputy Secretary of State, 169–
    70, 230–31
  Executive Secretary in
    California, 56
  flying by, 48–49, 261
  foreign policy formulation, 233
  Interior Secretary, 292
  judicial career, 56–57, 79
  Latin America, views on, 243
  Lebanon, U.S. Marines in, 292
  legal career, 49
  "mini-memos" for Reagan, 52
  National Security Adviser, 201–
    2, 223–24, 231–32, 289–
    93
  presidential campaign of 1980,
    116
  Nancy Reagan's campaign
    against, 233, 290–91
  Soviets, attitude toward, 241,
    290–92

Terra's appointment, 173–74
value to Reagan, 320
Von Damm hired by, 46
Von Damm's ambassadorial
  appointment, ix, 272, 276
on von Damm's divorce from
  Leeds, 302
Von Damm's move to
  Personnel Office, 206–7
on von Damm's second
  marriage, 74
Washington lifestyle, 229–30
as Westerner, 48
White House staff selections,
  role in, 143–44
worldview of, 232
Classified documents, 159–60
Clements, Bill, 128, 136, 258–59
Cohn, Roy, 102–3, 275
Communism, von Damm's attitude
  toward, 44
Congressional elections of 1982,
  258–59
Connally, John, 98, 101, 128,
  130, 138
Conscience of a Conservative, The
  (Goldwater), 38
Coors, Joe, 132, 133
Coro Foundation, 90–91
Corporation for Public
  Broadcasting, appointment
  of chairman for, 217–19
Cowen, Philip, 263
Cribb, Ken, 253
Crispen, Elaine, 86, 169, 310
Cronkite, Walter, 82
Cummings, Ted, 126, 129, 268
Czerny, Karen, 281

Dam, Kenneth, 130
Dana, Norma, 112
Darman, Dick, ix, 254

Dart, Justin, 62, 126, 130, 133, 138
Davis, Kathy, 59
Davis, Loyal, 72
Dean, Leamond, 287
Deaver, Carolyn, 47, 208, 287
Deaver, Michael K., ix, 33, 72, 75, 83, 94, 143, 156, 158, 165, 186, 213, 217–18, 231, 234, 310
  ambitiousness of, 196–97
  assassination attempt on Reagan, reaction to, 194, 195
  Baker, relations with, 168–69, 196–97
  Baker's selection as Chief of Staff, 143
  Chief of Staff, wish to be, 292–94
  Clark's deputy in California, 47
  Clark's selection as National Security Adviser, 201, 223
  conservatives, actions against, 225, 233, 234, 240, 249
  cooking, enjoyment of, 48
  decision-making by, 197
  Deputy Chief of Staff, selection as, 144
  Donovan affair, 237
  fickleness of, 47–48
  Frechette appointment, 242
  legal problems, 317–18
  letters and phone calls to Reagan, control of, 182
  political appointments, role in, 252–55
  power in the White House, 195–99
  presidential campaign of 1976, 80
  presidential campaign of 1980, 97, 98, 110–11, 118, 124–25
  press, relations with, 168
  public relations firms
    in California, 78, 87
    in Washington, 305, 317
  N. Reagan, friendship with, 70, 198
  staff of, 197–98
  state dinner guest lists, 176–77
  Stockman's interview, 223
  U.S.–Soviet relations, attitude toward, 291
  Von Damm's advance work, 87, 89–90
  Von Damm's ambassadorial appointment, 272, 276
  Von Damm's move to Personnel Office, 206, 207
  Von Damm's White House position, 145–46
  White House barbershop dispute, 163, 164
  White House office of, 160–61
Debates in presidential campaigns, 116–17, 122–23
Defense Department, personnel appointments in, 262–65
Dellinger, Dottie, 86
De Mille, Cecil B., 86
Deutsch, Armand, 220
Disclosure laws, 191
Dobrynin, Anatoly, 241, 291–92
Dole, Elizabeth, 128, 132–33, 180, 204–5, 229, 248, 251, 252, 266, 267
Dole, Robert, 127
Donovan, Raymond, ix, 72
  Labor Secretary, 130, 137–38, 139, 144–45
  legal problems, 142, 191, 236–37
  presidential campaign of 1980, 130, 137–38, 139, 144–45
Donovan, Wild Bill, 119

Dorrell, Claire, 86, 93
Duberstein, Ken, 158, 251
Dunlop, Becky Norton, 212–13,
    214, 235

Eagleburger, Larry, ix, 170, 245,
    274, 277, 279
East, John, 216
Eckard, Fred, 177
Economic Recovery Tax Act, 203
Elliott, Lee Ann, ix, 33–34, 36,
    37, 38–39, 95
El Salvador, U.S. policy toward,
    157
Emmerich, Klaus, 140
Empire State Building, 29
Enders, Thomas, 243
Erlangen, Germany, 19–24

Faillace, Tony, 103, 107, 286
Farrell, Mike, 212
Fenwick, Millicent, 150, 258
Fernandez, Ben, 130
Fielding, Fred, 149, 189–90, 208,
    213, 229, 251
Fine, Bill, 111–12
Fischer, Dave, 90, 169, 181, 194–
    95, 201
Foley, Tom, 204
Folger Shakespeare Library party,
    187–88
Ford, Gerald, 80, 82, 119
Foreign policy of Reagan
    Administration, 232–34,
    240–44
Fourth of July parties, 202–3, 286
Frechette, Miles, 242–43
Friedersdorf, Max, 158, 229
Fuller, Craig, 90, 169, 254, 312
Furino, Fred, 236

Galvin, John, 40
Gaspard, Leon, 276

Gayman, Pat, 59
Gergen, David, 157, 158, 193
Geyer, Georgie Ann, 316–17
Ginzburg, Douglas, 172
Goldwater, Barry, 38, 53, 138
Gorbachev, Mikhail, 241
Gottfurcht, Fred and Helen, 287,
    297
Gotthelf, Ida and Joe, 230
Graham, Katharine, 196
Grain embargo against Soviets,
    157
Granville, Bonita, 62
Gray, Bob, 132, 137, 149, 312
Gray, Solon, 58
Great Britain, U.S. Ambassador
    to, 151–52
Greider, William, 222
Gürtler, Peter (fourth husband),
    306, 317
    divorce from von Damm, 321–
    22
    first meetings with, 299, 300
    marriage to, 303–4
    Reagan, meeting with, 310–12

Hadad, Col., 209
Haig, Alexander, 201, 223
    assassination attempt on Reagan,
    reaction to, 193–94
    foreign policy frustrations, 232–
    33
    "power play" by, 156
    resignation of, 233–34
    Secretary of Defense,
    considered for, 128, 135
    Secretary of State, appointment
    as, 130, 145, 170
Hanley, Allie and Lee, 104
Hannaford, Peter, 78, 83
Hare, Mary, 32
Harlow, Jean, 113
Harper, Ed, 229, 251

Hartford Steam Boiler Insurance and Inspection Company, 27–28, 32, 33, 34
Hatch, Orrin, 138
Hatfield, Mark, 149, 154, 312
Health and Human Services, Department of, 259–60
Hearst, Patty, 66
Hearst, William Randolph, 66
Heckler, Margaret, 258, 259–60
Heldridge, Missy, 79
Helga (friend in Germany), 23
Helms, Jesse, 81, 148, 216
Herrington, John, 205
Hickel, Walter, 129
Hinckley, John, 194
Hitler, Adolf, 1
Hodsoll, Frank, 220
Hollander, Robert B., 215
Holocaust, the, 21–22
Holtzman, Evie and Seymour, 287
Holtzman, Marc, 79, 175–76
Hope, Bob, 154
Human Events magazine, 182

Inauguration of 1981, 153–56
Inman, Bobby, 138
Iran/Contra affair, 240, 306, 318, 319–20
Ireland, U.S. Ambassador to, 172–73
Israel, von Damm's visit to, 207–9

James, Pendleton, 147, 148, 151, 229
    Cabinet selections for Reagan Administration, 120–21, 126, 127, 128, 129, 130, 134, 136, 139
    Presidential Personnel Office, director of, 171–72, 173, 211, 212, 246, 251
Jeepers Jamboree (jeep race), 58

Jefferson, Thomas, 39
John Paul II, Pope, 282
Johnson, Lorraine, 59
Johnson, Lyndon, 177
Jorgensen, Earle, 62, 201
Jorgensen, Marion, 201
Judicial appointments, 213–14
Justice Department, political appointments in, 213

Kaminsky, Phyllis, 207, 208–9, 307
Kassebaum, Nancy, 267, 274–75
Kazanjian, Carol, 36
Kelly, Gene, 114
Kemp, Jack, 106, 204
Kennedy, Edward, 122
Kennedy Center, Presidential Box of, 161–62
Kingsbury, Heide, 57–58, 250
Kinser, Dick, 263
Kirschläger, Rudolf, 280
Kirkpatrick, Jeane, 122, 234, 240, 243, 266, 267, 286, 294
Kissinger, Henry, 130, 154, 163, 286
Kitchen cabinet, 61–62, 82, 126–31, 132–39, 146–49
Klestil, Thomas, 275
Kohl, Walter, 281
Kollek, Teddy, 209
Kruger, Helen, 59

Lake, Jim, 97, 111
Latin America, U.S. policy on, 241–44
Lautenberg, Frank, 258, 274
Laxalt, Paul, 63, 74, 82, 225
    Cabinet selections for Reagan Administration, 126, 127, 129, 130, 136, 137, 138
Lebanon, U.S. Marines in, 292

Leeds, Byron (third husband),
119, 120, 123, 141, 149,
251, 258, 286
breakup of marriage with, 297–
303
business, sale of, 270–71
in Germany with (1940s), 20–
22
honeymoon with, 199–200
inauguration of 1981, 154, 155,
156
Jewish heritage, 21–22
marriage to, 199
married life, 200–1, 236, 261
Pope, meeting with, 282
reunions with,
1963, 92–93
1976, 93–94
Von Damm's swearing-in
ceremony, vii–viii, ix
Leeds, Marsha, 92
Leeds, Michael, 154
Leeds, Warren, 154
Lewis, Drew, ix, 82, 105, 107–8,
123, 130, 132, 138, 139,
144, 166, 191, 305–6
Lewis, Marilyn, 123, 174–75
Liechtenstein, Prince and Princess
of, 287
Little Hoover Commission, 54–55
Lodge, John, 248, 249
Long, Preston, 103, 107
Louis, John J., Jr., 151–52
Lowe, Marvin, 29–32, 33, 36, 38
Lowe, Sylva, 30, 38
Luers, Bill, 246
Lugar, Richard, 274
Lyng, Richard, 127

Maazel, Lorin, 287
McCann, William, 104, 172–73
McCarthy, Joseph, 102

McDonald, Charles (first
husband), 24–25
divorce from, 30–31
marriage to, 24
married life with, 26–27, 28
McFarlane, Robert C., 294, 309,
320
McPherson, Peter, 189
Malone, Patrice, 121
Mann, Ron, 213, 238
Maseng, Mari, 267
Mason, Morgan, 175
Mathias, Charles (Mac), 247, 274
Mauthausen concentration camp,
22
Medical care, public and private,
38
Meese, Edwin, III, ix, 79, 132,
148, 156, 165, 217–18,
235, 266
Attorney General, 173
Cabinet selections for Reagan
Administration, 126, 135,
137
Clark's replacement at NSC,
selection of, 293
conservative views of, 198–99
Counselor to the President,
143–44, 195–96
Donovan affair, 236
Executive Secretary in
California, 68
Frechette appointment, 242
legal problems of, 307, 318
judicial appointments, role in,
213
political appointments, role in,
252–55
power in the White House,
195–96
presidential campaign of 1976,
80

presidential campaign of 1980, 116, 117, 118, 120, 121
Reagan, intuitive understanding with, 69, 198–99
Reagan's political action committee, 83
son's death, 237–38
speaking style of, 320
Stockman's interview, 223
Von Damm's assessment of, 68–69, 167–68
Whittlesey, defense of, 248
Meese, Scott, 237
Meese, Ursula, 208, 237–38
Menges, Constantine, 243, 244
Michel, Bob, 204, 258
Miller, Joe, 187
Morris, Jay, 131
Motley, Anthony, 243–44

National Endowment for the Arts, appointment of chairman for, 220
National Endowment for the Humanities, appointment of chairman for, 214–16
National Governors' Conference of 1968, 63
National Journal, 192
National Review, 119, 182
Newman, Bonnie, 212, 250
Nicaragua, U.S. policy toward, 233, 243
Niles, Tom, 245–46
Nixon, Richard, 79, 133
Nofziger, Lyn, ix, 79, 136, 143, 165, 191, 260, 266
    departure from White House, 225–27
    legal problems, 318
    political liaison position, 169
    presidential campaign of 1980, 97–98, 118

press secretary in California, 53–54
Reagan's political action committee, 83
Stockman's interview, 223
Nunn, Sam, 128

Ohland, Leslie, 86
Old Executive Office Building, 210–11
Olmer, Judy, 230
Olmer, Lionel, ix, 230
O'Neill, Thomas P. (Tip), 203, 204
Orfila, Alejandro, 275
Orr, Robin, 141
Orr, Verne and Joann, 123
Osborne, Kathy, 58, 205–6, 255, 310, 311
Osmond, Marie, 154

Party circuit in Washington, 187–88
Patrick, Dennis, ix, 212, 213, 235, 312
Pell, Claiborne, 274
Pentagon comptroller, appointment of, 262–64
Percy, Charles, 217, 218–19, 274, 275
Perle, Richard, 175
Perrin, William, 246
Pershing missiles in Europe, controversy regarding, 284–85
Perskie, Debra, 154
Peru, von Damm's visit to, 250
Pfautch, Roy, 187, 226, 276
Pierce, Samuel, 130, 138
Poindexter, Adm. John, 244
Presidential Personnel, Office of, 205–7, 210–21, 227–28,

238–40, 242, 246–48, 250–55, 262–65

President's Advisory Commission on the Arts, 220

Price, Mr. and Mrs. Charles, II, 287, 309

Professional Air Traffic Controllers' Organization (PATCO), strike by, 207

Puritano, Vincent, 263, 264

Quinn, Art, 131

Rabb, Maxwell, 101, 102, 107, 177, 309

Rather, Dan, 193

Raugh, Janet and Gary, 75

Ray, Robert, 127

Reagan, Maureen, 229

Reagan, Nancy, ix, 49, 165, 202, 317
  ambassadorial appointments, role in, 151
  Arts Commission chairman, 220
  assassination attempt on Reagan, reaction to, 195
  astrology, interest in, 229
  Baker's selection as Chief of Staff, 143
  Clark, campaign against, 233, 290–91
  conservatives, actions against, 225, 233, 240
  Deaver, friendship with, 70, 198
  demanding nature of, 70–72
  Donovan affair, 237
  elegance, sense of, 186
  friends, treatment of, 70
  letters and phone calls to Reagan, control of, 182
  Nofziger, attitude toward, 225
  personnel appointments, role in, 227–28
  as "power behind the throne," 228–29, 321
  presidential campaign of 1980, 98, 99, 111, 112, 117
  press secretary for, 141
  Reagan, relationship with, 71–72
  Reagan's image, concern for, 72
  resilience of, 186–87
  social secretary for, 186
  Soviet policy, influence on, 241, 290–92
  state dinner guest lists, 176–77
  unforgiving nature of, 294–95
  Von Damm, campaign against, 306–8, 313
  Von Damm, kindness toward, 85–86
  Von Damm's advance work for Reagan, opposition to, 89–90
  Von Damm's ambassadorial appointment, opposition to, 271–73, 288, 294–95, 296
  Von Damm's first meeting with, 69–70

Reagan, Ronald, 73, 75, 91, 132, 176, 191, 220
  Ambassador to Great Britain, selection of, 151
  assassination attempt on, 192–95
  Baker selected as Chief of Staff, 143
  Cabinet meetings, 53, 150
  Cabinet selections, 127, 135, 136, 137, 138–39
  Camp David weekends, 224
  capital punishment, attitude toward, 66
  chair used by, 155–56

Clark's replacement at NSC, selection of, 292–94
correspondence, publication of, 79
Donovan affair, 237
eating habits, 184
first days as President, 157
foreign policy formulation, 233
generosity of, 67–68
as governor, 52–53, 64–68
greatness of, 321
gubernatorial campaign of 1966, 61–62
Gürtler and von Damm, meeting with, 310–12
hair-dying controversy, 185
Harlem, lost in, 89
Heckler affair, 260
"inner self," 60–61
on Israel, 209
judicial appointments, 213–14
kindness of, 185
Lebanon, U.S. Marines in, 292
management style, 244–45, 320–21
Meese, intuitive understanding with, 69, 198–99
"mini-memos" for, 52
national security briefings, 231–32
Nofziger and, 226
PATCO strike, 207
personnel matters, approach to, 224–26, 255–56, 263–65
philosophy of government, 66–67
political actions committee for, 83
political success, secret of, 67
presidential campaign of 1976, 80, 81–83
presidential campaign of 1980, 111, 116–18, 122–23, 124

Nancy Reagan, relationship with, 71–72
religious beliefs, 61
security measures, disregard for, 63–64
Soviets, policy toward, 241
speaking tours (1970s), 78–79
speeches by, 39–40, 158–59, 204
Stockman's interview, 223
tax cut legislation, 203–5
taxes, attitude toward, 64–65
tax hike of 1982, 167
temperament of, 60, 184
Terra's appointment, 174
Von Damm, feelings for, 59–60
Von Damm, private conversations with, 184
Von Damm's ambassadorial appointment, viii–ix, 269, 270, 287–88, 313–14, 315
Von Damm's move to Personnel Office, 206
weaknesses of his presidency, 318–21
White House barbershop dispute, 164
wit and humor of, 61
women, attitude toward, 149, 267
work habits, 182–83
Reagan Administration
Cabinet meetings, 150
Cabinet selections, 120–21, 126–40
confirmation of, 169–70
Cabinet substaffing, 144–45, 146–48, 150–51
foreign policy, 232–34, 240–44
kitchen cabinet, role of, 126–31, 132–39, 146–49
tax cut legislation, 203–5

women in, 174–75, 267–68
See also White House
Reagan gubernatorial campaign of
    1966, 42–45, 61–62
Reagan presidential campaign of
    1976, 80–83
Reagan presidential campaign of
    1980, 96
    campaign managers, 97–98, 118
    candidacy announcement dinner,
        105–9
    debates, 116–17, 122–23
    finance operation, 98–106, 111–
        15, 118–19
    general election victory, 123–24
    infighting, 110–11, 115, 117
    Iowa caucus, 116–17
    nomination, 119
    personnel changes, 118
    primary victories, 118–19
Reed, Tom, 45
Regan, Donald, 61, 149, 193, 313
    book written by, 319
    Chief of Staff, 228, 229, 260,
        305, 306, 311, 312
    presidential campaign of 1980,
        103, 142
    Treasury Secretary, 142
Republican Convention of 1976,
    81–83
Republican Convention of 1980,
    119
Republican National Committee,
    92
Reynolds, Nancy, 53–54, 78, 86,
    94, 95, 99–100, 140–41,
    149, 229, 312
Rhodes, James, 129
Roberts, Wayne, 131
Robinson, Gil, 295
Robinson, Natalie, 202
Robinson, Paul, 177
Roche, George, 129

Rockefeller, Jay, 217
Rockefeller, Nelson, 55
Rockefeller, Sharon Percy, 217–19
Rogers, John, 266
Roosevelt, Selwa (Lucky), viii
Rostenkowski, Dan, 204
Rubel, Cy, 61
Rumsfeld, Donald, 128–29, 130
Rymer, Pam, 214

Safire, Bill, 229
St. Cyr, Lindy, 252
Salvatori, Henry, 61, 147
Savickas, Evelyn, 28
Scharffenberger, George, 128
Schiavone, Chris, 121
Schiavone, Ronald, 103–4
Schier, Wendy, 154
Schmidl (gardener in Austria), 297
Schmidt, Helmut, 135
Schrieber, Taft, 61
Schweiker, Richard, 82, 97, 130,
    133, 138, 139, 149, 203
Sears, John, 80, 81, 82, 83, 97,
    98, 110–11, 116–18
Secret Service, 160
Senatorial courtesy, 247
Sexism in government, 265–67
Shad, John, 102, 107, 173, 275
Shoup, Shirley, 36
Shultz, George, 130, 135, 140,
    306, 309, 313
    Clark's replacement at NSC,
        selection of, 294
    Lebanon, U.S. Marines in, 292
    Secretary of State, appointment
        as, 234
    State Department political
        appointments, 239–40,
        241–42
    U.S.–Soviet relations, attitude
        toward, 291
Silverman, Leon, 236, 237

Simon, William E., 101, 106
  Cabinet selections for Reagan
    Administration, 126, 127,
    128, 129, 130–31, 133–34,
    136, 140
Sinatra, Frank, 67, 104, 150, 154,
    287
Sincerely, Ronald Reagan (book), 79
Smith, Ben, 103, 107
Smith, William Bell, 185
Smith, William French, 62, 170,
    173
  Cabinet selections for Reagan
    Administration, 126, 127,
    128, 130–31, 136, 138,
    139
Soviet Union
  Austria, occupation of, 6–9
  disinformation activities, 281
  U.S. grain embargo, 157
  U.S. policy toward, 240–41,
    290–92
Sowell, Thomas, 129
Speakes, Larry, 319
Spencer, Stu, 62, 80, 236, 295
Stack, Robert, 109
Stahl, Leslie, 222
State Department
  ambassadorial appointments,
    246–49
  foreign service officers, 245–46
  independence from White
    House, 244
  political appointees, 235–36,
    238–40, 241–45
  Von Damm's ambassadorial
    appointment, reaction to,
    273
State dinners, guests invited to,
    176–77
Stockman, David, 129, 227
  Atlantic Monthly interview, 222–
    23

book written by, 319
OMB director, 133, 157, 175,
    203
  as opportunist, 122
Stone, Roger, 115
Svahn, Jack, 259–60
Switzerland, U.S. Ambassador to,
    247–49
Symbionese Liberation Army, 66

Taft, William Howard, III, 264,
    265
Tate, Sheila, 141
Tax cut legislation, 203–5
Taxes, Reagan's attitude toward,
    64–65
Tax hike of 1982, 167
Taylor, Elizabeth, 154
Terra, Adeline, 123
Terra, Dan, ix, 113–14, 123, 177,
    189, 276, 310, 313–14
  ambassadorship, interest in,
    151–52
  Cabinet selections for Reagan
    Administration, 120, 121,
    126, 131, 134, 135, 136,
    138
  Cultural Affairs Ambassador,
    173–74
  presidential campaign of 1980,
    98–99, 103, 115, 118
  Von Damm's assessment of,
    113–14
Tharp, Tad, ix, 106–7, 132, 217,
    235, 236, 252, 289
Thayer, Paul, 264–65
Tower, John, 129, 246–47
Trump, Donald and Ivana, 230
Tucker, Lem, 191
Tuttle, Bob, 190
Tuttle, Holmes, 61, 62–63, 126,
    131, 133, 268–69
Tuttle, Virginia, 63

Twain, Mark, 52
Tyson, Charles, 48, 79, 169
Tyson, Dorothy, 298

University of New Hampshire, 288
Urban, Maryann, 58, 211

Vienna, 12–13, 14–17, 18
Volkstimme (Austrian Communist newspaper), 284
Von Braun, Wernher, 57
Von Damm, Christian (second husband)
  divorce from, 86
  marriage to, 74–75
  married life with, 83–85
Von Damm, Helene
  advance work for Reagan, 86–87, 88–90
  Ambassador to Austria
    appointment as, 268–73
    confirmation hearings, 273–75
    embassy redecorating, 297
    "exchange of officials" program, 286–87
    "fall from grace," 306–14
    farewell parties in U.S., 275–76
    Fourth of July party, 286
    F-16 sales incident, 283–84
    fund-raising events, 287
    German language, problems with, 280–81
    NATO letter forgery, 281
    personal visit to Washington, 309–12
    political analyses for State Department, 282–83
    presentation of credentials, 279–80
      Nancy Reagan's opposition to appointment, 271–73, 288, 294–95, 296
      Reagan's foreign policy, promotion of ("public diplomacy"), 282, 284–86
      resignation, 313–15, 316–17
      State Department reaction to appointment, 273
      swearing-in ceremony, vii–x, 276
      trade-related work, 283, 284
      trip to Austria, 277, 278
      Washington visit with Austrian officials, 294–95
  AMPAC, employment with, 33–35, 38
  arrival in America, 24–25
  assassination attempt on Reagan, reaction to, 192–95
  boating adventure, 75–77
  brunch disaster, 230
  Cabinet, speech to, 256–57
  Cabinet selections for Reagan Administration, 120–21, 126–40
  California life, 57–59
  campaign school, 92
  car crash, 51–52
  career, need for, 95, 188–90
  in Chicago, 31–41
  childhood, 2–12, 17–18
  Clark's executive secretary in California, 46–47, 49–50, 56–57
  Communism, attitude toward, 44
  in Detroit, 26–31
  divorce from Leeds and marriage to Gürtler, 297–304
  education, 3, 11–12, 36, 84
  in Erlangen, Germany, 19–24

"fall from grace," 306–14
farmhouse in New Jersey, 261
fascination with America, 10
father, relationship with, 10–11
father figures for, 57
F-15 flight, 261
fortieth birthday, 93–94
fund-raising work, 100–6, 111–15
gubernatorial campaign of 1966, 42–46
honorary doctorate, 288
husband-hunting as young woman, 15
inauguration of 1981, 153–56
insane asylum job, 23
insurance underwriting job, 27–28, 33
Israel visit, 207–9
leadership training program, 90–91
marriages. *See* Gürtler, Peter; Leeds, Byron; McDonald, Charles; Von Damm, Christian
medical care, views on, 38
mother, relationship with, 9–10, 29, 199–200, 270, 296–97
mother's visit to America, 28–29
mountaineering course, 85
New Year's Day party (1981), 149
Nofziger's departure from White House, 225–27
party circuit in Washington, 187–88
Peru visit, 250
planes, dislike of, 2
politics, interest in, 50
Pope, meeting with, 282
pregnancy, failure regarding, 77

presidential campaign of 1976, 80–81
presidential campaign of 1980, 96, 98, 99–109, 111–15, 123–25
Presidential Personnel Office
  Assistant to the President position, 250–55, 262–65
  Deputy Assistant position, 205–7, 210–21, 227–28, 238–40, 242, 246–48
  women, recruitment of, 267–68
press coverage of, 140, 189–91, 208, 279, 303–4, 316–17
public relations work with Deaver and Hannaford, 78–79, 86–87, 88–91, 94
public speaking, 81
rape attempt on, 17–18
Nancy Reagan, first meeting with, 69–70
Nancy Reagan's campaign against, 306–8, 313
Nancy Reagan's kindness toward, 85–86
Reagan, dedication to, 40, 44, 53, 78–80
Reagan, first exposure to, 39–40
Reagan, private conversations with, 184
Reagan's correspondence, publication of, 79
Reagan's feelings for, 59–60
Reagan's gifts to, 64
Reagan's meeting with Gürtler and, 310–12
Reagan's secretary in California, 59–60, 63–64, 73
Reagan's secretary in Washington, 141, 145–46, 159–60, 163, 181–82, 188–90

personnel decisions, 171–76
as refugee, 3–6
regimented lifestyle, 36–37
"scandalette" regarding, 189–91
secretarial jobs, 14–15, 16–17, 27, 33
secret of her success, 95–96
self-improvement binge, 36
sexual harassment experienced by, 16–18
shopping habits, 141–42
Soviet occupation, life under, 7–9
state dinner guest lists, 176–77
Terra passed over as Ambassador to Great Britain, 151–52
two sides of, 18
U.S. citizenship, 37–38
in Vienna (1940s), 12–13, 14–17, 18
waitressing jobs, 40–41
wealth, admiration for, 63, 112–13
White House barbershop dispute, 163–64
White House office of, 155
White House staff meetings, 179–80
Who's Who form, 251
World War II, 2–5
Vranitzky, Franz, 304

Walker, June, 106
Wallace, Mike, 98, 99, 115
Watergate scandal, 77
Watt, James, 292
Weidenfeld, Ed, 131
Weil, Cary, 121
Weil, Lee, 102
Weinberger, Caspar, ix, 123, 124, 132, 144, 148, 149, 156, 183

assassination attempt on Reagan, reaction to, 193–94
Cabinet selections for Reagan Administration, 126, 128, 129, 130, 133–34, 136, 139
Clark's replacement at NSC, selection of, 293
Lebanon, U.S. Marines in, 292
in Nixon Administration, 79
personnel appointments, 262–65
Von Damm's assessment of, 54–55
Weinberger, Jane, 55, 123, 149
Wentner, Nita, 46
Weyrich, Paul, 167
White, Donald H., 263
White, Mark, 259
White House
barbershop dispute, 163–64
guest lists for functions at, 176–77
mess privileges, 162
perks of workers in, 161–62
press leaks from, 168
security measures, 159–60
staff, selection of, 143–44
staff meetings, 179–80, 252
"Troika" of Baker, Deaver and Meese, 195–99, 252–55
Whittlesey, Faith Ryan, 248–49, 267
Wick, Charles, 123, 132, 149
Cabinet selections for Reagan Administration, 126, 127, 131, 133, 138
presidential campaign of 1980, 105–6, 107, 108–9, 111
"public diplomacy" idea, 284
Robinson incident, 295
United States Information Agency chairman, 173

Wick, Mary Jane, 105, 123, 149,
229, 273
break with, 294, 295
Will, George, 122, 161
Wilson, Bill, 61–62, 126, 146,
147, 148–49, 150
Wilson, Pete, 37, 258, 312
Winter, Frau (mother), 3–4, 9–10,
12, 15, 22, 25, 28–29,
199–200, 270, 278, 296–
97
Winter, Herr (father), 3, 9, 10–11
Winter, Pepi (brother), 2, 3, 10,

11, 12–13, 18–19, 36,
199–200
Wirthlin, Dick, 117, 256
Women, discrimination against,
90, 265–67
Wood, Lynn, ix, 58–59, 86, 106,
112, 131, 212, 217, 307
World War II, 2–5, 21–22
Wrather, Jack, 62, 126, 128
Wright, Jim, 204

Zenzie, Henry, 103
Zipkin, Jerry, 112

*B*ORN IN AUSTRIA IN THE LATE 1930S, HELENE VON Damm emigrated to the United States in 1959. Inspired by a speech Ronald Reagan gave in Chicago, she moved to California to work on his campaign for Governor. She became his personal secretary in Sacramento, his advance person after he left the governorship, his campaign fund-raiser for the Northeast in the 1980 presidential election, his secretary in the White House, and, ultimately, his director of Presidential Personnel. Then, in 1983, President Reagan appointed her Ambassador to Austria. Ms. von Damm is now consulting for private industries in Austria and the United States, after having assisted the Republican National Committee's fund-raising efforts for the 1988 presidential elections.